THE CHAINING OF PROMETHEUS

The development of a national science policy for Canada – and the priorities to be set within any such policy – have been topics of a mounting debate within government and the scientific community. The questions involved are of concern in every country today: Can governments now afford to support laissez-faire 'pure' research to any extent? Or rather, should available resources be allocated to mission-oriented studies determined by government-established national goals?

Professor Hayes assesses the limitations and prospects for success of attempts to impose a pattern of planning on Canadian science and critically examines the reports of the Glassco Commission, the examiners for the OECD, the Lamontagne Committee, and the Science Council, as well as of several university-sponsored groups. The power of the Treasury Board and other parts of the control system also receive attention.

Most reports on Canadian science policy have been productions of federal agencies. Of the outside opinions, with a few notable exceptions, analyses and proposals about the natural sciences have been put forward by social scientists. The author, a scientist and former senior civil servant who has had experience in the research and administration of natural science both in the university and government, makes a unique, personal analysis of the attempts in Canada to impose national planning and controls over the historical free enterprise system of scientific research and development.

F. RONALD HAYES is Killam Professor of Environmental Science, Dalhousie University.

F. RONALD HAYES

The Chaining of Prometheus: evolution of a power structure for Canadian science

UNIVERSITY OF TORONTO PRESS

© University of Toronto Press 1973
Toronto and Buffalo
Reprinted in paperback 2017

ISBN 978-0-8020-1967-7 (cloth)
ISBN 978-1-4875-9151-9 (paper)
LC 72-97780

To my colleagues in the public service with the sincere hope that they will find this book too long to have it Xeroxed by their secretaries and distributed free.

Prometheus loved mankind and helped them to live on earth in happiness. Some say that he fashioned man out of earth and water. Prometheus took fire from Olympus, or from the sun, and brought it to mankind. He taught men the mining and working of metals and all the other arts. He granted them the gift of hope by which all enterprise thrives. But Zeus, when he observed fire glowing from the dwellings of men, commanded Hephaestus to fashion the girl Pandora (Senator Lamontagne) through whom many evils fell upon the earth. Also he sent the terrible eagle, offspring of Echidna (Secretary of the Treasury Board), to feed on the liver of Prometheus every day, for it grew again by night. Heracles (Gerhard Herzberg) shot the eagle which was torturing Prometheus. When Heracles had freed Prometheus he wreathed himself with olive, and the wreath was taken to represent the bonds of Prometheus.

Contents

Tables

Figures

Preface

The beginnings of this book are to be found in a paper, 'The development of science in Canada,' which I wrote for the *Dalhousie Review* in 1961. A few paragraphs from it survive in the opening chapter of the present volume.

The article concluded by comparing our several national science programs with the specialized parts of the brain. Each part reacts independently and is biased in a certain direction; for example, towards sight, hearing, smell, taste, balance, and so on. In the highest vertebrates and man, cerebral association areas are added, which extend and co-ordinate the senses, giving the power of long-term decisions or variable behaviour, and which are supposed to be the basis of success. These association areas were compared to the universities, with the conclusion that the key to a national science program was the development of mature, responsible universities.

That was in 1961. In the decade since, Canadian science has been kept continually on the couch pouring out its thoughts to one committee of social diagnosticians after another. Probably the scientific endeavour of no other country has endured so much scrutiny.

The analysts generally agree that our central problem is to harmonize, in the interest of the whole nation, the individual science programs now working independently. They do not, however, show any confidence that the universities are, by any extrapolation, likely to assume policy responsibility. This is to be controlled by some agency of the federal government.

After 1961 my own thoughts about science policy began to take a practical turn through the intrusion of administrative responsibilities, first in the university and later during five years as a government servant in Ottawa. I found myself in Ottawa in the position of C.P. Snow's narrator, Lewis Eliot, important enough to be present at senior meetings, but not important enough to attract notice. It was an instructive experience for an academic interested in the anatomy of power.

At the end Dalhousie, with much grace, offered me, through a Killam professorship, the leisure to filter the mass of accumulated evidence through my experience.

The first large piece of evidence was the report of the Glassco Commission on Government Organization. As its recommendations began to be adopted it became, for senior public servants, the hinge of fate. Anything or anyone that was there before Glassco was suspected of being old-fashioned or incompetent; anyone who came after was presumed to be efficient and high-minded. The men who had assisted Glassco in writing his report arrived in Ottawa to root out the old practitioners.

The Glassco report forms the natural centre of the time-scale for this book. What happened before Glassco is scientific history; what happened after is contemporary science policy. Reports subsequent to Glassco have moderated or developed its lines but have not changed its direction.

The plot of this book concerns attempts to impose national planning and controls over the historical free-enterprise system of scientific research and development. The opening chapter is intended to lay the foundation for what follows by defining the positions of the protagonists. This chapter is somewhat more theoretical than those that come after. I hope it will be found to have repaid the effort.

Chapter 2 gives a sketch of the federal world of science as it developed up to the time of Glassco. This is followed by an analysis of the three major reports which have ushered in the age of controls. Chapter 3 looks at the effectiveness of existing control mechanisms as they function at present. The remaining chapters, which make up half the book, outline the components from which any Canadian science policy will have to be built, and enlarge on some questions of current interest among them. My personal conclusions are offered in a final chaper. In addition, brief interpretations and opinions are inserted at the end of the discussion of major topics. This is not intended to be an exhaustive treatise or a technical book, or to be encyclopaedic. The number and content of tables has been restricted to the minimum necessary to develop the argument.

A word about quotations. The book contains a good many and there is scarcely one that has not been shortened. In particular Parliamentary debates are discursive and public hearings, where successive members of the tribunal question witnesses on the same topic, are repetitious. In quoting from these, I have used the dramatist's privilege of giving only the essential words of the dialogue.

A first draft of the book was read by my wife, Dr Dixie Pelluet, by Dr W.E. Ricker of the Fisheries Research Board, Nanaimo, and by Professor J.P. Atherton of the Classics Department at Dalhousie. Later drafts have had the benefit of comments by reviewers for the University of Toronto Press. The many suggestions resulted in extensive rewriting with, I hope, considerable improvement. I am very grateful.

Abbreviations

AECL   Atomic Energy of Canada Limited

Agriculture   Used, as the context requires, to refer either to the Canada
                Department of Agriculture or to the Research Branch of the
                department.

Bladen   V.K. Bladen et al. 1965. *Financing Higher Education in*
report   *Canada*. Association of Universities and Colleges of
                Canada.

DBS   Dominion Bureau of Statistics. Now Statistics Canada.

DIP   See 'Federal support for industry.'

DIR   See 'Federal support for industry.'

DM   Deputy Minister

DRB   Defence Research Board of Canada. As with boards and
                councils generally, the designation is used interchangeably
                to describe both the honorary management group and the
                employees.

EM & R   Department of Energy, Mines and Resources

Federal   In addition to contracts for research and development there
support for   are five special agencies:
industry   DIP Defence Industrial Productivity Program of the
                Department of Industry, Trade and Commerce
                DIR Defence Industrial Research Program of the Defence
                Research Board
                IRAP Industrial Research Assistance Program of the
                National Research Council

PAIT Program for the Advancement of Industrial Technology of the Department of Industry, Trade and Commerce

IRDIA Industrial Research and Development Incentives Act, essentially a form of tax abatement to encourage expenditure on research.

FRB Fisheries Research Board of Canada

Glassco report J.G. Glassco et al. 1963. *The Royal Commission on Government Organization.* 4 vols. Ottawa: Queen's Printer. Section 23 in vol. 4 is on scientific research and development.

Green Book *Federal Government Costs and Expenditures.* Ministry of State for Science and Technology. This is an annual publication which was started in 1971. It gives the federal government costs and expenditures for a ten-year period. The method of calculation differs from that of the DBS, but not sufficiently to affect any of the conclusions drawn in this book. Where both are available, the Green Book has been used. The Green Book is unique in that it deals with the social sciences as well as the natural sciences.

Health Department of National Health and Welfare

Industry Department of Industry, created by the Pearson government. In the Trudeau administration it was put in with the Department of Trade and Commerce to make a new department, Industry, Trade and Commerce.

ING Intense Neutron Generator

IRAP See 'Federal support for industry.'

IRDIA See 'Federal support for industry.'

Lamontagne See 'Sen. com. proc.' and 'Sen. com. report.'

Macdonald report J.B. Macdonald et al. 1969. *The Role of the Federal Government in Support of Research in Canadian Universities.* Science Council special study no. 7. Ottawa: Queen's Printer. (See also Science Council report no. 5, which is a commentary on the above.)

MRC Medical Research Council. Formerly a nominal branch of the National Research Council, it became, as part of the post-Glassco restructuring, an independent agency reporting to the Minister of Health.

NRC National Research Council of Canada

OECD report Organization for Economic Co-operation and Development. 1969. *Reviews of National Science Policy: Canada.*

PAIT	See 'Federal support for industry.'
PPB	Planning, Programming, Budgeting
PSC	Public Service Commission, which operates the civil service.
Queen's Printer	Now called Information Canada
R & D	Research and development
SC	Science Council of Canada
SCITEC	The Association of the Scientific, Engineering and Technological Community of Canada. Originally called Science-Technology Canada, from which the abbreviation originated.
Sen. com. proc.	*Proceedings of the Special Committee of the Senate on Science Policy.* Maurice Lamontagne, Chairman. There were fourteen numbers of the Proceedings during the session 1967-8; eighty during 1968-9, and three during 1969-70. The hearings included oral evidence and briefs, the former predominating in the early phases, the latter at the end. As an example, where the citation given is: Sen. com. proc. 68–9, 15, the full reference is: Canada. 28th Parliament, 1968-9. Senate. Special Committee on Science Policy. Proceedings no. 15. Ottawa: Queen's Printer.
Sen. com. report	M. Lamontagne et al. 1970. *A Science Policy for Canada.* Report of the Senate Special Committee on Science Policy. Vol. 1: *A Critical Review: Past and Present.* Vol. 2: *Targets and Strategies for the Seventies.* Ottawa: Queen's Printer. The pages in the two volumes are numbered consecutively.
SS	Science Secretariat of the Privy Council Office. Now called Secretariat for Science Policy.
TB	Treasury Board

THE CHAINING OF PROMETHEUS

1
Planned science

After the Second World War good fortune came easily to the scientific community which, as a result, had no incentive to develop the political instincts commonplace in other segments of society that are dependent on the goodwill and understanding of government. On the government side, lip-service to research is one of the virtues acclaimed by aspirants to public office, whether of the right, left, or centre. The science-government linkage developed because the war had demonstrated that it was in the national interest for science and technology to thrive. The politicians arrived at this conclusion not as a result of political pressure from scientists or through a deep understanding of research but as an act of faith, and this permitted scientists to build up over the years a distorted view of political reality.

What we may by this time begin to call the classical view held by scientists is illustrated by an American proposal in 1959 for support of high-energy physics research, in which the long range plans were described as follows:

It is not possible to assign priorities to fields of basic science, nor should they be placed in competition. Each science, at any given time, faces a set of critical problems that requires solutions for continued growth. Sometimes these solutions can be acquired with little cost; sometimes larger expenditures of funds are needed. Hence, the cost may not reflect the relative value but rather the need. Each area must be funded according to these needs.

4 The chaining of Prometheus

As the Lamontagne report remarks, 'In its purest and most elaborate form this doctrine holds that the scientific community – or in the economist's language, the suppliers of research – should determine the level and distribution of scientific activities, thus applying to science a classical law of markets, that supply creates its own demand.'[1] Scientists are, in other words, pictured as economic liberals, who believe in competition as the spur to excellence.

The statement which was quoted about high-energy physics may be contrasted with one made in 1968 by the Science Council:

Starting with the axiom that the value of any scientific enterprise is determined by the social, cultural and economic goals that society seeks, a framework could be built in logical order by identifying the goals, the factors determining their attainment, the contributions of science and technology to the goals and what conditions permit.[2]

An era of the history of science has passed between these two statements. The first assumes that science is so important and valuable that it should be supported purely on a basis of what it needs, and not in terms of its place among other competitors for national resources. The second says that science is merely another competitor for national resources, and that it had better state its case clearly and persuasively if it wishes to command public respect. It says that scientists had better come to terms with the cultural revolution which has made possible the advances of science and technology in our time.

In an age of socialism, it would seem that the social planners have much the better of the argument, with the scientists stumbling back in disorder. However, practical obstacles arise in both prediction and execution of a general science policy, which will be commented on in later chapters.

At this point it is advisable to define the types of scientific activity and indicate the defence offered for basic research whose magnitude in Canadian science has been a main target of criticism.

Three types of research can be designated even though they may not always be clearly recognized.[3] *Basic research* or pure science, frequently thought of by academics as university research, is said to include work undertaken to advance scientific knowledge without a specific practical application in view.* *Applied research* is the same but with a practical aim

---

* The Senate committee quotes the definitions of the Zukerman committee in the UK, which distinguishes between 'pure basic' and 'objective basic' research. About the Zukerman distinctions Lord Rothschild commented, 'One wonders for whom this elaborate taxonomy was necessary and to whom it is useful' (*New Statesman*, 31 December 1971).

in view. *Development* is the process of directing the results of basic or applied research to some practical use.

The government, looking at increased science costs, would like to be provided by the scientific planners with something along the lines of a breathalyser test by which to identify basic science. At the same time a cabinet decision would determine what percentage of the total research and development cost was to be devoted to basic science. All then would be plain sailing. But despite a great deal of analysis and classification, we remain as far away as ever from any definition by which a panel can select from among academic proposals those which will have some future application. The lines therefore remain blurred.

There are five main reasons given by science spokesmen for substantial support of basic science: its intellectual and cultural value, its ultimate usefulness, its value in training graduate students, its political or prestige value, and its high costs which put it beyond the reach of all but the federal patron.[4]

Since a great deal of the Canadian debate about science policy hinges on the place to be occupied by basic science, we may take a few paragraphs to evaluate the five reasons adduced in its favour. The first claim is the one traditionally made for Greek:

We delight in physics for the same reason that we delight in the arts, because it makes us feel good inside and because it takes us further along the endless road that is ours alone, the realization of Man as Man. The pursuit of physics is a deep contribution to Man's self-realization. It is for us to recognize that, in a deep sense, the world, life and joy are what we make them and finally to ask in concrete terms: 'Is this not worth two per cent of our Gross National Product?'[5]

To planners, the sting of this proposition is in the final sentence. It is difficult, they will say, to persuade the government to support science because it is fun, or a sort of amusement park for the scientific community. The cultural argument for support of science competes with similar arguments advanced for music or sport and it is hard to prove uniqueness for science in this sense.

The claim of ultimate usefulness is so far the best drawing card for basic research, which thus is offered as the foundation of all technological development. The directions of application, however, are observable only by hindsight. Even a man like Albert Einstein could not foresee the outcome of his work after he had completed at an early age his epoch-making discoveries on relativity and quantum theory. He spent the major part of his remaining years on what seems so far to have been a fruitless search for a unified field theory. If it is impossible for the people directly involved to foresee the practical uses that may arise from their discoveries, it must also be impossible for a science administrator to tell them whether they are on the right track. Dr Gerhard Herzberg has said:

The history of technology shows that many of the major developments of the last hundred years are based on discoveries made by scientists motivated by the quest for knowledge. If we want to ensure further beneficial development of technology in Canada, we shall have a much better chance of success if we support basic research with all possible freedom for the individual scientist than if we support only those missions in which we can foresee immediate advantages.[6]

In the training of graduate students pure science is said to have superior virtues; in recent years this element has come to be increasingly stressed. Formerly university research was defended as contributing in a by-product manner to the health of the universities. Now it seems that logic is pushing us towards the reverse position; that academic discoveries may be defended as the by-product of graduate education. In either case, the policy assumption is that a close relationship exists between research and university development, so that programs directed towards one of these goals must affect the other. The idea of research as an educational by-product is of special interest in Canada, since it is likely to form the basis for equalization claims by new universities and by Atlantic and French-language universities, and it gets some endorsement from the Science Council:

Support need not be given as a reward for mediocrity but allocations should take into account their potential contribution to 'research training' and general 'health' of the institution as well as their contribution to 'new knowledge.'[7]

The same idea is expressed in the Bladen report:

The smaller and newer universities must compete for research grants with the bigger, stronger, well-established universities, This is right and proper; research money must be placed where it is most productive. But, through trial grants, scholars who have not yet established reputations should be given a chance to develop to the point where they can compete without favour. In this way we will build up a stronger group of universities.[8]

While the 'general health' or 'by-product' argument enjoys considerable acceptance, the essentiality of pure science in the package does not. Indeed the Lamontagne report (see chapter 2) takes the view that students are made unfit for their careers by present programs and would be better off practising on research problems related to their future occupations.

The by-product argument moreover is blunted as a basis for federal support of research by the fact that education is a provincial responsibility. 'In matters of education the Canadian state is the provincial state and none other.'[9]

For the fourth argument, the contribution basic science can make to national politics and prestige, the best example came when we saw on our TV sets the American flag being planted on the moon by a clean-living white boy who had just said his prayers. In Canada we have nothing so classy. However, the geophysics of the continental shelf and the exploration of the Arctic provide two areas of prime political motivation.

But the political criterion, even when accepted by the state, requires choices between fields of science. For example, if contributions to economic growth are given great weight, it would be logical to support engineering, mathematics, and economics. If cultural progress and knowledge of the universe are the justifying values, high-energy physics, molecular biology, and astronomy might take precedence. Molecular biology offers fairly tangible predictions about areas of application, for example the potential replacement of defective parts of a person's genetic code. The utility of high-energy physics, on the other hand, turns on a rather intangible general prediction that all basic science eventually proves useful.

High costs, the final reason advanced in favour of federal support for pure science, has some overlap with political claims. Thus wind tunnels and ocean-going ships are large pieces of equipment which have military and political overtones. Somewhat more pure a field, perhaps, is astronomy, which has a critical manpower-equipment ratio. This subject could hardly exist today in the absence of a federal 'home' which possessed optical and radio-telescopes supported by technicians.

II FORECASTING AND PLANNING

In elementary planning, individuals, corporations, and institutions seek for themselves a course designed to maximize gain and minimize cost and loss. Social intervention in the process has the object of redirecting technology to reduce its undesirable consequences for others. Until recent years, social benefits were for small *élites* only, and effects on the population generally were not considered.

Contemporary planning holds in theory that decisions about the application of new technologies must not be allowed to rest solely on their immediate utility to their sponsors and users. Rather they should reflect the Benthamite doctrine of 'the greatest good for the greatest number.' There is, however, no agreed-upon algebra by which one can subtract the pains from the pleasures in order to arrive at a net index of social desirability. In practice decisions are made on the basis of a persuasive case which breaks into the consciousness of someone with political power.

'Technology assessment' means the evaluation of a proposed development with a view to forecasting its consequences. The contents of the notion vary with the outlook of its proponents. To some, concerned with the preservation of environmental quality, assessment will consist of focusing public attention on the long-range consequences. Others are concerned with the relation of technical to social goals; social impact often includes the physical and biological environment. To still others, technology assessment represents planning-programming-budgeting (PPB). Their emphasis is on defining objectives as they relate to national goals, assessing performance in cost-benefit terms, and seeking ways to modify old programs.

Among academic scientists there is an instinct that industrial development and innovation ought somehow to be capable of evolving, like basic research, by diverse processes of trial and error, which will allow different, inconsistent, and even opposing modes to be followed at the same time. Engineers and economists, on the other hand, tend to think that research, for the purposes of planning, can be lumped in as a part of development. The brief of the Engineering Institute of Canada to the Science Council is probably close to a good deal of government thinking. It pointed out that Canada is lagging behind the USA in its science expenditures, and that of the inadequate amount that we do spend, too little is going to innovation in manufacturing fields and too much is going to basic research and to government research, especially in agriculture.

Such views, which are widely held, lead to the premises of planning:
–Canada's component of basic research is inconsistently high in relation to national economic goals,
–research is to be supported because it is a necessary tool for the achievement of such national goals as economic growth and industrial development, and
–some national agency ought to sit like an infinitely wise spider, at the centre of a web which reaches into every science activity in the nation, tightening up here, slackening off there.
Our spider is supposed to be working on the assumption that research

can improve the quality of forecasting by reducing the costs due to uncertainty. The relation has limits, since no amount of research, however great, can ensure the commercial success of an innovation – think of the Edsel car. The object of planned science is to find a balance between research and development which minimizes the uncertainty of forecasts. The correct balance could be calculated in practice only for an industrial operation with well-defined aims; it might, for example, have saved $50 to $100 million if applied to the Nova Scotia heavy water project. But in so far as the content of a field lies outside engineering applications, in the area of more general science, the precision of planning declines. To put this another way; as planning becomes efficient the project is moving out of research into practice. The following examples show this. On the left is a list of basic discoveries which emerged as the result of somebody's mental effort. They then passed through an intermediate R & D stage in which science planning did take place. To the right are objectives for which plans lead to accurate forecasts; the aims, however, are social, military, or economic rather than scientific and the top planners are not technical experts concerned with science.

De novo discovery no planners	Plans produce
Insulin	Hospitals
$E = mc^2$	Power plants, bombs
TV	Networks
Radar	Aircraft routes
DDT	Pollution abatement

At one end of the spectrum, where basic science predominates, planning is ineffective because it is of no value in making predictions. At the other end predictibility is high but the object is application rather than R & D. It is in the intermediate zone, represented by the lines, that science planning has its place.

One would think that there ought to be some fairly standard pattern to be found in those research projects which have led to substantial economic consequences – in the selection, monitoring, and establishment of priorities, funding, and so on. Unfortunately no such pattern emerges, which is disconcerting to those who fund research and particularly so for those who direct it.

This conclusion about a lack of pattern could hardly be drawn *a priori* or from the experience of a single laboratory. It has in fact been verified in dozens of laboratories over the world that the study of R & D case histories does not lead to constructive proposals on how to avoid failures. The NRC brief to the Senate hearings includes this comment:

We have available a particularly useful background collection of some 60 case histories of technological innovations all of which impact our economy in a major way, and many of which originated in laboratory research. Each one is uniquely different in its whole pattern of selection, initiation, monitoring and funding.[10]

Despite the lack of pattern all sides agree that a major justification for support is that research pays. It is therefore natural to relate priorities to areas from which a pay-off is most urgently desired. With that premise, here is the priority pattern and set of categories proposed by M.D. Reagan:

First priority goes to those social objectives which are defined as most urgent politically and to which scientific research can most clearly make a contribution.
Second priority goes to science-related educational needs, from elementary schools to the graduate education-research laboratory level.
Third priority goes to undirected small-scale research – so-called little science.
Fourth priority goes to Big Science; those fields having very high equipment costs requiring large teams of researchers or large facilities, yet which are part of basic research.[11]

As examples of Canadian first priorities, one thinks of housing and improved urban transportation systems. With a country the dimensions of ours, next to a great neighbour, communications and the development of satellites could be added. And, of course, the deterioration of the environment is of great concern.

Reagan's second priority, in so far as it relates to elementary science teaching, lies outside the present consideration of R & D. University support is discussed in a later chapter.

In the third priority, the support of academic science, Reagan would allocate resources according to Alvin Weinberg's criteria, which join the competence of the scientists and ripeness of the field to its technological and social merit.[12] The questions to be asked concern:

INTERNAL CRITERIA
– Is the field ready for exploitation?
– Are the scientists in the field really competent?

- What is the technological merit or quality of each proposal or field as indicated by review panel ratings?
- What will be its probable contribution to other fields of science?
- Does it have social merit or relevance to human welfare and the values of man?

As an example from the behavioural sciences, take what is to many the most important problem of the times: how to find a way to limit the aggressive behaviour of man which leads to wars. Proposals to attack such a problem might include: increased support for the extra-scientific approaches of churches and welfare agencies, development of psychology departments in the universities, support for experiments with hallucinogenic drugs and tranquilizers, and increased research in human genetics leading to the breeding of better behaved people. In the Weinberg system, such proposals, and others in the behavioural sciences, would be judged to have high social relevance, but not yet sufficient scientific development to warrant much support.

To molecular biology, Weinberg gave high points, both for its scientific qualities and for its social merit in terms of potential applications to health problems. Fields of science such as this, that stood high on several counts, would then be placed above those with lower scores.

In Canadian practice, as evidenced by public judgments such as appear from the Science Council, the external criteria of social and technological merit have higher standing than considerations of scientific merit, the readiness of a field for exploitation, or the competence of scientists in the field. The latter factor in particular rarely appears. Scientists do not discuss the competence of their fellows because of their natural desire to live and let live – at least in public. It is easy enough to assert that one's own field is ready for exploitation, but it is socially difficult for anyone within the scientific community to say that another man's field is not. It would be even more surprising if scientists were prepared to state publicly that those in any field were incompetent. But the external criteria which weigh heavily with analysts like the sc tend to favour application rather than pure science. This is because the higher the component of development, the easier it is to see applications and to explain significance to non-scientists. For this reason researchers themselves often use the social utility pitch in public, although not often within their own fraternity.

The fourth priority, Big Science, is considered to include such things as oceanography, astronomy, and high-energy physics for which major facilities are required. Obviously some Big Science might relate to the first priority, for example, a radio-telescope might be essential to study communications satellites, or oceanographic equipment might relate to pollution. Judging from u.s. experiences, Big Science in Canada will likely be approved and geographically located according to political rather than scientific considerations, and therefore does not have a high place on lists prepared by researchers, except special pleaders.

Another approach to the design of policy is offered by N.H. Lithwick.[13] His model is intended to show how a national science plan could be drawn up via an extension of the theory of economic policy making. The scheme is interesting as showing natural scientists what is in store for them at the hands of economists. At the outset one assumes broad objectives and assigns to each what is called a notional shadow price; for example, national identity is worth .40, prosperity .25, freedom and justice .15 each, and international involvement .05. To each of these items another coefficient is assigned representing the ability of society to achieve the objectives. A third number assigned to each aim represents the degree to which it is related to science policy; justice and freedom, for example, are said to be unamenable to treatment by science and thus out of concern.

According to Lithwick, the first objective, national identity, can be partitioned into three components:

- Racial problems, in which the contribution of science is negligible.
- Regional disparity, for which the solutions will be mainly economic with marginal science input. There are three sub-divisions, resource development, industrial development, and depopulation.
- Finally the field of excellence, in which Canadian science does have some potential, but which is unimportant because the scientific community to which gains would accrue is small. It includes atomic energy, transportation and communication, and medicine, which together have a notional shadow value of .05 (out of the total of .40 for all of national identity).

The contributions of science to each aim are similarly identified and by use of the three coefficients (value of objective, ability of society to achieve it, component of science in it) an equation is worked out which yields the relative support to be given to any one branch of science.

Lithwick ends up with a list of notional science priorities, of which the highest (preventive medicine) is arbitrarily set at 100 and the others rated below it. Given his assumptions, the several areas of medicine taken together would aggregate 153, agriculture 89, industrial technology 77, resources 46, pollution 22, defence 12, etc., etc. According to Lithwick, one advantage of his method is that policies have their basis in the desires of society, not those of the technocrats; another is that the criteria are objective. As a long-term bonus, in other words, scientists will be stoppered from purple prose and fuzzy thinking about intellectual challenge and unforeseen benefits for their grand new projects.

About this proposal and others like it, one might ask whether there is any individual or committee of experts, or eventually perhaps a Gallup Poll, that can attach acceptable relative numbers to our national aims?

If the first two coefficients are more theoretical than practical, the third – which shows the component of science in each national aim – is ascertainable only by hindsight. To take an example, it might be said that science entered the military sphere with the First World War. A favourite story told by E.W.R. Steacie concerned a colleague who offered his services as a chemist to the u.s. government when that country entered the War. He received a reply stating that the government already had a chemist. However, by the end of the War chemistry was well established as a military adjunct. In the Second World War it was physics which came to the forefront. At the beginning Canada had two physical oceanographers, one for each coast. As the submarines and magnetic and acoustic mines began to take their toll the need for additional physicists became clear in that field, just as the development of radar and nuclear weapons summoned them forth elsewhere. More recently in Vietnam biology (crop destruction) and negative medicine (spread of disease) are coming in for their share of glory.

Lithwick's third coefficient in reality answers the question: What discoveries have already been made that are applicable to each national aim? To put it into use it would tend to freeze the existing level of effort.

III   SYSTEMS ANALYSIS AND PPB

In earlier times, when personnel and purchasing were unreliable, the prime consideration of budgets was how to prevent stealing. Control over objects of expenditure was the first motive; other objectives such as planning and functional accounting were subordinate. The budget was traditionally built up from the bottom by a sum of unit expenditures and tended to carry on from year to year with increments.

Currently there is a strong trend towards what is called performance budgeting with emphasis on systems analysis and planning. The operation begins with a statement of objectives and, theoretically, requires existing activities to compete on an equal footing with new proposals.

Systems   analysis   and   its   handmaiden,   Planning-Programming-

Budgeting, may be defined as a mental assembly-line technique which is supposed to bring information directly into relation with national needs and provide estimates of the costs and benefits of alternate treatments. Moreover, it claims to notch up the intelligence performance of public servants so that they can revise goals, change plans, reallocate resources, and avoid solving the wrong problems. It is in short a modern philosopher's stone which will transmute base metal into gold.

It is an assumption of PPB that alteration in the form in which information is classified and used will produce desirable changes in the behaviour of users, for example 'crosswalking' (jargonese for co-operation). The assumption remains untested; while the form of PPB has received slavish attention, the behavioural side has suffered from neglect.

PPB was developed in the USA by the Rand Corporation (Rand stands for R & D). It came into prominence when Robert McNamara put it into practice in the U.S. Defense Department, outraging the admirals by raising such questions as whether aircraft-carriers were worth their cost. In 1965, the U.S. president asked all departments to install a planning-programming-budgeting system. In Canada the Glassco recommendations triggered a similar reorganization of budgeting by the Treasury Board.

At Treasury Board instigation, groups of government employees, including researchers, are brought to Ottawa for short courses in cost-benefit analysis and PPB, given by a firm of chartered accountants.[14] The kind of situation in which the system is believed to work best is indicated by the topics selected for case history study by the trainees: deciding between alternative patterns of road-building to connect U.S. towns, efficiency of mail delivery by the U.S. Post Office, improvement in police protection against robbery in a small U.S. city, changing arrangements in the St Lawrence Seaway in order to get more ships through the locks. These cases have in common that the policy decision has already been made – to build roads, deliver mail, protect by police, use the Seaway. Given a plan, or policy, the method is set up to decide among alternative solutions. It is stated as an axiom of PPB that if you can't measure success you will never achieve the desired end. It is on this axiom that PPB founders when attempts are made to apply it to research.

We are fortunate in having an analysis of PPB, as used in the management of Canadian science, straight from the horse's mouth. On two occasions the secretary of the Treasury Board appeared before the Senate Science Committee.[15] Because the board's professional relations are confidential, these public events might be compared to an interrogation of the head of the Jesuit Order by the Inquisition, to document the nature of the true faith.

Senator Maurice Lamontagne, chairman: This morning we have the pleasure of receiving the Secretary of the Treasury Board. Perhaps, Mr Reisman, you want to make an opening statement.

Simon Reisman, secretary, Treasury Board: I would like to say a few words about science. In the eyes of the Board, science is not regarded as a thing in itself but as a means to an end. Scientific projects are not examined on their merits but as components of programs. Several agencies, including the National Research Council, carry on projects in science in order to further their defined program objectives. These mission-oriented departments have to be viewed within the framework of the programs that they have been allocated. This kind of thinking has enabled the Treasury Board to identify seiected areas of research and development that justified priority treatment.

Decision-making will be strengthened through planning, programming and budgeting. There are three key aspects to PPB. The first is to have clear objectives derived from national goals. The second adds the dimension of cost-benefit analysis, and the third is the need to examine alternative means. PPB should enable parliamentarians to compare expenditure proposals with objectives.

Chairman: If I may interrupt you for a moment, Mr Reisman, will there be a special figure for expenditures devoted to R & D in scientific activities?

Reisman: The answer to that is no. The notion that there is a relationship between all the bits of science is foreign to our thinking.

Senator Chesley W. Carter: In your brief you give an illustration of the decision-making process. You work out the cost benefit for system A and system B and conclude that the breakeven point comes after 40 years. After that the benefit ratio for B is greater, so the inference is that the decision would favour B. Where are you making allowance for technological advances during these 40 years? I would plump for A on the assumption that within 40 years they will both be obsolete.

Reisman: There are many problems, particularly in the government sector, which do not lend themselves to this kind of quantitative analysis.

Carter: This is an illustration though, in your own brief. I would not make decisions on the basis of the assumptions you have quoted.

Senator Hédard Robichaud: Who decides what R & D projects must have priority? In your brief you say: 'The Treasury Board staff is responsible for surveillance – but the power of decision remains with the Ministers.'

What criteria does the Board's secretariat use to decide which projects are not within the secretariat's jurisdiction and must be submitted to the cabinet ministers?

Reisman: That is a very tough question.

Robichaud: Where is the division line?

Reisman: You are asking how they decide what they put before the Board?

Robichaud: Yes.

16 The chaining of Prometheus

Reisman: As recently as ten years ago, some 20,000 cases a year were put before the Board. Since that time the device was introduced of vetting submissions. Those of a routine or minor nature were assembled in a book which was placed in the centre of the table at meetings so that the ministers would have an opportunity of leafing through it and raising questions about any case that attracted their attention.
Chairman: It was only theoretical.
Reisman: I think you are right, Mr Chairman, the ministers did not get too worried about the routine cases.
Chairman: The Treasury Board has, let us say, 55 professional people. Would they be assigned to specific divisions?
Reisman: Oh, yes, indeed. The major scientific programs are concentrated in the third division. There are nine people there.
Chairman: And, of course, they have to look at all the government. This is a pretty wide field so I suppose there is very little time to have a serious look at individual research programs.
Reisman: We have a great deal of work to do. We are a pretty lean organization and we work our people very, very hard.
Chairman: Mr Drury made a statement recently that the Treasury Board was looking almost exclusively to new programs.
Reisman: If the Honourable C.M. Drury made an observation, I am sure it was a correct one.
Chairman: Could you comment on what you do.
Reisman: We look at everything that forms the subject of government expenditures.
Chairman: You cannot look at everything with the same kind of attention. When I was in Northern Affairs there was the exercise of what we used to call 'going to confession' before Treasury Board. They were looking at new programs, assuming more or less that the money given to the department the previous year was all right.
Reisman: I suppose, sir, that that observation of yours has a certain general validity to it.
Carter: When it comes to priorities between one scientific project and another, how is the choice made?
Reisman: Let us take the satellite communications project as an example; is it to be looked at as a scientific project, as a communications project or as a national project unifying the country? The way I look at the problem, scientific research is to be understood as an instrument, together with other instruments, for achieving certain objectives.

Should one say, now in the interests of science we should be building a communications satellite and casting it up into space. Or should we say we are developing a national project and, of course, it will have a high scientific content. There is your dilemma.

Chairman: You have chosen a very good example to suit your own theories.

Carter: I would not regard Mr Reisman's illustration as being parallel or even related to the question I posed, because putting up a satellite for communications is not much more difficult than installing a telephone.

A project might have the lowest priority on the department's list, where it was competing with a host of other projects which that particular department were more interested in. It does not follow that on a national scale or in an overall context it would still be low man on the totem pole.

Reisman: It is not only a matter of one science project with another science project. For example, a program of the magnitude of ING has got to be offset against virtually everything that the government does – the causeway to Prince Edward Island or Medicare or the whole regional development program.

There is no logical way that I know of for making these choices, but we try to do it.

Senator Allister Grosart: Looking at your brief, I notice that recreation, for example, is one of the main considerations in the allocation of resources, whereas science is not.

Reisman: You are wondering why we put recreation together in one package but do not put research and development in one package.

Grosart: That is my question. The OECD makes comparisons between countries on the assumption that the total expenditures on R & D have some importance.

We have had departments before us and we have asked them 'When you decide to give grants to ABC universities for XYZ projects, do you know what other departments may be doing? And the answer has always been no.

Reisman: I do not think it makes much sense to lump together, say the research done on the sex life of the giant clam with scientific activities to promote technological development. Science expenditures should be regarded as a tool to achieve certain ends and can only be understood in relation to the objectives of a program.

Grosart: Does that apply to every single vote in the estimates?

Reisman: All expenditures are a means to an end. The interesting thing is not the thing itself but the means to which it is directed. The national science policy comprises a series of policies with respect to pollution, nuclear energy, fisheries, civilian and military industrial research and development, defence. Together they make up a national science policy.

Chairman: At the end we get a policy by accident.

Reisman: That is true, sir.

Chairman: If, in addition to having the science component of all our programs we do not have an overall science budget, we cannot see the imbalances.

Reisman: Mr Chairman, you know my prejudices in this field. I think that the notion of an overall budget for science is nonsense. The activities under all the scientific fields are so diverse that to talk about a single budget embracing them is an abstraction that my mind is incapable of grasping.

Chairman: I am tempted to make an analogy between microeconomics and macroeconomics. Your microeconomic approach does not give the whole story, but the other one does not tell you the whole story either; the two have to complement each other. Otherwise there are a lot of fools – a lot of people losing their time.

Reisman: I suppose, sir, there are a lot of people losing their time.

Chairman: Not in the Treasury Board.

Reisman: I think I understand what you are talking about. I can see some merit in that kind of approach as a means of focusing the attention of the public at large on the fact that the national resources devoted to an area of disciplines is not adequate.

Chairman: Thank you very much for spending this time and sharing your vast experience with us.

The committee adjourned.

Mr Reisman's evidence shows that the first fallacy in PPB lies in the initial P for planning. There is, as he admitted, no logical way to choose among national goals, especially scientific ones. If the issue is large, it is decided by the prime minister; if small by a Treasury Board official. The basis for decision may be political pressure, the quality of breakfast, or a leading article in the morning paper. However caused, decision on the first P stacks the deck, and the cards are passed on, usually to the Treasury Board, with an admonition to play fair with PB.

The second P for Programming introduces cost-benefit analysis, a tricky field for prediction of research application. In medicine, for example, every advance creates new needs which did not exist until the means of meeting them came into the realm of the possible. Every time a discovery is made, say in the technique of transplants, the horizon of need and cost is suddenly enlarged.

B for Budgeting, which includes the examination of alternative methods, is applicable to industrial or military operations with well-defined aims. Its usefulness enters science from the Development end of the spectrum and diminishes in proportion to the loss of predictability as we pass through applied towards basic science. The budgetary assumption of PPB is 'No science except from pre-existing economics.'

PPB may, for all I know, have considerable merit when applied to business operations. There is virtue in any system which forces people to re-examine the basic assumptions of their routines. As Samuel Johnson remarked, 'When a man knows he is to be hanged in a fortnight, it concentrates his mind wonderfully.' The PPB system, however, in more complex situations such as science, breaks down by reason of the general error of its assumption that the outcome of experiments is predictable.

IV COMMENTARY

The efforts of scientists to articulate bases for federal support of science have not gone very far towards providing a usable framework for decision-making. Too much of what scientists have said comes down to special pleading for university-based research or for special disciplines. It is evident that the scientific community has not yet faced up to the problem of priority in the allocation of funds for science. It is apparently still in a state of wishful thinking for the good old days of about 1950-68 when competing claims were handled by increasing funds sufficiently to satisfy all claimants at once.

In their political attitudes scientists should not be lumped together as a group. D.K. Price suggests that mathematicians and physicists have tended to be the most radical, chemists rather conservative, and doctors the most conservative of all:

Physicists have been more convinced than other scientists that their science possesses the key to the riddle of the universe, and they see no reason why, by bold and speculative thinking, the practical problems of politics could not be solved overnight. The chemists are much more accustomed to teamwork with engineers and administrators in relatively stable industries; they are more aware that abstract sciences do not always lead directly to practical application. And the doctors, of course, are trained every hour of their experience to see how hard and slow a job it is to apply the results of science to the affairs of human beings.[16]

If there is a general academic view of science policy, it has been that we should ensure excellence in basic science, from which applied science and development would inevitably flow. Political difficulties of supporting this view have arisen because it has not been possible to discern the appearance of the desired results within an acceptable time span. Consequently the attention of planners in leading countries has shifted towards an examination of the linkages in the whole research and development cycle, and the way in which the national effort should be divided up among them. This question has become more pressing as science costs have increased.

The core of the academic view is the assumption of uniqueness for scientific research. Because science at its best is highly creative, everyone practising science is assumed to be creative, and hence entitled to very special treatment by society. This doctrine of merit by association is not accepted by planners nor by leaders of industry. To them scientists are people of considerable variability in their aptitude, competence, training, and capacity for effective work. In the government-industry sector, J.K. Galbraith's remarks sum up a good deal of policy: 'Scientists are not without prestige in our day, but to be really useful we still assume that they should be under the direction of a production man.'[17]

Misunderstandings often arise from failure to identify the part of R & D one is talking about; thus university people when they talk about science generally mean basic research (however defined). When government planners are at work, they are more likely to be thinking about the D end, as the following comment by the Science Council illustrates:

A study conducted in the U.S. indicated that only 1.2 per cent of the population who possessed an intelligence score of 130, considered average for a PH D, actually got a doctorate. These figures indicate that we are not making the best use of available talent.[18]

What kind of scientific activity does the council envisage for this 98.8 per cent who are to be saved? Surely these are not the people for whom freedom is sought to pursue their own way. On the contrary, this is the group whose research will modify the fenders for the new model cars, ascertain what variety of tomatoes will do best in Prince Edward Island, or clock the incidence of an epidemic. They are the dentists of science, filling the cavities that appear in our knowledge; among our most useful and revered citizens, but not likely to be asked by society to work outside a plan.

Most of this book is devoted to an examination of two questions: How do we decide what policy to follow, and how do we get our decisions transferred into action? Let us first expand on the latter point.

For the past half century it has been the policy of the federal government in its own laboratories to harness science into the economic system. Currently the policy is seen to be extending to industry and the universities. Proposals in this direction are likely to involve a blend of force and persuasion, and introduce the great political dilemma of our times, which is much easier stated than resolved. It is quite easy to preserve individual rights and tolerate minority views, so long as we limit ourselves to reforms which make no challenge to established power structures. It is also quite straightforward, if not easy, to carry through reforms while dispensing with freedom and confining the determination of goals and methods to a few omnipotent men. The problem is to combine freedom with change; the dilemma presents itself when freedom permits resistance, which may frustrate the achievement.

In Canadian science the application of force is quite difficult, since the universities and industries are independent, education is provincial, and planning and financing are federal. Outside of some extraordinary condition such as war, there is no real possibility that Canadians would accept a fundamental and rapid shake-up such as might be possible in, say, China, or in a large u.s. business firm. Changes are more likely to be accomplished gradually, through a modest application of financial force, applied through the manipulation of support patterns.

Returning to the first necessity, which is to reach a decision about what to do, we encounter the idea of prediction; what will happen if a certain policy is adopted? Prediction is, of course, an ultimate test of scientific truth, whether in astronomy, genetics, or tomorrow's weather. Where prediction is imprecise the subject is unsatisfactory. This is the present status of science policy, in which experiments fail to show results quickly – if at all.

If the scientists have not faced up to their problem, the same is true of the planners led by the Treasury Board. These people have decided that the solution is to administer science as imitation business. This raises the danger that scientists may respond by embarking on a con game, in which their superior ingenuity and facility with the use of numbers would neuter the accountants. If you ask a recent science 'graduate' of the PPB course for his opinion, you are likely to hear 'Of course it's a bunch of crap, but all you have to do is ... ' Fortunately, so far, the university indoctrination that science candidates receive about the virtue of experimental truth has limited their predatory instincts. But the situation is unstable since no scientist likes to occupy indefinitely the position of court fool to the Treasury Board.

2
Government science and the national critics

People who work at science usually deplore suggestions that their activities have a national flavour. The scientific worker, with an objective outlook in his own field and able to meet those in other countries on common ground, is inclined to pride himself that he has established an international framework which can serve as a model for all other fields of endeavour. Every effort is made, for example, to make Russian periodicals widely known in Canada, and if possible to have them translated into English. The spirit of science may be contrasted with proposals that would prevent American magazines or TV programs from entering this country on the ground that they would compromise the ideals of our national culture.

But even with full allowance for idealism and the world aims of science, one could hardly believe that the political, historical, and social forces of a country could fail to show their influence. In Canadian public affairs, there have been three great phases; exploration, colonialism and self-government. These have been paralleled in science by a phase of description and inventory-taking, the development of technology and fundamental research, and the era of national planning. Science, however, has marched along historically a quarter of a century in the rear of political developments.

It is instructive to contrast the problems of government in newly independent African states with the advent of Canadian political and scientific

nationhood. To Canada our fathers brought with them the heritage of European political traditions and political maturity. There was no period of disorder in which primitive tribesmen were struggling to learn the rudiments
of the rule of law. This country was furnished, from the old land, with a
do-it-yourself kit including a Speaker's Chair and a mace. In the Congo,
by contrast, when freedom was achieved, there were only about a dozen
university graduates in the country. The national capacity in law and government would approximately coincide with that of early Canada in science. Nor does the parallel end there. Even in the old countries, science
in those early days was mainly the pursuit of the amateur with private
means. We would not have welcomed such gentry into Canada. We would
have preferred, as the Congo does today, so-called practical men who
could teach us practical skills. The egg-head has no place in a developing
country.

The problem of our new country was to recruit professionals and to
decide in which direction their work should go. Inevitably the first thing
to do in a new country is to evaluate the natural resources. In the nature
of the Canadian terrain this meant the development of geology, and there
was, in fact, an early flowering of this science.

The description of geological resources and the identification of animals
and plants is the scientific equivalent of the voyages of early explorers up
the rivers in their canoes. Like exploration it will never be finished, and
like exploration it tapers off. Today the main directions of the geological
drive are under the oceans and into the Arctic. The enhancement of interest
in the ocean is due to defence needs for improved submarine detection, to
commercial possibilities such as the search for oil, and to pressure on our
fisheries by foreign competitors. The opening up of the Arctic is also a by-
product of defence. After the War, under the threat of manned bombers
from Russia, the DEW line was set up with concomitant communications
and services. The cost would have been considered prohibitive except for
military purposes, but once it was going the incorporation of civilian enterprises was quite economical.

In the second phase of science, that of technology, the white-coated
laboratory worker came, like the red-coated soldier, bringing civilization.
What we still needed is what new African States like the Congo need today:
practical men in medicine, agriculture, fisheries, and engineering to show
us how to do what more advanced countries were doing. Eventually, of
course, any country expects to raise its own white-coats. I would date the
flowering of Canadian technology from the time of the First World War,
at the beginning of which we were a scientific colony of England. By the

end of it we were ready to embark on technology, and at that time there was a general development of laboratories – for example, the establishment of Fisheries Technological Stations at Halifax and Prince Rupert.

The object of technology is to find out what principles have been discovered and apply them to the local situation. It is presumed that principles are discovered by foreigners. Technology may yield great rewards, especially when it is possible to copy products from outside and place them on world markets at prices that ruin the original designers. It is very difficult to convince the public that there is any occasion for national science to progress beyond the level of technology. Surely, they say, the clever thing is to let the foreigners put in the tedious, unrewarding work while we wait to skim off the profits.

It is impossible, however, to maintain a good technological laboratory or a good university without the encouragement of curiosity among members of the staff. Whether we like to admit it or not, we could no more escape scientific maturity than we could escape political maturity. In contrast to the Congolese, we Canadians have been reluctant, because of strong reasons of sentiment, to face the implications of maturity, in both the political and scientific fields. The questions asked about Canadian university science after the Second World War were in essence the same as those which confronted proposals to assume political maturity after the First World War. Where could we find diplomats to equal the smoothly efficient British type? Was it worth the cost of setting up embassies? How could we ever manage to think out a Canadian foreign policy?

One of the effects of the 1939-45 wartime expansion of Canadian scientific work was the increase of pure science in government laboratories. Another was the introduction of technological activity into universities, where it is today often found easier to secure money for applied than for fundamental researches. Incidentally, this trend towards technology has changed the character of the universities as much on the arts side as in science. One thinks, for example, of Business Administration, Library Science, and Education.

Phase three, which we have now entered, stresses national policy rather than the management of science for itself. The problem of water resources, for example, takes in the whole of the science spectrum as well as economic and sociological considerations. Acceptance of phase three raises the question whether a national science policy can be developed effectively in the absence of equally coherent policies for economics, education, and social development. Science, it seems, has become too pervasive to be left to scientists.

TABLE 1

Distribution of current R & D expenditures by type and performer (percentages)

	Fundamental research	Applied research	Development	Total
Industry	2	12	30	44
Government	7	23	6	36
Universities, including 1% by non-profit institutes	14	5	1	20
Total	23	40	37	100

SOURCE: OECD report, table 7, which used data supplied by the Department of Industry.
NOTE: Based on figures for 1965, when the total expenditure was $0.7 billion; by 1969 it had reached $1 billion including capital. The distributions do not include capital costs, but these would not be expected to make much difference since capital is usually charged to its appropriate use.

As to performers of science, table 1 shows that most Canadian fundamental research is done in universities, most applied research in government laboratories, and most development in industry. The distributions are extremely subjective and can be shifted quite widely according to the prevailing climate.* The technical staff in business organizations may, for example, have to keep proving to the bosses that all efforts are related to application; yet the largest firms may then want to show a prestige fraction as fundamental research. In government, a department such as Agriculture may discover that life is easier for its minister in Parliament if the practical applications of its research are stressed. And in the universities the purity of scholarship has always been a status symbol. Current pressures tend to encourage all segments to stress applicability and relevance.

It has already been noted that the phases of dominant science expenditure are related to the maturity of the country, and follow something like this sequence – exploration, technology, government science, university research, and industrial development. For this reason it can be quite misleading to compare expenditure ratios in Canada, Congo, or the USA, in any particular year. To do so is as meaningless as to equate the relative limb

* As a Canadian example, private industry is stated to have performed, in 1958-9, 29 per cent of federal government supported research. The following year the 'private' part dropped to 15 per cent because the Arrow project was cancelled as a result of a federal government decision.

TABLE 2

Total federal government expenditures on scientific activities by performer

	1963-4	1964-5	1965-6	1966-7	1967-8	1968-9	1969-70	1970-1	1971-2	1972-3
	%	%	%	%	%	%	%	%	%	%
Intramural (current and capital)	74	72	68	66	66	62	60	59	60	61
Industry	17	17	19	19	16	18	18	21	19	20
Universities and non-profit institutions	8	10	12	14	17	19	20	18	19	17
Other Canadian and foreign performers	1	1	1	1	1	1	2	2	2	2
Dollar total in millions	301	337	410	465	543	622	656	728	800	881
Percentage increase from previous year		12	22	14	17	15	6	11	10	10

SOURCE: Green Book

or head sizes of a baby with those of an adult. There is in both a gradual change in the distributions as the system matures.

In Canada science has been influenced, along with everything else, by the financial restraints of the late sixties. It has been federal policy to hold back intramural expenditures, especially in construction. The results are evident in table 2 which shows the pattern of spending in the last ten years. The amount spent in government research establishments dropped from about three-quarters of the total to less than two-thirds. The avowed policy of stimulating industry seems to have borne little fruit. The universities show a steady increase as performers of research.

Ottawa's total science bill for 1972-3 is $881 million, up 10 per cent from the previous year. In earlier years the annual increases were larger, amounting to 22 per cent between 1964-5 and 1965-6.

II STATUS AND FUNDING OF FEDERAL LABORATORIES

Even before the end of the nineteenth century, several departments of the federal government had established national laboratories especially in relation to the exploitation of natural resources. Some of these, for agriculture, fisheries, and mining resources, have become large and scientifically advanced institutions. The size of the country, its low density of population, and the small proportion of secondary industry made it inevitable that the central government should play a major role in Canadian science.

Much government science is in areas of national interest which are not amenable to cost-benefit calculations, do not lead to economic growth in any direct sense, and are not of interest to the business community. Nevertheless if not adequately attended to they could choke off the whole economy. Examples are environmental pollution, transportation aids (water, land, and air), resource conservation (forests, wildlife), military science, and medical services. What research should be done in these social problem areas, and on what scale, are questions particularly difficult to settle.

Government agencies are supposed to be mission oriented and their general attitude towards planning is summed up in a brief by EM & R.[1]

To the proposal that scientific research should be directed towards economic returns, the traditional reply of the scientist has been that the results of research are unpredictable, and therefore criteria other than those of the scientist himself will destroy the creative process.

These statements have validity at the frontier of knowledge. But applied R & D,

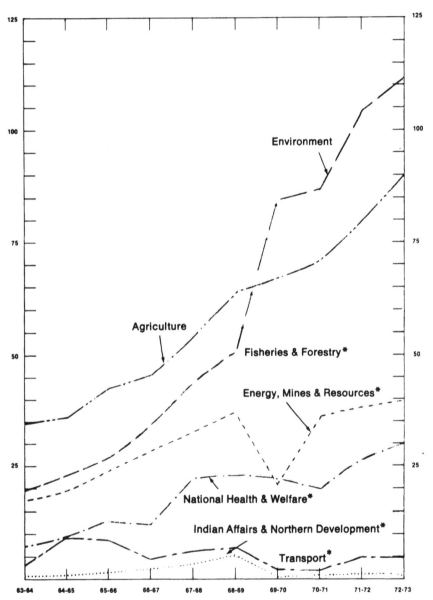

Figure 1 Total federal costs of R & D by department or agency, 1963-4 to 1972-3 (millions of dollars)

* Certain programs from these departments have been transferred to Environment.

SOURCE: Green Book

by its nature, is directed towards some criterion other than mere curiosity; the scientist in accepting an applied project, accepts at the same time the constraints placed by his employer on his activities, his scientific freedom consisting of freedom as to *how* he works, and freedom to report his findings regardless of preconceived ideas.

An important complicating factor is the individual scientific brain which happens to be available at a given time. To take advantage of the particular strengths and skills of a first class scientist, departments make adjustments in programs and priorities; failure to support him could result in the loss of important competence to Canada.

During recent years the federal intramural expenditures have risen steadily. In 1963-4 their science total was $227 million; in 1972-3 it was $641 million. There has been a marked change in the use of the money, as figures 1 and 2 show. We see military science declining steadily from the top place. Atomic energy enjoyed a rise to top position and suffered a more recent fall. The NRC has now begun to fall relatively while the environment emerges as the big winner. There will be occasion to say more about federal science in a later chapter.

Mention here may be made of a federal agency likely to grow in importance. This is the International Development Research Centre, which was set up in May 1970, and began work a few months later. Its chief sponsors and originators were Lester Pearson and Maurice Strong, who thought Canada should establish a centre that would attract scholars from over the world who would help to solve major problems of developing nations.

From the standpoint of science policy the venture is significant as a symbol of the shift away from the traditional promotion of Big Science by scientists. We have here a project whose inception rests on social and political considerations. Its origins contrast, for example, with those of the ING proposal discussed below.

It is recognized in the IDRC that the problems of countries with a glut of unskilled manpower cannot be solved by the introduction of modern, labour-saving machinery. What is sought is rather a kind of intermediate technology which raises the productivity of labour with minimum capital and without putting people out of work. Project grants to develop such technology are made to Canadian universities and in developing countries.

The plight of the rural populations in the developing countries is a more serious version of conditions found in the Atlantic provinces and eastern Quebec. Think of the Newfoundland fisherman in his dory suffering unemployment because of the introduction of modern trawlers. He becomes underemployed or unemployed, loses hope, and often drifts to the cities

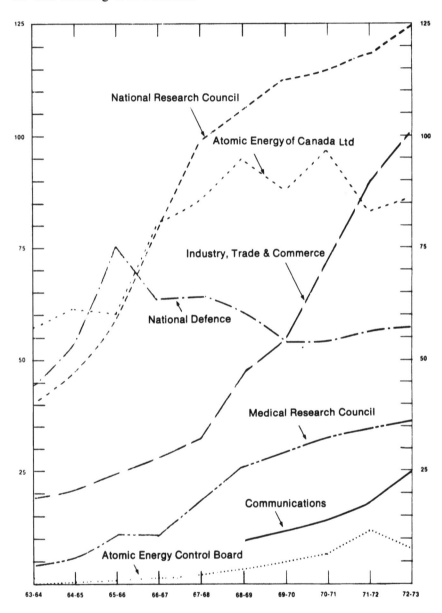

Figure 2 Total federal costs of R & D by department or agency, 1963-4 to 1972-3 (millions of dollars) (continued)

SOURCE: Green Book

where there is no work for him. Thus in a sense the IDRC might be considered an international version of DREE.

The IDRC expenditure for 1971-2 was about $5.5 million, of which $2 million went for management, including work of staff with non-centre agencies over the world, and for seminars. The remaining $3.5 million was assigned to the program areas of the centre as follows: agriculture, food and nutrition, 44 per cent; information, 2 per cent; population and health, 23 per cent; social sciences and human resources, 31 per cent. Clearly the program of IDRC extends over both the natural and social sciences.

The various federal agencies exhibit status differences which (like those of the old Halifax families) are not adequately appreciated outside the locale. It is almost impossible for anyone who has not worked in Ottawa to realize the immense importance which is attached there to the rating of each agency – whether it is certified to report *through* a minister (NRC, AECL) or *to* a minister (FRB, DRB), or, within the public service, to a deputy minister (EM & R, Agriculture).* There is nothing like it in universities nor, as far as I know, in business. There may be a parallel distinction in the army between the staff function and the line function, and the Roman Catholic church has had historic struggles as to whether monastic orders were authorized to report to bishops or directly to the pope.

The Right Hon. C.D. Howe shared the low opinion of the old Civil Service Commission and its doctrinaire methods of appointment, promotion, and management. Reform of the whole system, however, was beyond even his powers and was not yet in sight (it began eventually with Glassco). So when he had anything important to start, like Air Canada, Polymer Corporation, or AECL, he set it up as an independent agency outside the civil service. Some science activities were already independent and to these Howe added the NRC's post-war offspring, the DRB.

Traditionally the so-called exempt agencies, which were outside the Public Service Commission, have had advantages of flexibility and better salaries. Also their technicians and scientists were advanced on the merit plan rather than on the job-rating plan. Here, for instance, is Yves Pratte speaking of the 1970 reorganization of Air Canada:

---

* In a late 1972 restructuring of Environment, the FRB lost its independent status and was brought into line authority, reporting to the new assistant deputy minister for marine and fisheries. This will not immediately affect the work of the laboratories but the Honorary Board becomes a dead duck. While it is unlikely that a minority government would face the fuss of attempting to repeal the FRB Act, the transaction does offer a forecast about what is in store for other boards and councils. The government simply cannot contemplate the control of policy and funds by any but its own employees.

We don't have to run like the civil service. Ability, not seniority, should be the reason for promotion. I want to see the best people getting ahead.

In the civil service, the system is to evaluate a job and say 'This janitor of a small building is worth so much and the only way he can get more is to become janitor of a larger building.' The system was more or less workable for scientists in the Ottawa district, where there was a large concentration and transfers were possible, but it was quite difficult with dispersed laboratories where a scientist, in order to get a pay increase, might have to move from one coast to the other. Now the differences are disappearing. Since Glassco the public service has begun to enter the age of enlightenment, and in 1968 introduced conditions of employment for research scientists that compared quite favourably with those of the boards. In addition the advent of collective bargaining has made it difficult in practice for a board to institute any personnel policy which diverges from that of the public service generally. As the scientific and technical competence of the line-authority agencies has been climbing, they are losing their traditional antagonism to the Public Service Commission.

Chairman: Do you think your research operation could be better organized, more flexible, and more efficient, if it were to operate outside the authority of the Public Service Commission?
James C. Woodward, head of research for Agriculture: If you had asked me this question a few years ago, I would have said 'Yes.' We would have more flexibility and it would be easier to keep salaries relevant. But now that we have the research scientist class which is based on the merit system, and the tools to keep salary scales modern, I think we will be able to accommodate them very well under the Public Service Commission.[2]

It is also noteworthy that the deputy ministers, formerly largely 'practical' men, are becoming a Treasury Board-selected managerial class who, as 'decision makers' are not expected to make policy on research programs. It used to be said that while the minister was political, the DM really knew something about the work of the department. Now the knowledge requirement has been moved down to the lower classes.

Line authority is in origin a military development which, no doubt, has practical value in determining quickly who is to take command when the colonel falls in battle. As a civilian exercise the system retains classical purity in the public service. It derives from the deputy ministers, of whom C.P. Snow has observed:

Administrators are by temperament active men. Their tendency, strengthened by the nature of the job, is to live in the short term, to become masters of the short term solution. They do not relish the complexity of brute reality, and they will hare after a simple concept whenever one shows its head.[3]

The effect of line authority on a research agency is to substitute development work for research. Gradually the research content becomes reduced, the scientific reputation sags, recruitment is impeded, and eventually a new man has to be summoned to restore the old quality. Here, for example, is a statement by Agriculture about some of its units:

The pressure of service work and extension activities seriously interferes with research, which tends to be a start-stop operation not conducive to output. Fundamental studies are often put aside indefinitely although they are likely to have greater impact on the economy. Glassco commented that in the Economics Branch, with the largest economics organization in the government, the pressure of *ad hoc* projects is so great that virtually no economic research is done.[4]

In the mid thirties, Agriculture underwent a reorganization designed to separate the scientists from the 'practical' men on its farms and to provide a climate that would attract good specialists. A separate unit called Science Services was set up to be independent of the farms. A quarter of a century later, in 1959, the parts were put together again as a Research Branch in the hope that team-work could go forward while still maintaining the quality of the research arm.

I have cited Agriculture not because it is unique, but because it is important and illustrates the tendency of line authority to cleverly slip sawdust into the oats of the research donkey until the animal is becoming moribund and drastic recuperative measures are needed.

The 'exempt' agencies have the opposite tendency, namely to drift away from their missions into pure science, which they euphemistically call prerequisite science. The charge against them is not bad research but lack of total relevance. For instance, the fishing industry attempted in the years immediately after the First World War to get the then Biological Board abolished because it was too academic. The result was that industry members were put in to augment the professors on the board, and product research was initiated. Another hard attack along the same lines came in the thirties when the name was changed to Fisheries Research Board. Skirmishing continues till now.

In practice the boards have not functioned in immediate or emergency decisions because of the tendency of each minister to use the chairman as a staff assistant and the permanent employees as consultants – a procedure that can make board members feel that they are being by-passed. Probably the best balance for management of government research is a board with enough academics to keep the science from getting rotten and enough vocal industry members to question continually the retention of the mission for which the agency exists.

As working conditions for scientists in the departments have improved and the 'exempt' agencies have come under increasing scrutiny, the differences between them, as noted, have tended to disappear. Despite residual suspicions of the civil service mentality, the current policy trend is to bring all science agencies under central control. The FRB became part of the public service in 1970 and other independents seem likely to follow. Crown corporations like AECL are a legal step further from assimilation.

Galbraith, describing a modern corporation, observed:

Power is passed from the owners to the managers, scientists and technicians. And they now exercise full and autonomous power and, not surprisingly, they exercise it in their own interests. Growth is more important to the managers than maximum earnings, because those in charge do not get the profits. But they – the scientists and technicians – do get the promotions, enlarged opportunities, higher salaries and prestige which go with the growth of the firm.[5]

The belief in growth as synonymous with progress has been fully taken over by government laboratories and has often led them to focus on areas where the departments have the greatest role rather than where the social needs are greatest. It also relates to their historical lack of enthusiasm for developing university or industrial research.

The SC and its Macdonald report have recommended that the government transfer some or most of its R & D to the universities. This proposal was motivated more by the financial plight of the universities than by any thought of improving government research. Indeed one of the key criticisms levelled at government agencies, that they have difficulty keeping Pegasus hitched to the plough, has greater validity for the universities. It is extremely doubtful whether faculty members would accept the government system of annual progress scrutiny leading to changes and cancellations of programs. The illusion of freedom from planning is one of the attractions of university life. Others appear in evidence given by research leaders from Agriculture.

Senator Allister Grosart: Is the university environment really more attractive to scientifically-minded people than mission-oriented projects?

James C. Woodward: Our officers have had more attractive offers from universities; we may provide a distinguished scientist with one technician, but he knows that if he goes to a university he will have three, four or five graduate students pushing him.

Dr Bert Migicovsky: We have to increase the activities at universities so that they will produce the type of people that our research requires. The universities are not as well-fitted to do the kind of research that we do in-house.

Chairman: Why do they move then?

Migicovsky: Each man has his own reasons. He might not like living in Lethbridge or Swift Current, and when the opportunity arrives for him to move to wherever the university is, his wife says: 'This is much better. You will be known as a professor and you will live a better life'.

Grosart: Maybe you should start having your own titles and degrees.[6]

III THE NATIONAL RESEARCH COUNCIL

The National Research Council was set up in 1916, modelled on developments of the time in England. At that period Canada already had reasonable facilities to serve the primary industries of agriculture, mining, fishing, forestry; the need was mainly to provide for those secondary and manufacturing industries that had begun to emerge.

Its Act gave the council general responsibilities which governments over the years have gradually made inoperative. The Act was based on the principle that there should be two types of government scientific effort, one serving the general needs of the country and the other the departmental development programs. The broad non-departmental areas of science were to be assigned to the NRC. The principle was nullified by government action in accepting items in departmental budgets that led to the building up of general scientific strength.

This tidy proposal for R & D, with the R to go to the NRC and the D and near-D to the departments, must have looked rather naive even in 1916. Whether in government or industry, it has proved impossible in practice to recruit a competent scientific team who are willing to restrict their activities to development work.

Section 13 of its Act provides that the NRC should promote scientific and industrial research and 'without restricting the generality of the foregoing' goes on to list what its founders had in mind: natural resources; technical processes; industrial waste; standards of measurement, of instruments, and of materials; agriculture. It was intended that the council should have general oversight of science policy in Canada. Owing to strong rivalries it never attained any control of the policies of other government agencies, such as Agriculture. Its own functions have been gradually reduced by giving away bits of science to other agencies, notably atomic energy and medicine. Thus the NRC has been tending towards the restricted area of engineering and industrial research, and in this way coming to resemble other government agencies.

The NRC Act contains no mention of any program of university support. The council was originally supposed to undertake and co-ordinate research, but there were so few trained people in the country that it was soon decided as well to provide training for research. NRC began offering scholarships in 1917 and soon added research grants to professors. The council also made a decision of basic importance; unless the scholarships were made tenable only in Canadian universities, the students would go abroad, there would be little development here, and Canada would remain a colony as far as science was concerned.

Senator Allister Grosart: Would it be fair to say that the NRC saw this gap and persuaded the government to have the NRC fill it?
Senator Norman A.M. MacKenzie: The NRC is supporting research, not supporting universities and not filling a gap. It has found the most efficient vehicle to do it for certain purposes is the university. If you want the NRC to create other research institutions for the work, this can be done at a cost to the taxpayer.
Grosart: Senator, I am only asking questions.
MacKenzie: But they are loaded questions.[7]

When created, the NRC was given control of its own budget, and reported to the minister who was chairman of a cabinet committee on scientific and industrial research (at that time the Minister of Trade and Commerce). The struggle between the council system and line authority began at once: 'Mr F.C.T. O'Hara, Deputy Minister of Trade and Commerce, never really understood the legal freedom that had been given to the new organization. His need for power made him seek to dominate the NRC, which he regarded as a portion of his Department.'[8]

The first row was about furnishings for the new NRC offices, and dozens of others followed.

From the government departments engaged in science the new council at first received a friendly reception. It was calling attention to low salary scales and making objective suggestions. However, the friendly attitude disappeared suddenly in 1919 with a draft of a bill to set up NRC laboratories which, it seemed, would be rivals of the departments. Later the government declared its intent 'to gradually coordinate research work of government departments under one controlling organization.' Although the coordination was widely supported by parliamentarians of both parties, it was rigidly opposed by the deputy ministers and never did come about. The ecumenical movement runs into the same human obstacles in science as it does elsewhere.

The NRC's action in 1920 in starting an Associate Committee on Industrial Hygiene evoked this letter from the deputy minister of public health (quoted *in toto*): 'You are not so smart as you think you are.'

Gradually the council came to the policy of avoiding any sort of work that could conceivably fall within the range of interest of a government department.

In 1928, money was voted to begin the new laboratories at Ottawa. Dr H.M. Tory determined to make himself their director as well as president of the council and was able to overcome the objections of other council members, who desired a double-jointed institution. Their reasoning foreshadowed criticisms offered many years later by the Glassco Commission.

Hume Cronyn was a business man, and he said it was foreign to business ways for the chairman of the board to be also president of the company. J.C. McLennan was professor of physics at the University of Toronto, one of Canada's top-line researchers and a formidable man disposed to animosity. He feared that trouble would arise from groups of technical civil servants. The new laboratories would be one more institution among equals, but more equal than the others because of its advisory council. The NRC and its president should be above all that. A.B. Macallum, professor of biochemistry at the University of Toronto, became the first head of the NRC, holding the post until 1921 and remaining on the council thereafter. A man of strong views, he was the sparkplug who fired up the first NRC-sponsored researches in the universities.* His opposition was based on a belief that Tory simply was not competent to direct the laboratories.

In the end, the council, by accepting Tory's power drive, laid up for itself one of the troubles that were to assail it in the sixties.

In another confrontation, which had an ironic sequel, the council forced Tory to pay increased attention in his planning to long term fundamental science. Tory had a fine sense of timing in public relations:

---

* Macallum was also addicted to Shavian prose and is credited by Thistle with a 1919 aphorism often attributed to Churchill: 'Engineers should be on tap, not on top.'

We remain the only country in the world which does not provide laboratories for the standardization of its own materials. If this state of affairs is allowed to continue we will find ourselves a nation of peasants and traders while the wealth of our natural resources goes to swell the coffers of people having greater initiative.[9]

He tended to favour short-term practical problems that would make a noise, and he made science look like a head-on race for utility. The other members of council would not stand for this solid-usefulness sales pitch; they felt strongly enough to instruct Tory to make definite and unmistakable provision for some pure research in the new laboratories. The irony is that this pure research component, which came to be rather flaunted, also fell under the eye of Glassco. The council, in a public relations gesture a few years after the Glassco report, quietly dropped its divisions of pure physics and pure chemistry.

At the present time the council has two major activities, university grants and scholarships and intramural research programs, and two minor activities, industrial research assistance and promotion and its information service (table 3). The first three of these operate under non-transferable parliamentary votes, so that there is separate political and financial decision making in each area. The council declares that its most important role today is to promote a consolidation of research in the university, industry, and government sectors and to forge stronger links between them. The OECD report commented:

The system of co-ordination which has developed around the NRC stems from the pragmatic approach so typical of the Canadian mentality. It is based on the principle of temporary free association and the rejection of rigid coercive institutionalization. Like so many other organizations in Canada, it is a mixture of personal contacts and the community spirit. The system consists of a series of standing committees, national committees, and associate committees.[10]

The program of university support has been designed to bring research in the graduate schools up to a level comparable with that in the council's own laboratories. As the effort has succeeded, the university people have felt increasingly confident and independent of their patron. The development might be compared with that of the British Empire, in which the Mother Country, after generations of endeavour to make the colonies self-governing and independent, was a little shocked to discover that its efforts had been successful.

The general principle governing the distribution of NRC awards is that

TABLE 3

Distribution of expenditures by the NRC in
the late sixties

	%
University support, including grants, 43%, and scholarships, 8%	51
NRC laboratories	40
Industry support	5
Information service	4
Dollar total in millions, 1967–8	104

SOURCE: NRC brief in Sen. com. proc. 68–9, 3
NOTE: The total was $143 million in 1972–3.

applicants are judged on their merits as scientists. This principle of quality as a standard for awards has been tempered, however, with the object of getting research started in newer universities, departments, or fields of science. No attempt has been made to evaluate university research projects according to the contribution they might make to national targets. The council decides how its funds shall be divided up among the various branches of science; then the applications are judged by a number of grant-selection committees whose members are university scientists.

When the NRC laboratories were opened in 1932, Tory predicted that their work should be 'paralleled by definite research developed within the industries themselves.' As it turned out, Canadian industrial R & D was paralyzed by the great depression and did not get started until the War. Its development since the War has been in specialized directions, and federal stimulation has been largely through agencies other than the NRC.

By 1963, the year of the Glassco report, the NRC was, in its own laboratories, mainly engaged in technology. Radio, electrical, and mechanical engineering, together with building research and the national aeronautical establishment, made up 57 per cent of the budget (table 4). Fractions of the other activities might bring the total of applied research to three quarters of the whole.

Biology has been poorly represented in the NRC, partly because the resource area has been occupied by other government agencies; partly because the NRC was expected primarily to forward industrial development; and partly because Tory had a low opinion of biology except when it was tarted up to look like physics.[11]

TABLE 4

Distribution of NRC costs to
operate its own laboratories,
1963–4 (percentages)

Engineering and technology	57
Physics, applied and pure	17
Chemistry, applied and pure	13
Biosciences	6
Prairie regional laboratory	4
Atlantic regional laboratory	3

SOURCE: NRC brief in Sen. com.
proc. 68–9, 3
NOTE: The total in 1963–4 was
about $19 million.

Another notable feature of table 4 is the weak development of NRC activity outside Ottawa. Both the regional laboratories owe their origin to pressures from outside the council, which never developed a policy of decentralization. There is a Prairie Regional Laboratory at Saskatoon and an Atlantic Regional Laboratory at Halifax. Neither has ever functioned regionally in the sense that people were bringing local problems to it. The PRL was set up to find a use for agricultural waste, but soon moved into the area of general plant biochemistry. The ARL was officially described by the NRC to the Senate Committee as 'a free enterprise system whereby the scientists develop their own projects.' It also has been strongly oriented towards basic research in biochemistry and physical chemistry. During the last few years its program has come under increased scrutiny in an effort to find a mission.

In the operation of its own laboratories the council has been able to minimize the congenital disease of government research – bureaucracy – and other government science organizations have benefited from having the NRC operating in their midst. Gradually the departmental agencies have organized their internal affairs to give their scientists a working environment which has approached that of the NRC.

From the beginning the Civil Service Commission has attempted, more or less continually, to tidy up the council by removing from it the power to do its own hiring and firing. The government has several times agreed to transfer the NRC to the civil service, but on each occasion, when the council has objected, has rescinded the order.

By 1963, the merit of the NRC was recognized throughout the world of science. To sum up some of its accomplishments, it had:
- developed in its own laboratories such applied science divisions as Building Research, the Aeronautical Establishment, and Transportation,
- conducted fundamental and applied research in selected areas of chemistry, physics, and biology,
- got university research started in such new fields as dentistry, oceanography, psychology, and radio-astronomy,
- initiated programs leading to the creation of such mission-oriented agencies as AECL, DRB, and MRC,
- set up one of the series of government programs to stimulate applied research in industry (for non-defence areas),
- represented Canada in international science as the counterpart of the Soviet Academy of Science, the Royal Society of London, etc.,
- sponsored the spread of PH D programs in universities across the country and initiated postdoctoral training in Canada.

With all its accomplishments and with its national and international reputation, it came to the council as a shock that the Glassco Commission should offer as its key recommendation the transfer to other agencies of the functions assigned to the NRC for planning science and advising the government. It was as though some commission looking into improved law enforcement should recommend as a first step to diminish the RCMP. To take over the force's international functions and communicate with the FBI and Scotland Yard, a new group would be recruited, chaired by a prominent cop from, say, Vancouver. Another council would take over planning the strategy against crime; they would be nationally representative, including the Chiefs of Police of a few cities, a smattering of law professors and business leaders, somebody from Brink's, and from Ottawa the heads of the Army Provost Corps and the CNR Police.

What was the climate, what were the causes that led men to conclude that the NRC was inadequate? Why was it thought easier to start all over again than to ask the council to re-read and act on its Act? The reasoning on this question, of the Glassco and other national reports, is reserved for succeeding sections.

IV   DR E. W. R. STEACIE

Dr Edgar William Richard Steacie, FRS, was the man on whom the postwar reconstruction of the NRC chiefly rested, and who gave it its contemporary character. He was a first-class scientist and a first-class administrator, with a personality at the same time forceful and attractive. He was always sympathetic to research workers and outspokenly critical of the administrative obstacles of bureaucracy. These qualities and the clarity of his thought and speech earned him a high regard from everyone. At his death in 1962 he was the accepted leader of Canadian science.[12]

Had Steacie lived he would undoubtedly have responded to changes as they came. His death, however, disabled the council and it remained frozen In His Steps for half a dozen critical years. By the time it began to adapt, the environment itself was in rapid transformation. Since then it has taken all the running the council could do to keep in the same place.

Steacie described himself as one of the guinea pigs in the development of graduate education in Canada. The usual thing for good students in his time was to get out of the country, but he took his PH D at McGill, supported in his final year by one of the early NRC studentships.

After teaching for a few years at McGill, he joined the NRC as director of the division of chemistry in 1939. He had expected to build up chemistry, but as it turned out all activities were concentrated on the War effort. In the latter part of the War he was deputy director (to Cockcroft) of the Atomic Energy Project which later became AECL.

When the War was over, Steacie returned to his plan to build up chemistry. About half the enlarged division worked on applied problems, while the other half enjoyed officially recognized freedom to follow purely academic research. The scope of his influence increased when he became vice-president in 1950 and president in 1952.

Steacie observed that in a government laboratory, with its fixed establishment, it is difficult to maintain the lively atmosphere that a university enjoys by reason of the continuous flow of students. To overcome the drawback, he started the NRC postdoctorate fellowship scheme, which was later adopted by other government laboratories and extended to university departments active in research. These developments moved the educational system a notch upward as postdoctoral education became a recognized part of the process.

To Steacie science was a scholarly pursuit and the scientist a creative individual. He could accept no image that did not leave to the scientist his independent initiative. From this belief came his aversion to all attempts to plan or co-ordinate science, his objection to professionalism, and his abhorrence of secrecy. Informal mechanisms like the scientific meeting and the expert committee were as far as he would allow the NRC to go in organizing Canadian science.

He gave precedence to university research because he believed that in the long run this was the best way for the NRC to fulfil its responsibilities to industry. He could not conceive of an effective industrial research complex in the absence of graduate schools which would ensure the proper scientific climate and technical outlook. He had grave doubts about whether speed-up procedures would be effective in the transfer of research activity from universities to industry.

It does not appear to have been part of Steacie's view that appropriately designed cost incentives might work as effectively to stimulate industrial research, as they had for, say, medical research. This was the experiment which others initiated in the sixties, the results of which are not yet evident. His failure to introduce industrial incentives is the base of the Lamontagne criticism of Steacie:

Very few people even today would question Dr Steacie's views if he had been in charge of a laboratory engaged only in fundamental research. But he also had responsibility for an industrial laboratory complex and for advising the Privy Council committee on the whole spectrum of mission-oriented R & D, both as NRC president and as chairman of the Advisory Panel for Scientific Policy.[13]

Of the three leading presidents of the NRC, Tory was born with an instinct for public relations which impelled him to stress the practicality of the NRC and its works; C.J. Mackenzie, through the pressures of war, achieved a very special kind of practicality; and Steacie, an academic chemist who inherited the great postwar laboratory complex, had practicality thrust upon him.

The policies which he held to be essential for the operation of the NRC and the welfare of national science, can be deduced from the following few extracts from his speeches.

It is important to support people, not projects. If a man is good enough to be supported, surely he is good enough to decide what to work on.

The important thing is to realize that we have now grown up sufficiently that we must recognize second-rate work as second-rate and give up the idea that such work may be 'good by Canadian standards.'

There is no reason why an engineering student should ever have seen a plant or a mine before he graduates. 'Practical' knowledge can be acquired on the job and is certainly not a proper part of a university education.

Financial pressure has caused universities to accept 'sponsored' projects with a technological motive. This often leads to lack of freedom for the worker. No matter how fundamental, there is still an element of ulterior motive which is regrettable.

An efficient organization is one in which the accounting department knows the exact cost of every useless administrative procedure which they themselves have initiated.[14]

These views are emphatically academic, of the 'Here I stand' type. They are not unique, being indeed the opinions of professors of science generally. What is surprising is that in these days, when the emphasis is all on co-ordination and priorities, a scientist expressing such views so forthrightly should be permitted to determine, for a decade, the science policy of his own country. To the leaders of science he was a man 'whose singular praise it is, to have done the best things in ye worst times, when all thinges Sacred were throughout ye nation, either demolisht or profaned.'[15]

V THE GLASSCO ROYAL COMMISSION AND
THE MACKENZIE REPORT

In 1960 the Diefenbaker government set up a Royal Commission on Government Organization under J. Grant Glassco, which reported to the Pearson government in 1963. Its recommendations began to be put into force gradually and, in the Trudeau era, more rapidly. The commission was required, in general terms, to propose measures destined to increase efficiency and economy in all departments. As to the casual directness of the C.D. Howe era, the findings were severe:

The existence of suitable machinery for informing and assiting the Prime Minister and Cabinet with respect to major scientific policy decisions is of paramount importance. Such arrangements as exist on paper today are, because of their narrow compass, less than adequate. But the real concern is that in fact they have been virtually inoperative and the whole postwar expansion of government scientific activity has proceeded on a piecemeal basis without adequate coordination. There has been no effective mobilization of advice and counsel from outside the public service, and responsibility for the expansion of various activities has been borne by individual ministers without any evidence of their relation to national policy as a whole.[16]

In the federal sphere, the ultimate authority for policy on science, as on all other matters, resides in the cabinet. There was a cabinet committee to deal with science policy, with an advisory panel of science agency heads, but, as Glassco noted, both were inactive. Glassco might have identified the root of the trouble as the lack of interest of successive governments in seeking scientific advice, notwithstanding the fact that the mechanism existed through which advice could be obtained. The commission, however, preferred to make the NRC the scapegoat for our national defects in planning. The NRC, they said, had concentrated its attention on the university grants program in which the members had a high personal interest, to the neglect of broad national policy. It was also suggested that the impartiality of the NRC on national issues was compromised by the operation of its own laboratories, in competition with other government and university research agencies. The council had also been unsuccessful in its role as a promotor of industrial research.

One of the original purposes of government in devoting money to research was to encourage and stimulate Canadian industry. From being a primary goal this has, over the years, been relegated to being little more than a minor distraction. At present there is a wide-spread feeling that fundamental research is the only activity adequately recognized within the National Research Council.[17]

Following their conclusion that 'in practice the system has failed to function as intended,' the Glassco commission envisaged a new institutional framework with the following general division of functions:
- A minister responsible for science, an issue on which the government hedged.
- A permanent Science Secretariat under the immediate authority of the president of the Treasury Board, having a director with the rank of deputy minister, and provided with a small staff.* The ss was to advise the government on immediate problems and implementation of decisions. It came into being in 1964.
- A Science Council, to offer advice to the government on national science policy. It was to outline publicly its views on major programs and technological contributions to economic and social needs. Presumably the new council was somehow to escape the weakness noted by Glassco in the old regime, that the decision makers 'had not been entirely disinterested' because they were concerned with implementing their own decisions. The SC was set up in 1966. It now reports to the minister of state for science and technology.
- The NRC continuing to act as a co-ordinator and performer of R & D.

* I am following the titles which ultimately came to be used. Glassco and Mackenzie used different terms for the ss and sc.

On the Glassco recommendations, the Senate report comments: 'Although the commission did not mention its source of inspiration, its plan was remarkably similar to the French model.' Glassco would have given the sc more power than it ultimately received; he wished it to be called upon each year to review all government programs and report its views to the Treasury Board.

Glassco noted that government laboratories have a tendency to drift away from their missions towards more broadly based research in the same general field. The commission recommended the periodic review by advisory groups of all federal programs, whether intramural or contracted out to universities or other bodies. Despite a good deal of discussion since, the problem persists. Where does one find in Canada the critics who are technically expert, independent, and dedicated enough to make an adverse judgement on the work of a colleague? There is also the practical consideration that veterans who are carrying on with obsolete programs are often not adaptable to change.

Glassco had many further recommendations dealing with individual agencies. They were aimed at improved organization, from which it was assumed would flow improved science. The assumption is reasonable as applied to surveys, engineering applications, exploration, and development, but it does not lead to discoveries. If the commissioners had carried their reasoning to first principles they would probably have said that fundamental discovery was a second order correction on the corpus of government R & D, and need not be considered in deriving a first approximation to policy. Leave it to the universities.

Dr Gerhard Herzberg has commented on the Glassco philosophy:

The Glassco Commission was really not interested in good science. It was interested in good accounting. There is, of course, nothing wrong with good accounting, except that it does not necessarily lead to good science. The Glassco Commission considered the NRC in the same way as the Post Office or the Justice Department. Of course, these are important government departments, but their way of working is quite different from that of a research organization. What the Glassco Commission should have done was to enquire what particular organizational features were the reason for the high international standing of the National Research Council and how this standing could be further improved. Instead, the Commission recommended reorganization aimed at making the set-up tidier and more amenable to accounting.*

* G. Herzberg, 'The dangers of science policy,' Convocation address, York University, 7 November 1969. Herzberg might have added that the application of Glassco precepts to the Post Office has also been baneful.

Upon receipt of the Glassco report, Prime Minister Pearson asked Dr C.J. Mackenzie for an opinion on it. Mackenzie at seventy-five was a father figure in Canadian science. At the beginning of the War he had succeeded to the presidency of the NRC and had led the great expansion of the war years. As a former engineering student of C.D. Howe, and later his confidant, he was the nation's leading wartime science adviser. After the War he launched AECL as its first president.

When the Mackenzie report appeared, Mr Pearson was in charge of a minority government and his ministers were preoccupied with problems of survival. Had Mackenzie failed to endorse the Glassco recommendations the government could hardly have acted to set up the SS and SC. Thus the Mackenzie report enjoyed, in its moment, great leverage.

Mackenzie endorsed Glassco's proposal for a Science Council and Secretariat. He thought the NRC Act should be amended to 'bring it into conformity with the realities of 1964' but he would not, as Glassco had suggested, abolish the cabinet committee and its subsidiary panel of science agency heads.[18]

Mackenzie's proposals were a compromise which weakened both the future and existing science policy machinery. With one hand he pulled the teeth out of Glassco's Science Council, which was reduced to advisory status and was not to 'interfere with the normal channel of communication and recommendations to the Cabinet and Treasury Board.' In this way the 'rights and privileges' of the science agencies would remain intact. With the other hand he effectively removed the NRC from its central position. His proposal according to the Senate report was for 'science-policy machinery closely resembling the American model and much less influential than that envisaged by the Glassco Commission.'

The scientist-philosophers of earlier times used a simple classification for living creatures, which were known as either animals or vermin. Nearly all of us since have had a more or less submerged inclination to divide science in the same way. For Mackenzie the animals were his own promotions, the NRC and its offspring, the AECL, MRC, and DRB. These were to be the agencies with reserved seats on the SC. They had, in their own laboratory programs,* the common primary purpose of providing engineering back-up for civilian or military industry.

It is surprising that Mackenzie, with all his experience, should not have foreseen that his endorsation of a Science Council would initiate the removal of the NRC from its commanding position in Canadian science. His attention, however, was focused on the historical distinction which he evi-

---

* Except for the MRC which existed solely to make university grants.

dently thought would persist. On one side was the NRC 'serving the general needs of the country' and in contrast 'the other, serving the special responsibilities of departments.' In so far as these latter were doing research of a general character they were 'a deviation from the Haldane concept' and 'anomalies which cannot easily be changed.'

Mackenzie proposed some 'suggested types of studies' for the SS and SC which included:

- the supply, demand and disposition of scientific manpower which, in its top echelons, is likely to be the ultimate limiting factor in our scientific effort,
- total support for R & D and its balance between the sectors – university, industry, federal, provincial,
- priorities for federal laboratories,
- relation of civil to military policy and the expansion of civilian research.

The force necessary to translate studies of this kind into action would only be available to the federal government under wartime conditions. In war the aim is simple: give us the tools and we will finish the job. The wartime expansion of science, with which Mackenzie was familiar, had been one of personal relationships and quick decisions. This, as he recalled, was what made it possible in just a few minutes to take such a capital decision as to begin nuclear co-operation with the UK:

In response to a question by a journalist, 'Was it difficult getting the go-ahead from the Government?' Dr Mackenzie said: 'It was surprisingly easy. In those days the NRC reported to C.D. Howe. C.D. was a particular friend of mine. We all went to C.D.'s office and discussed the idea with him. I remember he sat there and listened to the whole thing, then he turned to me and said: "What do you think?" I told him I thought it was a sound idea, then he nodded a couple of times and said: "Okay, let's go." '[19]

Further unforeseen bugs in the proposed new machinery included the initial take-over of council functions by the secretariat; the domination of the council by its government representatives; and its inability to arrange science aims in any order of priority. We return to these later.[20]

As to the university response, concern of the academic community with the Glassco proposals was small. Professors generally were not interested; if they thought about the science of science at all it was to conclude that enlightened planning would result in doubling or trebling everybody's grants. The administration, and in particular the deans of the graduate faculties, regarded the NRC system of personal grants as conferring independence on individuals at the expense of the system. To them planning meant getting some money for disposal by deans. Everybody agreed that the research funds available for university use were insufficient and that planning would probably result in some improvement.

VI THE OECD REPORT

The Organization for Economic Cooperation and Development, of which Canada was a member, undertook as part of its overall program to conduct a survey of science policy in its member countries. Canada, through Mr C.M. Drury, who was *de facto* minister for science policy, requested that Canada be included, and arrangements were made by the Science Secretariat for the necessary tours of Canada.

The OECD report, which was published in 1969, contains an extensive array of information, and I have drawn freely on its tables. The background of some 350 pages was prepared by an international team which spent some months in Canada. Then there were two visits by three examiners, headed by Dr Alexander King, the OECD director general for scientific affairs, a former professor of chemistry. The other examiners were an economist from Japan and a French industrial scientist.

The examiners wrote a forty-page commentary on the background report and made suggestions about policy. Finally on 27 June 1969 there was a Confrontation Meeting in Paris at which Mr Drury and a half-dozen advisers from government science debated the issues with the examiners. Delegates from OECD countries were in attendance and several of them spoke. The account of this meeting occupies some twenty pages.

The report offers opinions on the work of many individual agencies. Some of the comments are cited in later chapters.

What is especially interesting in general, and new to academic scientists, was the disclosure of the underlying political philosophy of professional OECD planners. The examiners pointed out that during the Second World War Canada by a concerted national effort was able to marshal its substantial scientific capabilities and weld them into an effective force directed towards achieving the national goal of victory. We must today, they said, similarly incorporate our national goals into a broad plan of action that would utilize the creative ability of our scientists and engineers. This sounds very much like Mr David Lewis talking about poverty or inflation. Obviously there are difficulties in implementing such comprehensive political strategies in a democratic society, especially in times of peace.

In the paragraphs to follow, I shall identify briefly the means proposed by the OECD to attain its aims, as they apply to the various segments of science.

The report rejected a controlling ministry of science at the top as running contrary to world trends. It stressed the importance of large research programs, such as fisheries or agriculture, being as close as possible to their operating departments. A central science ministry would inhibit the free flow of science from research through to practice, and might make creative research more difficult.

The report did, however, recommend that a senior member of the cabinet be appointed as a minister for science policy, but without being in charge of any activity. This would be, like the chancellor of a university, a position of dignity without responsibility. At the confrontation meeting, Mr Drury pointed out in rebuttal that it was unlikely the prime minister would delegate just science policy but no other portfolio to a senior colleague. If the function were assigned to a junior member of the cabinet, it would be unlikely that his views would strongly influence departmental policies of more senior ministers.

As to industry, the examiners accepted the widely held thesis that economic growth is of primary importance and determines everything else. To secure growth, they said, we must give priority to scientific activities directly related to economic and scientific goals. The task of science policy must be to strengthen the technical potential of industry. 'The Canadian Government expects national scientific activities to contribute to the quantitative and qualitative progress of the economy.'

The report commented in some detail on the incentive plans for industry and how they might be improved. These are discussed in chapter 5.

Looking at government science the report questioned the validity of the historic distinction between university research (pure), government research (mission oriented), and industrial research (applied). It suggested that government should concentrate on the formulation of problems, relying on outside agencies of all types to solve them.

The Canadian consensus on this problem which had been developing among planners for a decade received official recognition in August 1972, when Mr Gillespie declared that it would be government policy to farm out government science jobs to industry wherever possible. It is recognized that the program of contracting out research will be strongly resisted by those public servants who fear the erosion of their power base, and that they may be able to defeat the cabinet plans. The credibility of the minister's announcement was reduced by his statement that the Ottawa scientific establishment will remain intact, and not be cut back as several investigatory commissions have recommended. Reporters also noted that the budget for 1972-3 gave the lion's share of increase to the in-house activities of the federal departments, especially the Green Giant Department of the Environment. This agency will have a budget of over $200 million, over 90 per cent of it intramural, with hardly anything for industry and only $3.4 million to universities.

In Britain the government was a little ahead of Mr Gillespie. A White Paper in July 1972 approved the recommendations of Lord Rothschild to apply the customer-contractor principle to all government applied research.[21] As Rothschild had put it, 'the customer says what he wants; the contractor does it (if he can) and the customer pays.' The government will also gradually transfer the funds now devoted to applied research by the Councils (Medical, Agricultural, etc.) to the departments concerned, which will contract them to industry.

Since control is to rest with the departments, no minister in control of science will be appointed.

In its remarks about the NRC the OECD report reflected the drift of contemporary thinking from the age of elegance to the age of practicality, from R to D, from analysis of the universe to cost-benefit analysis . Here are some sample observations:

The NRC has grown to such proportions that it may have become less conducive to innovation and initiative. The lack of formalism and the almost day-to-day pragmatism are no longer in keeping with the importance of an agency from which a tangible contribution to the future of the nation is expected. Canadian research is unduly dependent on federal departments and agencies whose generally benevolent sponsorship does not always pay sufficient attention to stringent economic requirements.

For its future, the NRC should: 1 / consider the separation of its grant-awarding activities from the management of its own national laboratories, 2 / shed its basic research activities which should be turned over to the universities [as already noted the NRC had deleted the word 'pure' from its terminology even before the report appeared], 3 / expand its scope to take charge of the new, largely multi-disciplinary activities of the seventies, either in its own laboratories or preferably through other institutions.

In their remarks on universities the examiners noted that Canadian higher education, like that of other countries, has not yet managed to take full account of current trends. The most recent structures still follow conventional models. It will be necessary for the graduate schools to make the distinction between culture and skill in order to avoid a flow of PHD candidates to branches where there is no demand by society. Efforts at interdisciplinary study still exist largely on paper.

The review advocated a uniform grants system for university research, taking in the functions of the NRC, MRC, and Canada Council. The system of grants should have the object of orienting the fundamental research programs in our universities towards the problems from whose solution Canada can obtain direct economic and social advantages. Only universities that show themselves responsive to national science policies should receive major federal support.

In their reception of the report scientists were more resigned than enthusiastic. As Professor Harry E. Gunning wrote:

The proposals will strike many research scientists as a recipe for creating a bureaucratic monster in Ottawa – the Canadian equivalent of the Great Leap Forward. Scientists in general will not take kindly to the authoritarian philosophy underlying the examiners' recommendations. However, the mature research scientists among us will realize that the examiners have rightly sensed the trend of the times.[22]

A couple of years later, when he had seen the Senate report (see next section) the OECD effort began to look considerably better to Professor Gunning. Compared to Lamontagne

The OECD examiners showed a deeper understanding of how our scientific potential can be committed toward the solution of our social and economic problems. The Senate report falls into all too many of the typical parochialisms that scientists associate with the great mass of scientifically illiterate politicians. As usual the void of ignorance is filled with prejudice.[23]

With this introduction we pass on to consider the works of Senator Lamontagne.

VII   THE LAMONTAGNE COMMITTEE

The committee chaired by Senator Maurice Lamontagne had twenty-two members, while retirements and replacements brought the total who served up to twenty-six. The quorum of eight was usually the maximum attendance. Although in each session the honour of being the opening questioner was rotated, most of the members were, in truth, sleepers. The most effective was Allister Grosart, a rough-tongued, witty ex-advertising man and a Conservative. He did not exhibit complete public docility to the

Lamontagne line. If he had any effect on the report, as distinct from the hearings, it is not evident. The vice-chairman, Donald Cameron, took little part in the public hearings. Norman (Larry) Mackenzie, an ex-university president, played his life-long role of professional hayseed. His questions were often excuses to reminisce about his past experiences.

The chairman, Senator Lamontagne, was in complete dominance. He was once a professor at Laval and some of his fellow Senate committee members report that in the private sessions he tended to smother them with his professional mantle, pointing out that they as laymen could hardly be expected to understand the mental operations of a university economist. My own impression of Lamontagne at the hearings was of a witty, cultured, urbane, civilized man. Consequently the report, when it appeared, was a disappointment. Judy LaMarsh observed that Lamontagne was ineffectual often, and added, 'of him economists said he was a good politician and politicians that he was a good economist.'[24]

The committee began by hearing the views of some wise men from Canada and abroad who were concerned with policy in natural science. These were followed by federal agencies supported by extensive briefs prepared according to Senate guidelines. Next came the provincial, professional, learned society, industrial, and university representatives. Finally the committee visited the u.s. and seven European countries.

All the dialogue heard by the Senate committee, together with the supporting briefs, make up ten thousand pages of proceedings which have been the largest single reference source for this book.

By the end of their second year of hearings, the Senators were beginning to equate science with all knowledge and they invited surprised professors in the humanities to appear. As Professor P.B. Waite of the Humanities Research Council remarked: 'I put the brief together in five days. The word science led me to think there was no reason to come before this Committee. It was only on Senator Lamontagne's express invitation that we are here.'

Once there the professors gave a strong account of the unity of all knowledge.

Professor K. Hare: Geography throws a bridge across the gaps between the natural and social sciences. It deals intellectually with problems strikingly like those confronting the legislator. It is closer to policy formation than any of the analytical disciplines.

Professor P.B. Waite: Professor Hare has geographically synthesized the natural and social sciences. I suggest that history synthesizes the social sciences and humanities.

Professor C.M. Wells: The study of Classics embraces the interests of all humanities and of many disciplines outside. It includes history, anthropology, architecture, philosophy, art and archaeology. The brief of the Classical Association contains eight main requests, all of them for more money.

Professor Roy Wiles: I need not argue that English deserves attention. The brief of the Humanities Research Council is a kind of umbrella representing the various disciplines of which English is one.
Chairman: We may have too many umbrellas at the end.

Senator Allister Grosart: It is an unfortunate semantic fact that because of the prestige of the word science in getting money, everybody is saying 'We are a science.' Are the performing arts going to be in on it? They would like to be included in the term 'science' if that is the only way to get money.
Professor P.B. Waite: We would rather not call ourselves scientists.[25]

Chapter 16 of the report extends the universality theme still farther, dealing with trade and tariff policy, fiscal and monetary policy, foreign ownership, procurement policy, competition policy, standards policy, industrial relations and manpower policy, patent policy, and regional expansion policy. Indeed it is hardly an exaggeration to say that in the eyes of Senator Lamontagne science policy takes in every activity of the government except for the judiciary and French-English relations.

No doubt it is helpful for all of us to be reminded occasionally of the interdependence of national policies, but the value of seeking a master plan to deal with them all at once is rather dubious.

The committee's report is to be in three volumes, of which the first two have appeared as this is written. Half of volume 1 is taken up with a historical review of Canadian science and half with a review of the evidence from the proceedings. The essential framework round which the volume is built is the need to increase production and innovation in industry, which is to be secured by the control mechanisms proposed in volume 2. A third volume to which we may look forward is to cover 'social R & D and social innovations and is designed to enable Canadians to improve their welfare and the quality of their lives.'

The report is not the kind of document that scientists expect to see in a symposium or a review article, namely an attempt to present an objective account of the present state of knowledge and indicate future directions. Rather it is comparable to a prosecuting attorney's brief or to an attack by a member of Parliament on the opposing party. This would normally be followed by a rebuttal and eventually (in a court) by a judicial decision. But

Senator Lamontagne appears to be offended when scientists undertake to present their side of the case.

Lamontagne's principal target is government science in its engineering and industrial aspects, especially the NRC and AECL. The NRC, it seems, has been doing everything wrong since 1919, latterly led by its Pied Piper, E.W.R. Steacie. The favourite cliché in volume 1 is 'conventional wisdom' which pops up dozens and dozens of times. For instance in a four-page description of the policy of Steacie (one of Canada's most unconventional thinkers about science) the expression occurs three times. The term is, it would seem, intended to convey that the NRC and others lacked in their foresight the enhancement of vision enjoyed by the Lamontagne committee in hindsight.

The 'conventional wisdom' on which the NRC policies have foundered since 1919 and with which Lamontagne disagrees, is as follows:
– Canadian industry was not developed sufficiently to institute enough research of good quality to satisfy its needs,
– there were not enough scientists to investigate and solve industrial problems,
– fundamental research in strong universities was to be the seed-bed for industrial development, but the research programs of the universities were not to be oriented towards industrial applications.

Under the policy which derived from these premises, the NRC undertook to assist students to get advanced scientific training in Canadian universities. The graduates were largely employed in earlier years in the expanding government laboratories and latterly in the expanding universities.

Few scientists would agree that this was, in retrospect, a faulty base on which to build Canadian science. True, the English innovations of the early nineteenth century had come from 'practical' men outside the university system; but the more recent German dominance in drugs and optical and electrical apparatus had all arisen directly out of pure science.

Volume 1 portrays Canada led by the NRC and Steacie into an orgy of fundamental research. The truth is that all we have done is to bring this one aspect of our science up to a reasonable international standard. In the leading countries fundamental research expressed as a percentage of GNP is as follows: Netherlands, 0.49; USA, 0.42; UK, 0.29; Canada, 0.29; France, 0.28.[26] In total R & D, as a per cent of GNP, Canada is the second lowest of the ten leading countries.[27]

The Canadian policy of 1919 worked slowly, but by the late 1960s it was at length succeeding, with the production of sufficient PH DS to staff the expanding universities. The 1970 PH D surplus was the overshoot which usually marks the end of successful economic interventions; by that stage it is apparent to all that some changes are needed. It would, of course, have been better if the universities and the NRC had combined to introduce a gradual readjustment of the direction of graduate work, but foresight rarely is manifested in a successfully expanding enterprise. We return to the unversity problem in chapter 7.

According to the Senators, the faulty thinking of the early days, combined with our chestiness as a 'middle power,' led us into a series of postwar blunders.

– Like Britain and France we tried to force the challenge of fabulous technology and made costly mistakes. We should have built on a less glamorous and more realistic capability, as did Japan and West Germany.
– We should have suppressed our desire to be independent of other countries in developing industries for aircraft frames and engines and nuclear power. 'Other countries negotiate special arrangements with the United States.'
– We should have carried out our industrial R & D by contracts to private companies, where it would lead to innovation, rather than attempt it in government laboratories.
– We educated our scientists and technologists for an unreal world, especially in the PH D cycle. Academic support should have been designed to produce scientific technological skills (presumably analogous to hospital training in medicine). Fundamental science would be correspondingly depressed.

Volume 1 of the report contains this comment:

The new wisdom prescribes that the additional R & D effort be devoted to the life sciences and social sciences rather than the physical sciences, to engineering and development activities rather than scientific disciplines and fundamental research, to economic and social objectives rather than curiosity and discovery. Finally the new wisdom concludes that these proposed changes cannot be effected without a coherent overall science policy.[28]

The overall policy is expected to develop controls which, by the application of systems analysis, will readjust our R & D effort to increase market-oriented technical innovation. From there we will go on to define and solve our social problems.

The Lamontagne proposals carry their conviction by plausibility rather than by experience. Readers of the report are likely to assume that somewhere in the world a successful experiment has been carried out in the application of 'new wisdom.' This is not true.

The fact is that all leading Western nations have a strongly developed base of fundamental science. As to total R & D or any component of it, no significant relation can be found between this and the level of economic growth in the leading nations (see chapter 4). All we know of R & D internationally relates to input, i.e., costs, etc. There are almost no measurements of comparative national output of R & D.

Of nine leading nations whose science expenditures were compared by the Senate committee with those of Canada there were five in which the measurements of R & D as related to industrial growth did not fit the Senators' theoretical requirement that industrial performance be proportional to R & D. These were France, Japan, the Netherlands, Sweden, and Switzerland.[29]

British success in science planning is taken as the Lamontagne model, supported by lengthy quotations from speeches by the last Labour Minister of Technology. Here is a sample from a single two-and-a-half page quote from a speech by Anthony Wedgwood Benn.

Five years ago we decided that science could not be confined to a particular sector of our national life. We have developed new priorities. We have set it as a major objective of our policy – I am speaking of my Department – that science should be harnessed to the job of earning our living as a nation.

We have set up a Programmes Analysis Unit. In evaluating many projects we use calculations based on forward market analysis, as good, if not better, than those found in many firms and industries. Science seen as an arm of economic advance must be demand-oriented and not self-generated.

A positive policy must mean concentrating on where we can succeed and not in dissipating our efforts in the endless financing of work that is undertaken simply because it lies within the intellectual capacity of the scientific community.

It is the task of the Government, facing competition from other countries, to put a lot more effort into the exploitation side and not to think that research, however well organized, can solve our problems.[30]

Readers of the foregoing may be scratching their heads as they compare the oratory with the reality of Britain's export position, or think about the Concorde, the Rolls Royce collapse, and the absence of atomic power to alleviate the miners' strike.

A more sober historical account is given by Nigel Calder.[31] In 1959, according to Calder, the Labour Party, then out of office, produced a report, *Science and the Future of Britain,* which provoked the Conservative government into appointing a Minister for Science. When Labour came to power in 1964, the Ministry of Technology was set up but no provision was made for co-ordinating academic research and technology. The first minister, Frank Cousins, a trade union leader, resigned within two years over wages policy and from then on:

High hopes were thwarted and technological renewal seemed in retrospect an electoral gimmick. There was little evidence that the growth and implementation of science and technology was much faster or more effective than it would have been under the Conservatives.[32]

Volume 2 of Lamontagne appeared in February 1972. In volume 1 we had been led to expect that the second number would contain an extensive pattern for the reorganization of science. But the Senator, perhaps stung by his critics, had become more cautious. He now suggested that 'any important organizational changes be delayed until the specialized communities immediately concerned have had the opportunity to react.'[33]

Following a general introductory chapter, volume 2 attempted, as the Science Council and others had also done, to establish a system of priorities for national goals. One of the goals is cultural enrichment, and the report pointed out, correctly, that most scientists are too preoccupied with their own research to think about science itself. It urged, as do so many convocation speakers, that the relation of science to culture should be more widely stressed.

The priorities were not listed in an order of importance, with the first at the top. They are all to be followed. A second goal, thus, is to secure enough industrial innovation to make Canada prosperous, and linked to this is the maintenance of a balanced supply of manpower. This means in the near future a shift towards the training of more engineers and monitoring types of technical personnel, at the expense of the traditional products of our graduate schools. It has been noted by many people, but not apparently by the Senator, that manpower forecasts for even ten or fifteen years ahead are very dicey; for instance the advent of penicillin brought a sudden and totally unexpected demand for pharmacologists. And we seem at the moment to be on the verge of a huge assault on environmental problems, which was not evident even five years ago.

Other priorities included a national information network accompanied by an appraisal of the progress of technology and fundamental science. This latter perhaps looks easier to an economist than to a laboratory worker. Everyone deplores lapses like the forty-year gap that intervened between Mendel's discovery of the central principle of genetics and the realization of its significance by biologists, or the ten-year gap between the discovery of the principle of penicillin and its application. But would a committee of evaluators have spotted the possibilities at once?

Volume 2 continues with further detail on the framework for establishing targets for the seventies. There is to be a committee of the Economic Council to look into the prospects for 1985-2000 and a conference sponsored by the Senate to establish a Commission on the Future. The government is urged to adopt an overall plan for the seventies. This recommendation will be welcomed by scientists, who have found it disturbing to have their funds turned on and off like the tap. Scientists are very vulnerable because they are not numerous enough to be an appreciable political force. Thus when Mr Diefenbaker ran into hard times he turned science off. Mr Trudeau turned government science off with equal abruptness as soon as he was elected, pending 'restructuring ' by the Treasury Board.

The committee would also like to see a gradual increase in science expenditures from the recent level of 1.3 per cent of the GNP, to reach 2.5 per cent by 1980.

In the research sector we should maintain only enough workers to be able to recognize discoveries made elsewhere in the world, and our own efforts should be largely in application, especially to industry. As for graduate schools,

if, as is now widely claimed, a good teacher must have the opportunity to carry on his own research, in close association with his students, this is a reason to support academic R & D as an adjunct to teaching. This aspect of academic research should reflect the whole spectrum of the national R & D effort.

Here are a few examples from the recommendations about academic research:

Support for curiosity-oriented research should emphasize quality rather than quantity.

Research grants should be provided only to applicants who have demonstrated international quality standards, and to these should be more generous.

The new minister of science should re-appraise scholarship and fellowship schemes.

The order of priorities should be: first the social sciences and humanities; second the life sciences especially medical.

The main thrust of volume 2, comprising its second half, is towards increased industrial innovation and the strategy of getting more government support into R & D by secondary manufacturing industries. This is to be accompanied by relative restraint on academic and government science. The committee would like to see the R & D performed by industry increased from the recent level of 37 per cent to 60 per cent of the national effort. They would like to see industry take steps to improve its innovative capacity and would like to see the Ministry of Industry form a cabinet committee to consult with the provinces. An Office of Industrial Reorganization should also be formed. Numerous task forces to improve the performance of resource-based and primary manufacturing industries are also to be formed, as well as a national conference of all sectors.

In our industrial strategy we should not try to do big things, like hydrofoil ships, military aircraft, or atomic energy plants. What we want is more 'mini-inventions' which may be sold abroad. (It is of interest that the current 'mini-invention' which has almost single-handedly restored our favourable trade balance with the USA is the snowmobile, strictly a brainchild of one innovative business man.)

In the brave new world of planned science, some government laboratories will still be necessary where industries are composed of a large number of small firms, such as those attached to Agriculture, Fisheries, and the North. The rest should be pretty well wiped out.

Federal agencies now offer some $91 million annually to industry, and Canada has the most elaborate system of grants among all advanced countries. To make the system work better the committee advocates 're-structuring' the industrial grants into a single multipurpose program. The program should be broad but at the same time specific and it should include an efficient system for auditing the results of projects that have been supported.

It is difficult to escape the feeling that before an Ottawa committee has had time to get around to certifying that an industrial innovation is OK, the people directly concerned will have long since made up their minds about it. The real purpose of auditing is to prevent agencies from drifting away from their missions into pure science, as they undoubtedly have a tendency to do. The best way to accomplish this is to put a little dollar squeeze on the system, which forces a re-examination of priorities.

The committee recommended that a Canadian Innovation Bank be set up to provide venture capital to private industries.

In general, the Senate report had the same drift as those of Glassco and the OECD. Similar proposals advocating a shift towards increased technology at the expense of basic science have also been made in other countries (for example, the Rothschild pronouncements in the UK). The very small proportion of working scientists who read these reports have tended to see them as oversimplifications and infringements on academic freedom. The even smaller fraction of the educated public who read them have tended to be impressed with their plausibility.

In my own view there are three things basically wrong with the Lamontagne approach. The first might be called the Egyptian syndrome. If only we could destroy all that the Israelis have built up and reduce Palestine to a desert everyone would be equal and we could start to build a better world for the Arabs. Thus Lamontagne wants to destroy the NRC, the body that has nurtured and launched much of the government research and got the graduate programs going in our universities.* It is a fault of the Trudeau administration, which Lamontagne echoes, that in its 'restructuring' it never makes the initial quality enquiry: 'Is this agency doing good work or bad work?'

The whole report exhibits a belief in organization and re-organization as a basis for improving research and industrial innovation. Having destroyed the NRC, Lamontagne proposes 'to set up a Canadian research board ... to support basic research done in universities.'[34] For industry 'all existing fiscal grants should be integrated into a single, multi-purpose program to be administered by the Department of Industry, Trade and Commerce.'[35]

Lamontagne's second error lies in his implicit point of view that the crucially important part of science is applied research and development. Fundamental discovery is thought of as a side-order correction. Thus, while the Senator would allow a limited number of pure science people to be supported, he has not grasped the reason that Professor Roentgen, say, turned up, not in Brazil or Spain, but in Germany where there was a large pure science effort, most of it pedestrian. To change the example, Canadians are good at hockey because a lot of young people are interested. The Senator is looking for a way to find the Bobby Orrs without bothering with the neighbourhood rinks from which the stars emerge.

The Senator has more excuse for his second error than his first one, since he may simply be overreacting to a view commonly held by university faculty members. This is that research is always to be treated as a special,

---

* The intensity of the Senator's attack on the NRC invites the hypothesis that he must at some time have smarted under a remark by the outspoken Steacie. If so, the hurt was lasting enough to carry the vendetta beyond the grave.

highly imaginative profession whose practitioners should be supported by society to do work of their own choice. It will, in my view, be necessary to place research personnel, including those in universities, in two groups. One group will be judged on their originality and supported by some agency like the NRC. The other, larger group will be judged on their ability to cope with problems assigned by society, and will be supported by mission-oriented agencies. A good deal of our trouble with science policy has arisen from failure to accept this important distinction. As Bishop Blougram put it:

> All we have gained then by our unbelief
> Is a life of doubt diversified by faith,
> For one of faith diversified by doubt:
> We called the chess-board white – we call it black.

The third basic error in the Senate report lies in its arithmetic, to which attention has recently been drawn by the Science Council.

The targets proposed for industrial R & D expenditures are that these should account for some 60 per cent of a Gross Expenditure on R & D projected to be equal to 2.5 per cent of GNP by 1980. These would undoubtedly transgress a fundamental rule: no company should spend more on R & D – or, indeed, on any other innovative activity – than it is likely to find profitable. The targets, when coupled as they are with a proviso that the federal share of funding the activity will remain unchanged, are in any case totally unrealistic. They imply an additional annual R & D funding by industry of $2 billion by 1980. At a research intensity of 1.2 per cent of sales – the current level in R & D-performing companies in Canada – this presupposes a sales increase of $170 billion. At 4 per cent of sales – the US intensity – $50 billion additional sales are needed. Neither is likely: the whole of Canada's GNP in this period is forecast to increase by only $100 billion, and in 1970 sales of manufactured goods accounted for only about 25 per cent of GNP.[36]

VIII   RUSSIAN SCIENCE POLICY

Perhaps the most bizarre omission by Lamontagne, which he shares with most of his counterparts in other Western countries, is his failure to compare the proposed Canadian organization of science with existing practice in Russia, where his system has been under test for half a century, or in Czechoslovakia which has a quarter-century of experience with his methods. The deliberate fostering of advanced technology ever since the revolution has made the USSR the apotheosis of the 'new wisdom' and the pioneer country in the development of science policy. Arrangements whereby research and design organizations created technology and channelled it to the Soviet factories have been the heart of the system. Since the Russians were doing all the right things while we were doing all the wrong things, it is of interest that the Soviet difficulties today bear striking similarities to those of Canada, according to an OECD report.[37]

During the War, the Academy of Sciences engaged in military research and planning, and it expanded rapidly in the decade following the War. The prestige and good physical conditions in academy institutes have drawn the most talented scientists there while other sections, unless concerned with defence and space, have found it difficult to obtain high-quality staff.

'Branch of the economy' establishments, with their practical R & D activities, have tended to be regarded as of lower status than academy establishments and there is less public regard for applied science than for fundamental science.

Until the 1950s there was an overwhelming concentration of institutes and facilities in Moscow. Beginning in 1957, a number of establishments were transferred to regional authorities; they were, however, quite small, so that no substantial decentralization of administrative structure occurred. In the same period the academy was criticized for failing to maintain sufficiently close connections with industry, and many of its institutes doing applied R & D were transferred to the industries concerned.

The OECD report on Soviet science policy identified two factors responsible for the present poor application of research results. One was the fact that planning was originally production-oriented: thus innovation came to be regarded as competing with output.

The second factor, actually a group of factors, arose from faulty linkages within the system. Except in priority projects, the planning of the cycle from research to production has not been properly integrated. The research institutes of the academy have been organizationally separate from industrial R & D and have been given preference and priority. Industrial R & D is divided among several ministries, between which administrative barriers retard communication. Within each ministry the factories are administratively separated from the research and design bureaus. There are also strong barriers between military and civilian R & D.

The foregoing description closely parallels Canadian scientific history as outlined in our three major reports. Now if the human and organizational barriers between the phases of the research-production cycle can span the gulf between capitalism and communism, between planned and unplanned science, between 'conventional wisdom' and 'new wisdom,' they must be less superficial than the reports would indicate. They are in truth rooted in fundamental differences in the distribution of talents and outlook among people, which do not lend themselves easily to quick and clean solutions. We return to this topic in the discussion of universities; it is in the universities that opinions are moulded.

It is interesting to note that in Russia, after half a century of experimenting with science policy, the special status and autonomy of fundamental research is universally recognized. Officials concerned with planning concur that it is impossible to apply economic yardsticks in order to measure its value. No one has seriously questioned that the bulk of academy research must be financed without expectation of measurable economic return.

IX   SUMMARY

At the outset of this chapter it was noted that Canadian scientific development has followed a typical, indeed inevitable, pattern beginning with the identification of natural objects. Thus in 1609 Champlain published an exact description of a gar pike taken from Lake Champlain. This method for beginning science is one which we have recently seen repeated as the first men landed on the moon.

As Canada matured, new areas of scientific effort were started up, competing with and sometimes overwhelming the earlier ones. After the First World War there was a great flowering of federal laboratories, which came to dominate the scientific effort. It had been intended that the direct federal efforts of the thirties should include the stimulation of research in private industries, but the great depression, followed by the War, threw such plans out of phase. With the end of the Second World War, it was the universities which began to emerge as new centres of research.

Now, for the past decade there has been increasing pressure to seek means of enlarging the role of business in the national team. Recommendations to this end have formed one of the cornerstones of three reports dealing with our science policy. In promotion of this aim the government is urged to offer more support to industries, to allow the federal laboratories to decline by transfer of their activities to the private sector, and to restrict the effort under support in the universities. The universities are also to undergo a diversion of most of their natural and social science into areas related to secondary manufacturing. By all these treatments it is hoped to improve the linkages between the segments – universities, government, and industry.

A second cornerstone of the reports represents a trend of thought which is observed in many Western countries. This is to do for science what has been done for so many other activities, namely, to subsitute socialism for free enterprise (without using the word socialism). Socialism would stress national policy rather than the management of science for itself. It implies that science policy cannot be effectively developed without equally coherent policies in economics, education, and social development.

Most Canadians approve of socialism (provided it is described by a suitable euphemism) for every activity of the country except their own profession. Thus all but professors may be expected to approve of social control of university research. Outside of the academic world, there is not likely to be any widespread support for the maintenance of the free enterprise system in science. The concerned public is more likely to say that it should have been done twenty years ago.

3

The apportionment of policy control

It is a constitutional principle that the proceeds of taxation must be expended by those who are responsible to the representatives of the tax-payers. C.P. Snow said:

> We can draw diagrams which make us feel that everything can be reconciled with the principles of parliamentary government. But if we do, we shall not even begin to understand what is really happening. We shall fool ourselves with that particular brand of complacency which is one of the liabilities of the West.[1]

In addition to its national parties, Canada has a political force which has attracted some of the most ambitious and influential politicians. This is the party of management, system, expediency – government, as opposed to policies or ideology. The management group has obtained its great power because voters do not trust elected representatives to carry out complex operations. Similarly the stockholders of large corporations do not leave management to the owners who are perhaps the nephews or grandchildren of the founders. As Galbraith put it, if we are to have capitalism it must be without capitalist interference.* Similarly, the voters expect that public

---

* J.K. Galbraith, *The New Industrial State* (Houghton Mifflin, 1967). Galbraith notes that even the most patronage-ridden states leave the national airline to non-political management because the leaders have to travel on it.

corporations will not be allowed to suffer from intervention by ministers. Thus if we are to have socialism it must be without social control.

In a modern, large industrial corporation decisions are taken, not by any individual, but collectively by groups. In technical areas, governments have similarly tended to remove the decision-making function from control of parliament. Such publicly owned Canadian businesses as atomic energy, railways, steamships, air lines, and broadcasting, as well as film making and the research boards, are supposedly free from parliamentary control of policy. So is university support.

Parliament tends to restrict its intervention to small policy decisions where autonomy does not matter; questions centre about the morals of CBC programs and the closing of railway stations or village post offices. While I was writing an early draft of this section in February 1967, a broadcast announced that members were protesting in Parliament that the Board of Transport was allowing the Confederation Train to blow its whistle only once daily. They felt it should be allowed to reverberate its special 'O Canada' notes several times per day.

Within Parliament, there are recurrent expostulations over the surrender of management. In this the arts provide a safer whipping boy than science, since they are held to be understood by all and not essential to national survival. When it was announced in June 1966 that the new National Arts Centre would be run by a board of directors, independent of the government, the Hon. Gordon Churchill commented in the House that he hoped the directors 'would not attempt to stir up public interest by putting on performances calculated to make people think.'

Parliamentary committees are supposed to look at past performance and to make suggestions about better management. Since the government retains a majority in each, no committee can, in fact, override a minister, any more than Parliament itself can do so without bringing down the government. Through the standing committees, Parliament examines the civil servants in their new and increasing range of activities. No committee could, however, extract from a civil servant any indication that he had at some time or other expressed views different from those of his minister.

The powers of parliamentary committees to investigate are extremely limited. Unlike congressional committees, they have no counsel or research staff. When twenty-five politicians, few of whom have done their homework and all with their own axes to grind, try to ask questions at once, the result is bound to be discursive if not chaotic.

There have always been standing committees to examine the various departmental estimates. This was a pretty casual system in the Pearson era, and the money was usually spent before the estimates were approved. Since the Trudeau government took office, the committees have been much more prominent, and from this it is sometimes inferred that they have increased in importance. If so it is in the sense that the United Nations is important, i.e., for the publicity it can focus on a current issue. There is no evidence that the committees have been able to influence government policy in any major way.

The standing committees are portrayed in the press as bloodhounds of economy, sniffing out extravagance and waste. Actually the balance of effort is the other way; each member tends to be concerned with the interests of his own constituency and this makes for rather locally oriented questions to public servants. As an example, take half a dozen representative questions put by the Fisheries Committee to the FRB during consideration of the 1968-9 estimates:

MP: Are the present methods of harvesting Irish Moss on the Atlantic Coast detrimental to the industry?
Witness: It is possible to destroy the holdfast and kill the plant if care is not exercised.
MP: I want to ask about an experimental shrimp fishery that operates out of the Nanaimo biological station.
Witness: We have been exploring for new fishing grounds and studying the population dynamics of shrimps.
MP: Do you think that the large herring catches in the Bay of Fundy tend to reduce the numbers of other types of fish which feed on herring?
Witness: The evidence is rather the reverse. There is nothing to suggest that leaving the herring in the water would result in a greater catch of cod, etc.
MP: If female lobsters were not allowed to be caught, do you think this would help the population?
Witness: There appears to be no good relationship between the production of larval lobsters and the eventual production of adults.
MP: The oysters of New Brunswick were destroyed by a disease 10 years ago. Have you any progress report on how the new stock is taking in the area?
Witness: There was a small stock of disease-resistant oysters and from this a new disease-resistant group has been built up.
MP: What research has been conducted on the effects of logging right down to the banks of British Columbia salmon rivers and creeks?
Witness: It is well established that removal of trees causes an alternation of freshets and dry periods instead of a regularly flowing stream and that the removal of brush shelter is detrimental to the survival of young fish.[2]

The Senate special committee on science policy has been much more serious. In addition to developing a vast mass of evidence, it has put the science community on the defensive and caused it to re-examine its aims. To what extent its recommendations will be implemented remains to be seen. Its thrust, like that of almost every investigating agency today, is towards the suppression of fundamental research in favour of development.

In the theory of British parliamentary tradition the only active force in the process of government is the minister. This piece of mythology inhibits a clear view of what is actually going on in the administration. Here is an analysis of a minister's job by a former British Minister of Health.

The idea that members of a government extort by their weight and personal influence a larger or smaller share of national resources for their respective charges, is grotesquely unreal. The complex balance of pressures – electoral, social, practical – that determine the rate at which a branch of public expenditure grows are little accessible to individual sway.

Another popular fallacy is the expectation that a minister should either have a deep knowledge of the subject-matter of his department or at least remain there long enough to acquire it. A politician's job is politics, and his function is to handle the issues that are political in character, where the management of public opinion and the interpretation of actions and events in a political sense is involved. His skill or lack of it would be in evidence whether the subject-matter is pensions, or prisoners, or practitioners. He moves from one field to another as a barrister would put down one case and pick up another.

When a minister begins to think like his officials, he is losing the power to see the issues in a political light from the outside, which alone is what he is there for.[3]

A large government department is full of powerful men with initiatives, ideas, objectives of their own, and what a ministry does often expresses a consensus of these persons. Within the consensus a strong minister is, of course, a very important person, who will occasionally ignore his advisers and proceed as an inspired amateur in policy decisions. Also because he has to run an election every three or four years, it is imperative that he be continually presented to the public as a superman acting alone.

In theory the ultimate responsibility for policy rests with the cabinet. In fact, however, as disgruntled ex-ministers have recently been pointing out, decisions are made from within a group of about three associates of the prime minister and a small number of senior public servants. Cabinet members generally are kept informed.

Recommendations about science policy were for many years supposed to come from a standing committee of the Privy Council which included the ministers of science departments. This august body, as Glassco noted, met infrequently 'and between 1950 and 1958 was not called together at all.' More recently attempts were made to reactivate the committee, as appears from a debate in the House on 17 March 1969.

The presiding minister (Mr Drury): The Privy Council Committee on Scientific and Industrial Research met more often last summer than it had in the last year or so.
An honourable member: That would be three times.
Drury: Well, three times zero is infinity.

In May 1969, on the eve of the confrontation with the OECD examiners, the prime minister directed that this committee (PCCSIR) meet regularly once a week, and it was thought to be busily considering large science problems. Evidently, however, the small flicker of ministerial interest petered out again and the committee was abolished in October 1970. Shortly thereafter its chief science adviser resigned to return to university work.

There is a suggestion common among Western nations that general and especially cabinet interest could be enhanced by the establishment of a ministry of science which could bring together the various government development activities. When advocates of such a ministry define the functions of the office, it is evident that what they really envisage is a ministry of industrial technology. The minister is expected to lead scientists away from their romantic notions about exciting new discoveries, about excellence, and about the hope of possible 'spin-off' from pure science. The touch stone of research is to be its commercial purpose, and, through the new methods of analysis and forecasting, cross-checks on the cost-benefit and market potential of new discoveries would become available before the research was authorized.

In Canada the federal government has been proceeding slowly with the consolidation of science policy. During the Pearson administration, Mr Drury became the key minister in science matters, and with the Trudeau administration he became president of the Treasury Board as well. He was the chairman of the Committee of Science Ministers (PCCSIR), the Science Secretariat reported to him, and so did the NRC. In addition to his formal responsibilities he also became the minister to whom the Science Council reported, as indicated by the following exchange during the Senate committee hearings:

Chairman: When you want to deal with Cabinet to whom do you go? I know that officially and formally you go to the Prime Minister, but ...
Dr Omond Solandt, chairman, SC: We discuss problems with the President of the Treasury Board because he is the principal adviser to the Cabinet on scientific research.
Chairman: Your channel is through the President of the Treasury Board at the moment?
Solandt: Yes, on major discussions the Prime Minister has said, 'These are unresolved problems. Discuss them with Mr Drury.'[4]

Mr Drury's conflict of interest, in which financial considerations seemed always to outweigh scientific merit, has been a frightening aspect of Canadian science planning. Under the Drury regime, government scientists made the discovery that the only subject they were ever destined to discuss with their 'minister for science' was money.

During the 1970-1 session of Parliament the government moved to appoint a minister of state for science and technology. Although seven hours had been reserved for debate on the act, the Commons spent only ninety minutes discussing the new ministry. The appointee was Alastair Gillespie, who was elevated from the post of parliamentary secretary to Mr Drury.

In the post-election cabinet changes of late 1972, Mr Gillespie was succeeded in the Ministry for Science and Technology by Mrs Jeanne Sauvé. The new minister is well known as a radio and television broadcaster and as a writer on public affairs in both French and English.

II   THE SCIENCE SECRETARIAT AND THE SCIENCE COUNCIL

The Science Secretariat came into existence on 1 July 1964. It was supposed to 'assemble, digest, and analyze all information concerning the government's scientific and technological activities and their interrelation with university, private industrial, and provincial establishments.' When its first director, Professor Frank Forward, got the ss under steam with this program, the nation's scientific community began to wonder just what duties were supposed to be left for the future Science Council. Very few, it seemed.

More than two years later, in the autumn of 1966, the original membership of the council itself was named. After a further year and a half of trial marriage this is how the secretariat-council relations were developing, as seen by the Senators.

Dr Robert Weir, director, SS: The Science Council is composed of very busy, senior people who devote one or two days every couple of months to its meetings. So therefore the Secretariat has to develop much of the background for the Council to discuss.

Senator M. Wallace McCutcheon: What happens if the Council commissions you to make a study in a field where you have already been asked for advice by the Prime Minister? Does that condition your staff work?

Weir: In that case the Council would approve the consultants and we would do the administrative work for them.

Senator Allister Grosart: Is there a danger that the direction of your work for the Science Council might be influenced by your political responsibility to the Privy Council, so that a recommendation of the Science Council actually reflects the current political thinking of government?

Weir: It is a question that does concern us.

McCutcheon: There was only one fellow who looked both ways, and his name was Janus.

Grosart: And Lot also.

Chairman: You mean Lot's wife.[5]

Three months after this, in June 1968, the Trudeau government was elected with a clear majority and addressed itself to operation clean-up. In November 1968, the secretariat was formally separated from the council, which was provided with its own staff.

The Science Council is supposed to 'assess in a comprehensive manner Canada's scientific and technological resources, requirements and potentialities, and to make recommendations thereon,' to engage in 'long term planning for research and development,' and to advise on 'the responsibilities of departments and agencies of the Government of Canada in relation to those of universities, private companies and other organizations in furthering science and technology.'

The selection of members for the Science Council illustrates one of the entertaining fictions arising out of the BNA Act, namely, that members of boards or councils never represent any organization. If the SC happens, as it did when it started, to include the heads of the NRC, AECL, DRB, MRC, and several other government agencies, it is to be presumed that these gentlemen have been selected from the population at random for reasons of personal wisdom. C.J. Mackenzie recommended that the proposed SC contain a majority of outsiders but 'I feel equally as strongly that for the immediate future the presence of government scientists is essential.'

As originally set up, the sc had among its associate members the DM, Finance, and the secretary, Treasury Board. This practice, somewhat akin to having a couple of cats to watch the canary, has been discontinued.

The sc seems to be equilibrating with about equal numbers (eight to ten of each) of university, industry, and government members. Of the last-named group, those connected with research tend to be full members and those in administration or outside science tend to be associate members. There is no one from a provincial science establishment.

Even with its cautious approach to reporting, the sc has caused concern to its government members by saying things of which one or other of their ministers did not approve. It is obviously difficult for a government member to sign a report which goes contrary to the policies of his minister and his department.

In the u.s. there are no government members on the president's Science Advisory Committee. In England, the government people on such committees are called assessors; they attend meetings and participate in discussions but do not vote or sign reports. For Canada it may be expected that as the proportion of 'outside' science increases nationally, the government representatives will be phased out of the sc.

The chairman of the sc, Dr Omond Solandt, began his scientific career as a Toronto medical physiologist. In England, with the outbreak of War, he became interested in military applications of physiology and eventually the new field of operational research. When the DRB was created in 1947, he became its first chairman. Subsequently he has been vice-president, R & D, for the CNR and for de Havilland Aircraft of Canada. In 1966 he became chairman of the Science Council and vice-chairman of the Electric Reduction Co. of Canada. He resigned from the latter post early in 1971 because of conflict of interest (pollution).

Solandt's views are well recorded from his lengthy appearances as a witness before the Senate science committee, from sc reports, and from speeches. Here are half a dozen samples:

There is no longer any need to advance science. The need is rather to understand, guide and use science effectively for the welfare of mankind.

We must be careful that we do not spend all the money that we have for research on the early stages, which do not produce profits, and then have none left to complete the innovation, which is profitable.

The most unproductive government research is in applied R & D. A useful product or service is developed, and the project is then abandoned and industry berated for its lack of enterprise. We must starrt putting emphasis on profitable innovation rather than merely encouraging R & D expenditures.

We can only be pre-eminent in a few fields, which should be selected to avoid head-on collision with the United States of America, Russia or other major industrial nations. We should try to identify those fields in which our priorities are different from others and concentrate on these.

While there is need to enhance productivity in all parts of the economy, the problem is particularly acute in the service industries, especially where there are no market forces at play. The non-competitive service areas are led by the triumvirate, government, education and health services, and the greatest of these is government.

I have always felt that the Science Council should cover the social sciences as well as the natural sciences. When you look at problems like the development of our cities, you cannot hope to tackle these separately from the point of view of the natural and the social sciences.

In 1972, Dr Solandt resigned as Chairman of the Science Council. He was succeeded by Dr Roger Gaudry, who is also Rector of the University of Montreal. Dr Gaudry is expected to serve for one year after which the government is expected to make the position a full-time one.

In the early days the Science Secretariat initiated a series of disciplinary and sector studies intended, when completed, to be an encyclopaedia of the needs of Canadian science. The series was later taken over by the Science Council. Each of the so-called inventory reports was drawn up by specialists in the branch involved, and, predictably, put forward its claims. The physicists, practical and precise, recommended that 'the normal expenditure on physics research should rise at a rate of 23 per cent per annum.'* The psychologists took a loftier tone: 'Although among scien-

---

* While some of the slow disciplines, like biology, were still loading up to fire off their first study, the physicists, who in enlightened self interest led all the rest, had already produced their second directive on how to support physics. They had planned to enumerate priorities but found, as is usual, that it is impossible for any professional organization to agree that any of its branches should have second place priority. See G.C. Laurence, et al., 'Purpose and choice in the support of university research in physics,' *Physics in Canada*, vol. 27, (1971) no. 5. There is also a mimeo appraisal of the document by Vogt and others.

tists, psychologists have a higher than average educational level ...' In their general conclusion the reports all look alike, whether the field is water resources, a neutron generator, or a space program: despite limited resources the achievements have been outstanding, the promise is superb, and needs are expensive. The university department or faculty in the branch should receive substantial and sustained financial support. The theory of the preparators is that each field should put its best foot forward, leaving it to some hypothetical higher body to arrange the priority list among them.

The studies have been followed, or more usually preceded, by reports which offer the imprimatur of the sc.* The reports usually moderate the proposals in the studies; when examined in sequence, they reflect, by the increasing modesty of their recommendations, the relentless pressures of the slump.

The sc has found it comparatively easy to collect facts, but impossible to place recommendations about them in a priority list that the government can use. In this the council reflects a historic problem of our legal system, namely, to find mechanisms by which to focus independent judgment on problems in which there are strong vested interests. The creation of the sc represented an extension of this search to the field of science. But the Canadian scientific community is so small that qualified independent people are hard to come by. And non-scientists are often made diffident by the technical vocabulary.

The built-in difficulty which the sc faces in reaching definite conclusions arises from the care with which all shades of interest have been balanced among its members. In its failure to offer priorities it resembles the Economic Council of Canada. In both, goals were established without any view of the relative importance of each, and those things on which reports first came to hand – for example, space and water resources programs – were endorsed just because detailed proposals on them existed.

The behaviour patterns in the sc were described in the Senate hearings:

Chairman: Since most of the members of the council representing universities and industry are greatly dependent on government assistance to finance their research activities, does this incline them to constitute a lobby for the private sector, or does it frustrate them when they have to appraise and criticize government programs in the presence of public servants responsible for the allocation of grants?
Dr Omond Solandt: You have a gift for asking difficult questions. In general

* There are long delays in printing the studies, said to be due to slowness in obtaining French translations for simultaneous publication.

people from the universities find themselves in a very difficult position in dealing with government officials because they would like to be critical of what the government is doing but they recognize that most of their support comes from the same people.

Where everybody's interests are kept under close scrutiny, recommendations of the sc tend to be hedged so as not to disturb existing activities. An acceptable format used throughout report no. 4 is 1 / a general affirmation of the virtue of spending more money, with which all agree; 2 / a ringing declaration of a rather general principle, e.g., 'federal scientific organizations should have a particular responsibility for fostering the growth of the scientific community within the fields encompassed by their respective missions'; 3 / a carefully ambiguous proposal for action, e.g., 'the future of government laboratories devoted principally or entirely to fundamental research must be carefully considered.'*

The saving afterthought of part three calls to mind a little verse about certain gigantic dinosaurs that were stilted upon colossal pillar-like hind legs. They had, in consequence, an enlargement of the spinal cord over the hind legs that was larger than the brain itself, which inspired the late Bert L. Taylor, columnist of the *Chicago Tribune* to write:

> You will observe by these remains
> The creature had two sets of brains –
> One in his head (the usual place),
> The other at his spinal base ...
> No problem bothered him a bit.
> He made both head and tail of it ...
> And if in error he was caught
> He had a saving afterthought.

III   THE TREASURY BOARD

The term Treasury Board, like many similar expressions, refers both to the committee of cabinet ministers who compose it and to the group of public servants who operate it as a department of government. The board has

---

* The cautious writing continues till now. Here, for example is an extract from the executive director's foreword to special study no. 10 on Agriculture, which appeared in October 1970: 'The authors have produced a report whose conclusions might seem controversial to some.'

broad powers of supervision over all departments and agencies in the performance of their functions. Several years ago, the decision was made to
'restructure' the process of reviewing the estimates by the introduction of
a 'planning-programming-budgeting system,' the operation of which has
already been described.

The TB, originally a financial organization, has recently begun to recruit
its own scientific staff, and has also established liaison with the Science
Secretariat. This introduces close supervision of science at both the financial and the research level, and works in the direction of increasing the component of development, as opposed to research in scientific enterprises.

The importance as well as the size of the Treasury Board has greatly
increased in recent years. Always powerful, it is today the central command post of the government's internal operation, with responsibility over
the whole public service. Its heightened power and influence date from the
changes in government structure recommended by the Glassco report.
Since then its scope has been further increased by the introduction of collective bargaining.

With the unionization of public employees, the various scientific groups,
as well as others, are supposed to bargain about their wages and working
conditions; the 'employer' with whom they negotiate is the Treasury
Board. Government statements that no guidelines are imposed on its
negotiators present a strong credibility gap to the president of the Public
Service Alliance, C.A. Edwards. There are guidelines, he says, which stan-
dardize bargaining and make it impossible for groups that have lagged
behind to catch up. He goes on:

All of the agreements that have been negotiated by all unions in the public service
in the first round of bargaining, have adhered to a pattern of 7, 7 and 5 1/2 per cent
over a three-year period. We have always failed to break the barrier of 5 1/2 per
cent increase for the third year. Treasury Board negotiators have flatly told us that
regardless of evidence, anything above that level would have to be obtained through
strike action or arbitration.[6]

There is a small number of science agencies, like the NRC, outside the
public service. Examination of their settlements of wages and working conditions shows the same uniformity observed by Mr Edwards.

The exercise of power by the TB begins when all budgets have to be
negotiated with the board. These are in theory approved by the ministers;
in practice the cabinet provides an overall target within which individual
items are decided by the officials. Next, for all ordinary government

agencies in the public service the duties of every employee have been redefined since the Glassco report by a special branch of the TB, the Bureau of Classification Revision. Within the lists of duties and salary scales provided, appointments are made by the Public Service Commission. When the employees come to negotiate their wages and conditions of employment, the 'employer' is the TB. Finally, in case of disputes, the PSC provides the arbitration machinery.

Within the so-called 'exempt' boards and councils, whose employees are not under the PSC, the definition of each job is drawn up by the board or council, but then, with its salary scale, must be approved by the TB. Each council negotiates with its own employees, subject to TB guidelines, the existence of which is officially denied.

To the common reader the foregoing description would imply a rather detailed level of control. According to Mr Drury, however, the TB is moving in the opposite direction. The endeavour of the past few years, he says, has been to decentralize control of detail to the departments, and have the TB occupy itself with policy. It exercises its function in selecting priorities.

Management of the Treasury Board rests with its secretary, who is, by any reckoning, almost at the top of the Ottawa mandarin pecking order.* He has more impact on the daily lives of more than a quarter of a million federal civil servants than any other official, and he is necessarily under pressure from all departments as they push their needs and projects. The Treasury Board processes some twenty-five thousand submissions each year. The secretary frequently attends cabinet meetings as adviser, particularly on spending priorities. This puts him close to policy making and gives him the advantage of watching cabinet members in action.

One of the policy aims of the TB is the development of a managerial class of people who will carry its methods into all departments. Now people divide naturally between those who believe in line authority – the army, the church, the Treasury Board – and those who believe in community judgment and personal responsibility, including the universities and practising scientists generally. The ideological posture of the Treasury Board towards science is that of King Charles (or rather his adviser, Archbishop Laud), according to whom the 'right of private judgment' was an anarchistic principle, so that differences could be safely indulged only within the unity of a basic creed. The creed of systems analysis and PPB was examined in an earlier chapter.

* A mandarin is defined by the *Oxford English Dictionary* as a grotesque toy figure in Chinese costume that goes on nodding after it is shaken.

The most subtle exercise of power, which obviates the necessity of close control, is infiltration by reliable people – the creation of a ruling *élite*. Our most familiar example is the public school Englishman, whose numbers increased rapidly in the nineteenth century as the spread of public schools, following the Rugby of Dr Arnold, obliterated regional accents and gave a general upper-class speech to all.* These Englishmen, identifiable by the public school accent, became known the world over as the rulers of the British Empire.

With somewhat similar aims, the Public Service Commission is grooming future Canadian government managers to follow the general policies and precepts of the Treasury Board. They are not, of course, taken as schoolboys, and will come out with a uniformity of vocabulary rather than a uniformity of accent.† They are selected in groups from various agencies and given initial immersion courses of three months' duration. During May 1969, the press was invited to look in on one of these courses, which the folllowing extract describes. Similar reports appeared in all the newspapers.

Thirty-eight middle bracket civil servants are sweating and jogging through a Government Management Preparation Course here in a Smith's Falls hotel. The Public Service Commission has packed everything imaginable into a recently established twelve-week intensive course being offered three times a year as part of the career assignment program.

In their first week, the trainees are confronted with problems in logic and ethics posed by the Head of the Philosophy Department, Queen's University. The idea is to start them thinking about the prerequisites for decision making and about 'man as a decision maker, in part sub-rational but capable of learning.' After it had undergone this mental rinsing, the class moved on to the format for decision, the discipline process of analysing and reaching conclusions.

The course is structured to focus on the internal workings of the bureaucracy and the external factors and systems that affect it, and on modern management and

---

* Outside the Labour party the last important Englishman with a regional accent was Gladstone, who came from Liverpool.

† In his essay on the principles of Newspeak, Orwell identified the B vocabulary consisting of political words intended to impose a desirable mental attitude upon the person using them. Somebody ought to try this for the managerial class. Here are a few samples: conceptual framework, co-ordinate, freeze, global, integrate, lay-off, offset, override, restructure, surplus, task force, on-going.

information techniques. The big assignment is a group study of some major national problem such as the role of the CBC or the status of the Indian.

Most graduates are transferred to other departments for successive two-year stints to give them a broader experience in the public service. Most will eventually return to their own departments; the rest will become mobile managers and available wherever the need arises.

The course is modelled upon teaching methods developed in the General Electric Company, and its objective is said to be the development of decision-makers.

It might be observed that each fresh assistant professor, as he joins a university faculty, believes that he has newly discovered that the object of education is to 'make them think' rather than merely to impart information. Perhaps 'decision making' is a variant of this worthy aim.

An *élite* administrative corps comes to look on scientists as properly subordinate, and science as a way of thinking that should deal with the means to support its policy or ideology rather than as an end in itself.

In time of war most scientists would agree to place their knowledge at the disposal of the government, to put it to whatever use is judged best. In peacetime fewer of the scientific community feel that their ultimate moral responsibility is to the nation. Those that do should be working directly for the government as part of the *élite* corps.

British science, as C.P. Snow described it, is still under the charge of career administrators trained in the classics, who can snub the scientists and maintain a professional monopoly over the organization of government departments. It has no interest in moving scientists into its membership or working with universities on major policy problems.

In the United States the Revolution wiped out the hereditary ruling class and left the field free for scientists and engineers to move into managerial positions. Consequently, in all the fields in which scientific and technical knowledge is important, scientists and engineers have tended to rise into positions of executive responsibility. As D.K. Price put it:

In Great Britain the scientific civil servants have always complained that they were kept out of positions of top authority by the administrative class. In the United States the complaint is more likely to be the opposite – that good scientists are ruined by being taken from the laboratory and given administrative responsibilities for which they may be poorly suited.[7]

In Canada the historic practice has been like that of the USA. As D.K. Price observes, the system has probably made for poor management in little things but for dynamic administration in big issues. However, in 1968 the new Trudeau administration authorized the Treasury Board to go into high gear in implementing the Glassco report, and the switch-over to a managerial class began. Management does not, of course, exclude people with scientific training, but this is not a main qualification. As an illustration of the current policy, take the sequence of senior appointments in EM & R, a science department. In the past the deputy ministers have been earth-science oriented, usually geologists or engineers. The last of the breed, W.E. Van Steenburgh, was succeeded by an economist, C.M. Isbister, and in 1970 a Vancouver lawyer, Jack Austin, was appointed. *Sic transit* ...

IV GROWTH OF THE SCIENCE SECRETARIAT

In section 2 of this chapter we left the Science Secretariat surgically separated from its Siamese twin the Science Council and groping for nourishment, perhaps at the dry breast of the Treasury Board. It is a pleasure to report that the operation was ultimately successful beyond expectations. In May 1969, Dr R.J. Uffen was appointed as director of the ss, chief science adviser to the cabinet and secretary to the cabinet committee on science.[8] The secretariat, as an arm of the government, was supposed to co-ordinate presentation to the cabinet of proposals from science agencies. It was also to determine priorities and establish a mechanism for making logical choices between support for different fields of science, and to respond quickly to queries from the prime minister and cabinet members.

Unfortunately the scheme foundered, like every scheme of the kind since the beginning in 1916, by reason of the inability of the secretariat to hold any attention from the Cabinet. Mr Drury was concerned with money, and the ministers of the science departments with progress in their respective areas, and none of them could care less about general policy. At the end of 1970, Dr Uffen returned to his university and the secretariat became a *de facto* arm of the Treasury Board.

In August 1971 Alastair Gillespie was appointed as science and technology minister with the ss as his staff, and in September a new secretary (or deputy minister) took office. He was Dr Aurèle Beaulnes, previously professor of medicine at McGill and co-ordinator of the federal program on the non-medical use of drugs.[9] The ss was enlarged from about ten science advisers to fifty or sixty.

There is no evident intention of giving the ministry an operational role. Essentially it remains as the scientific arm of the Treasury Board to which its confidential advice is primarily tendered.[10] There are few clues so far as to what direction the advice will take. On inspection of a batch of press clippings reporting interviews and speeches during his first year, this is how Mr Gillespie's views came out:

The government will likely make an announcement on industrial R & D policy within a year.

In future industry will be hired to do more R & D for government.

I am prepared to question the assumption that teaching and research should always go together in universities.

I'm dubious about our ability as a society to quantify everything of value.

Whatever basic science is done should be related to national goals.

V THE ROYAL SOCIETY AND SCITEC

The professionalization of science and the consequent separation of science from society may be dated in England from 1847, the year in which the Royal Society was reorganized to eliminate from election to membership those who were not actually researchers. As of 1830, only 106 of 662 Fellows had published a paper in the society's journal, and the others were not providing much financial patronage in substitution. The reorganization of 1847 'transformed the Society from an eminent body of men interested in science, containing a minority of research workers, into a body of carefully selected specialists.'[11] And specialization increased, since only fifteen new members were to be elected each year. With competition intense, one's best chance lay in ploughing a narrow field. Interest in the wider aspects of science, including its relations with general society, came to be deprecated in consequence, and in the early part of the twentieth century, as science was really beginning to make an impact on the world, the Royal Society reached a low point in its attention to the social relations of science.

The Royal Society of Canada, since its formation in 1882, has been made up of 'selected and representative men who have themselves done original work of at least Canadian celebrity,' and remains 'exclusive in its membership but inclusive in that it offers its benefits to all.'[12] Fellows of the society have always hoped that it might attain a national importance comparable to that of its model, the Royal Society of London, or of various national academies of science, but they have been perennially disappointed. The fact is that the national academies generally have lost their position as authoritative government advisory bodies. The position of the Royal Society of London is anachronistic; its power has diminished but it has to a large extent maintained its influence. It maintains its outlook as a working society, not merely as an academy to which it is an honour to belong. In Canada most of the functions of a National Academy have been discharged by the NRC and more recently by the Science Secretariat.

When the Science Council was being formed, the society attempted to get the minister, Mr Drury, to ask it for advice on membership. However, 'the Minister was reluctant to request the Society for specific recommendations, since many professional organizations were eager to render similar assistance.' Names were sent in anyway, but evidently no notice was taken of them. Here again is an offer to the Senate Science Committee:

One of the most arduous responsibilities of the Government is the shrewd, dispassionate apportioning of public funds to support research. Situations arise periodically in which this Society might prove singularly fitted to advise and assist the Government. In such circumstances any invitation to make the services of Fellows freely available to the Government will receive a prompt and ready response.

Nearly every year the Royal Society gives itself a session on the couch to ascertain why it is not achieving power as well as glory, but the remedies proposed have not been effective. Perhaps the real reason is that science has grown so much, in people and dollars, that governments wish to keep control in the hands of employees. Also the society's restriction in number of Fellows has, with the growth of science, left more good people outside than inside. The outsiders include the new breed of science entrepreneurs, people who have little research accomplishment in their own right but are forwarding large science programs; chairmen of university departments, deans, directors of laboratories. Finally, the method of election of new Fellows by old ones perpetuates classical skills and retards novelty. The Geological Section, for instance, includes nearly all the senior classical types in the country but hardly any geophysicists or geochemists. And it has been easier for a camel to pass through the eye of a needle than for an engineer to enter the Royal Society.

Although lacking public power, the Royal Society is still respected enough to arouse jealousy from those on the outside. The society's presumption in disagreeing with a section of the Macdonald report elicited a letter-to-the-editor which read, in part:

It is unlikely that this opposition will carry much weight with those scientists who cannot share in the fellowship of the Society. What would be more instructive, would be a breakdown of its vote according to certain categories: the distribution of votes as between those who are in a position to receive the external support and those who are not; or, in the former category, between those who are at the peaks of their productive research careers, those who are now on the downslide, and those who are beyond real productivity.[13]

The Royal Society of Canada is somewhat less selective than its counterparts in other countries, as the following list shows. (Numbers are the ratios of membership to total population.)

USSR, Academy of Science	1:400,000
USA, Academy of Sciences	1:235,000
London, Royal Society	1:115,000
Australia, Academy of Science	1: 83,000
Sweden, Royal Academy of Sciences	1: 50,000
Canada, Royal Society	1: 28,000
Canada, Science Section of Royal Society	1: 42,000[14]

The chances of becoming a Fellow of the Science Section of the Royal Society of Canada are about equal to those of being elected in Sweden, about three times as great as in London, and about ten times as great as in the USSR.

In 1969, shortly after the Royal Society appeared before the Senate committee, that body received delegations from the Chemical Institute of Canada, the Canadian Association of Physicists, and the Engineering Institute. The leaders of these organizations, impressed by the Senators' evident frustration in determining 'who speaks for Canadian science' got together a conference leading to the formation of a super-association that would be fully representative of Canadian science and technology. Its objectives would be to solve the problems of intercommunication between science and government, between science and the public, and between scientists in different fields; in effect, this proposed super-association would speak for Canadian science. I quote now from a newsletter of the Royal Society:

The impression conveyed by the literature was that the Royal Society of Canada did not exist. Every effort was made by your representatives to correct this implication, by illustrating that the Society was not only viable but had special qualifications for exercising leadership in just these proposed directions. The response was most discouraging. Ignorance about the Society and prejudice against it are evidently rampant. Among the epithets one heard applied to it were 'irrelevant,' 'inadequate,' 'ineffective,' 'politically immature,' and – again and again – 'unrepresentative.' A popular-science newspaper reported as follows: The one institution that got gored badly in the revolutionary fervour of the conference was the Royal Society of Canada ... After the conference, one delegate maintained, 'They got what they deserved. The only people they speak to are themselves and God.'[15]

After this the Royal Society decided not to join the 'Who speaks' brigade, but to preserve an independent voice in matters of national concern. These experiences were hardly exhilarating but, as the president continued 'we cannot hope to rectify an unworthy image without realistically trying to appraise and remedy the reasons for it.'

SCITEC, Canada's answer to the AAAS, went into business in January 1970.* National societies which offered founding support included those for chemistry, physics, engineering, agriculture, and biology. The new body also won the immediate support of ACFAS – l'Association canadienne française pour l'avancement des sciences, Canada's original multidisciplinary scientific society, founded half a century ago. ACFAS is built out of thirty adhering societies, with both corporate members and individual members. It includes the social sciences as well as the natural sciences. At a recent annual meeting, 1,250 participants registered and over five hundred papers were presented in some thirty-six disciplines.

The prime objective of SCITEC is 'to marshall the scientific and technical community to provide leadership, and to communicate, co-operate and work within itself, with government and the public in the national interest.' SCITEC hopes to reach a membership of thirty thousand and an annual budget of $200,000. The membership elects a congress of two hundred, from which, together with the ACFAS assemblée, a council is formed. This smaller group will be expected to participate in the development and implementation of science policy. It is intended to hold annual conferences open to the entire membership. Anyone can join. Getting 'one voice' from thirty thousand people in a highly individualistic group of professions will be quite a job. Dr Claude Fortier, head of Laval University's physiology department indicated that he was doubtful and sceptical on the role of the

* The word SCITEC originated as an abbreviation of 'Science-Technology Canada,' the name first proposed for the society. Later it was decided to call the organization 'The Association of the Scientific, Engineering and Technological Community of Canada,' while retaining the abbreviation.

proposed society as the unique spokesman for science in Canada; it would be too broadly based. By admitting technologists, he said, the membership door could be logically opened to morticians and plumbers: consensus in such a group would be so general as to be useless. There was, he argued, need for two organizations; an élite group and a broadly based group.[16] SCITEC's usefulness is more likely to be, like that of the labour unions, the offering of opportunities to ambitious scientists to rise in the political sphere.

And what will SCITEC look like when it becomes fully representative and flourishing? Better, let us hope, than the future envisaged some years ago for one of its components:

(a) meetings will be so much bigger than they are now that they will hardly be worth coming to, except for the purpose of meeting salesmen;
(b) non-research people will inevitably be in control of the society, and there will be many complaints that the scientific sessions are not sufficiently suited to the practical man;
(c) professionalism will have risen strongly and the society will be more interested in the status of physicists and in surveys than it is in physics; and
(d) there will probably be compulsory licensing, and no one will be allowed to do research in physics without a certificate from a dubious group in Toronto.[17]

VI SUMMARY AND COMMENTARY

At this stage I must expect to be charged with being wholly negative in attemping to show that Parliament does not manage science and that the Science Council suffers from congenital lack of authority. The Treasury Board, on which the government has bestowed all powers, is in undoubted command; whether the government's procedure of using its accounting department as the final arbiter of science policy is a wise one may be questioned.

The Royal Society has largely occupied the role of spectator of science policy decisions, and there appears to be little ground for anticipating that it will attain increased political influence. As for SCITEC, the level of its influence is still to develop; its prototype, the AAAS, has an effective lobby in Washington and access to influential elected representatives, as well as a journal of prestige. The problem of SCITEC will be that of choosing priorities from the wide spectrum of interests of its members.

The promotion of R & D in industry was assigned chiefly to the Department of Industry which, as Darwin would say, still bears in its bodily frame the indelible stamp of its lowly origin. Set up by Simon Reisman, its first deputy minister, it is the very model of a modern system of cross-walking, cost-accounting, and science-without-scientists that the TB holds up as an example to other agencies. Its activities are discussed below.

With the universities, the NRC had developed voluntary relationships which were so well adapted to the postwar state of science that they served as a world model. Doubtless the council could have innovated within the changing pattern of academic and industrial science. But since the Glassco report the NRC has not enjoyed the confidence of the government as a chosen instrument of policy and has not advanced effectively.

The government's response to the eclipse of the NRC was to create the Science Council and I turn now to an examination of the potentiality of this body. C.P. Snow has suggested three requirements which must be met by a committee if it is to be 'as sharp a tool for doing business as government can find', and which may serve us as a standard for judging the SC.[18]

– The objective must be clear and not too grandiloquently vast. A committee set up to advise on the welfare of all science is not likely to get very far.
– The committee has got to be 'placed' within the government structure. It has to be in touch with working scientists, to have links with ministers and top civil servants, and to satisfy questions of academic status.
– To be of any real good the committee has to possess or take powers of action. If it does not at least have the powers of inspection and follow-up it will never get near the point of action and will fade away.

The SC seems potentially able to meet only the second of Snow's three requirements, namely, keeping in touch. The third power, of inspection and follow-up, has been assigned to the Treasury Board, backed up by its own scientific advisers and the SS. As to the first objective, the difficulties arising from the impracticably broad terms of reference given to the SC are evident from part of a debate on report no. 4:

Senator Andrew Thompson: I was looking at your goal of world peace and your approach to foreign aid to tackle the question of poverty and hunger. You also emphasize new industries and say they must get established on a viable footing. By that criterion you might limit your research with respect to world famine.

Dr Omond Solandt: There is no doubt that the whole report is full of conflicts. The problem of policy is to decide just how much of each you want. If we want to help the 'have-not' nations we are going to have to restrict our own growth in some areas in order to avoid competing with them.

Thompson: In your concept of setting up a commission to handle, say, this factor

of world famine, who would be included in that commission?
Solandt: We have not really defined our mechanism of action. That is one of the things we are starting to work at.
Chairman: Do you not think you will be a bit late?
Solandt: We are going to be late with everything.
Chairman: But in this specific case? The Government has already announced that it would set up a research institute or council on external aid.
Thompson: You placed a lot of stress on aid to developing areas. What were you planning to do about this? Were you going to set up a commission?
Solandt: No. We have always envisaged we could just work with the External Aid Office.

As the Lamontagne report summed it up: 'The Senate Committee has the impression that the Science Council has been working in a vacuum and that its impact on Canadian science policy has been minimal.'

The OECD report also expressed the view that the conditions which had been given to the SC did not permit its influence to be fully exerted. It does not have, for example, automatic access to government information and is, therefore, not always in full possession of the facts which would enable it to give essential advice on scientific questions which the government requires. At the same time the council is attempting to provide advice through publicly issued documents rather than directly to decision makers at the moment when such advice is essential. The SC is impotent to give the deep, timely, comprehensive advice on scientific questions which contemporary government requires. As the report says:

Our feeling is that the functions of the Science Council fall between two stools. It is not part of the active machinery of government and on the other hand, its members being appointed by the Prime Minister and its support coming from public funds, it does not have the complete independence of a learned society in unique representation of the views of the scientific community.

The OECD proposed reforms in the SC which would make it equivalent to the U.S. president's Scientific Advisory Committee, whose advice is offered confidentially. The reforms are now only of historical interest since the government has chosen to leave the SC on ice and operate via the Science Secretariat, as a confidential advisory group to the Treasury Board.

There was a quip which not long ago enjoyed wide currency in Europe; it was said that the optimists were learning Russian and the pessimists Chinese. Canada's scientists might similarly divide, with the optimists looking to the Science Council and the pessimists to the Treasury Board. Let us see what grounds for optimism arise from a comparison of the outlook of the SC with that of the TB, and the ability of the latter body to discharge its national obligations to science.

The Treasury Board does not accept that science is, for budgetary purposes, an identifiable national objective, and in this view it is apparently supported by the Science Council, which says: 'Canada should not fall into the trap of allocating this or that percentage of GNP to R & D and then dividing up this 'budget for R & D' between the contenders for funds.'[19]

To those who propose a science budget the TB reply is: you are advocating that we should similarly have a budget for economics; that we should tell the Bank of Canada, the Privy Council Office, the Department of Finance, the Department of National Revenue, and so on, that there is only so much money for economics, and that they have to go and ask whether they can have another economist, because the decision has been taken that there is only so much economics to be done in this country.

The economic parallel, they say, is rejected by sensible people because they know that economics is an integral part of the function of departments concerned with finance. In the same way science is an integral part of departments such as Agriculture or EM & R and you cannot budget for it separately any more than you can with economics. The decision on how much money is spent on R & D by, say, Agriculture, is part of the broad general decision on what the nation is going to do about agriculture.

There is no real difference between the ideologies of the SC and the TB. The former organization, however, has a strong representation of scientists, hence a more enlightened understanding of the problems of science. Also the SC shows an awareness that the prospect of homogenization with U.S. technology must be a factor in determining what to do about Canadian science. Its weakness is that it has never been equipped with authority to grasp the priority nettle. Some of the distinctions between the two bodies were evident in the Senate hearings.

Senator Harry Hays: To whom do you make recommendations on programs you have carried through?
Dr Omond Solandt: To the Prime Minister. And they are published at the same time.
Hays: Are these on a priority list, 1, 2 and 3, in relation to the amount of money that you have to spend?
Solandt: No.

Hays: Are they looking for that sort of information?
Solandt: Yes, the President of the Treasury Board would like to have a list with every scientific activity in order of priority with a running total of expenses down the column, and when he decides how much to spend he takes a pair of scissors and cuts off the list at that point.
Chairman: That is a typical Treasury Board approach.
Solandt: But this is a totally unreal idea because so many of the projects in science are interdependent. The Treasury has to say, 'Well, we have only got so much money. What things do you think we should cut off? You come back with a list and they say, 'Well, that is not enough, cut off another.'[20]

Treasury Board management was strongly criticized by the OECD, which noted that the board was not sufficiently qualified in matters of science and technology to make informed judgments of the departments before the budget was submitted to Parliament. Programs and projects worked out by the research workers themselves were subject to amendment, in the budget review process, only in the light of non-scientific considerations, such as the levels of the establishment or of expenditure which were considered as generally satisfactory in the current financial year. The final filter for scientific decisions is the government's accounting department.

There would be general 'agreement in principle' that a mechanism should exist through which national objectives having significant science components could be identified and approved, including the necessary research program for their implementation, and that decisions regarding the conduct of those scientific activities should be made by people with a proven background of research and science administration. Only at the most general level of planning should the effect of political, economic, and social constraints be introduced.

The most comfortable arrangement for the government, towards which it is headed, would be to use the Science Secretariat as the scientific arm of the TB. This would have the advantage that all the government's advisers would be its own employees, and the apparatus of publicity would be under complete control. The Science Council would be retained as an anodyne for the scientific community.

It was the hope of its founders that the SC would devise the pattern of future Canadian science – the *Bluenose* in the mind of her builder. Instead the SC is turning out to be the decorated nameplate of the vessel which is manned by the TB and SS. Where policy decisions are concerned it is doubtful whether the SC would be missed. The TB has the power and the SC the glory.

But the system of complete internal control has one drawback; it cannot extend to university science, which includes recruitment. Treasury Board methods lack the sublety necessary to coax professors to heel. Industrial R & D also, which is the area especially marked for stimulation, is both independent and refractory. The Canadian constitution of science provides that the universities and industries must advise *and consent* to manipulations originating in Ottawa. The consent must come not only from the abstract organization but from the working individuals concerned. Federal 'task forces' dedicated to scientific Vietnamization, peering into 'futurology' with the aid of a few academic advisers, will have little effect on the consent of working scientists.

Considerable finesse will be needed to think out a pattern for the segments of our science and then to get the parts working together. For this it seems that some outsiders may have to be incorporated into the working team. The agency which has best understood the technique of persuasion without coercion is the NRC. An industrially strengthened NRC with functions transferred to it from the Department of Industry would be a logical centre round which to build an enlarged science program along lines of national desire.

It must be admitted, however, that all signs point in another direction. Extrapolation of present tendencies suggests that future science policy will be initiated as the government from time to time encounters a priority, as for example when the Arctic suddenly became prominent in the summer of 1970. Word will then pass round that the TB may be letting a little money out for an expanded science program in the North. If the SC has prepared a report on the needs of Arctic research it will be looked up. (As it happens the SC in report 4 did not rate the Arctic among its topics for early consideration.) The federal agencies will prepare their own recommendations as to what is to be done and the TB will introduce some process of co-ordination designed to prevent overlap.

This system has not, in the past, worked too badly as a means of getting government agencies to respond to government needs. It has, however, been a major cause of the concentration of research in government laboratories, which was not in the plans. It has also failed to alleviate the schism between government science and that of the universities and industry. The federal formula for bringing the independents into the national league is by manipulation of grant patterns, which are described in later chapters.

4

National objectives

It is difficult to compare Canada's science effort with that of other countries because R & D spending is so greatly influenced by the extent of military research, atomic research, and space research. These last two are in most countries, but not in Canada, carried out with the object of strengthening military potential. To compare the national effort for economic and social purposes, one should subtract the military component. This is done in table 5, which shows R & D expenditure on a *per capita* basis to be highest in the United States. Next in order, with expenditures lower by about one-third, are the Netherlands, the United Kingdom, Canada, and Sweden. A little behind come Germany and France; other countries lag far behind the leading group. For a proper assessment of Canada's position, it should also be remembered that Canadian nuclear and space research are not defence-oriented. The volume of civilian research in Canada is thus more than is implied in table 5.

A variety of evidence suggests that a modest increase in Canadian R & D to perhaps 1.5 times the present level (excluding defence) would place us about equal to the USA and well ahead of all others. Military R & D should be considered as a separate item because of its variability from country to country.

For industry a larger increase would be required, with a continuing high proportion of D. A doubling of industrial research would probably bring the Canadian effort up to the U.S. level if defence and space are excluded. In these areas so-called private or company research is a fiction.

TABLE 5

Annual expenditure on R & D *per capita* in the mid sixties

	Economic and social purposes $U.S.	Military, atomic and space purposes $U.S.	Economic and social as % of total
United States	35	76	31
Netherlands	26	1	95
United Kingdom	24	16	60
Canada	24	8	74
Sweden	22	11	66
Germany	20	4	83
France	19	15	56
Japan	9	0	100

SOURCE: OECD report, table 3

The university component, in order to reach the utopian situation of total identity with U.S. practice, would require an increase in the areas of applied research, mainly engineering and in interdisciplinary research.

Federal government laboratories would tend to be frozen at their present levels.

One frequently hears assertions such as: 'Much of this expenditure [for R & D] demonstrably leads to increased productivity and greater profits for industry.'[1] According to the chairman of the Science Council, economic growth is of primary importance and determines everything else: 'First of all, we must support economic growth because it is the growth of the economy that pays for everything else. If our economy is not healthy and expanding, there is no use talking about even fundamental research.'[2]

Economic expansion thus appears as a fundamental common goal towards which all national efforts should tend. This means giving priority to scientific activities directly oriented towards economic and social objectives. The SC is expected to define a series of priorities capable of being identified with long-term national aspirations. It is assumed that the logic of these priorities will suffice to ensure acceptance in all circles concerned.

Lithwick, however, compared the total R & D with the economic growth rates of nine Western nations, but failed to establish correlation.[3] The leading countries in growth rate, but not in R & D, are Japan and Germany, from which it might be inferred that the key to industrial success is defeat in a war with resulting release from military commitments and removal of the national debt via inflation. Japan was also helped through a critical time by the outbreak of the Korean War, which brought her a stream of u.s. dollars in the form of procurement contracts and troop spending.

Within individual industries, however, there does exist, both in Canada and the USA, a highly significant relationship between exports and the number of scientists and engineers employed. Lithwick pointed out that it is deceptive to concentrate such enquiries on manufacturing since, in Canada, a large share of our exports are non-manufactured, e.g., wheat and mining products. The OECD report adds that the Canadian belief in a general formula for progress is attributable to hope rather than evidence:

It is surprising to see how enthusiastically Canadians accept the quasi-mathematical hypothesis of a close correlation between scientific effort, technical progress and economic growth. The steady growth of foreign interests provokes a reaction reflected in an emotional desire to find a body of precepts capable of orienting the country along more specifically Canadian lines.

Of Canada the OECD examiners said, 'It would be hard to find any country whose scientific structures and attitudes towards science are more clearly rooted in geography and history.' Our structures, certainly, are British in origin with recent American modifications. But what of attitudes? The highest common denominator of Canadian current attitudes to be found in Science Council report no. 4, which lists what we think our science can do. For comparison, we might look at a similar 1969 report by the Science Policy Council of the Netherlands, giving the criteria for priorities in that country. Since Canada and Holland are differently rooted in geography and history, it might be concluded that where the lists coincide they reflect a general attitude of Western nations. Where they differ we may look for some especially Canadian attitude.

The comparison is made in table 6. In one column the Canadian aims are given in order and opposite each entry the nearest Netherlands equivalent is shown. There are five Netherland goals which cover the same ground as the Canadian six. The scientific contributions to each are strikingly similar and represent in fact the aims of Western nations generally. More interesting are the two Canadian residuals at the end of the list, dealing with resources and with efficiency.

TABLE 6

Canadian science goals compared with those of the Netherlands

CANADA	NETHERLANDS
National prosperity	*Economic potential*
Industrial productivity of selected manufacturing industries; motivation and decision making in industry	Economic growth; equilibrium in balance of payments
Regional economic disparity	Sufficient geographic spread of employment
Health	*Physical living conditions*
Group behaviour in relation to health; medical research; pollution	Environmental hygiene and health care
Urban and rural living	Infrastructure and housing; physical planning
Education	*Moral and cultural standard of living*
Teaching and information services; curiosity directed approach; student motivation	Knowledge and insight; quality at all levels of education
University research; urge to explore and know	Quality of scientific education
Freedom, security, and unity	
National defence	National prestige
Criminology and forensic science	Justice and police
Leisure and personal development	*Social living conditions*
Communications and transportation; inexpensive and easy travel	Traffic and transport
Communication between groups or regions; billingualism	Communications between various social levels; social mobility; Netherlands social values
Accessories and hardware of leisure	Creation and decentralized provision for cultural needs
World peace	*Position of Netherlands internationally*
Foreign aid with technology, food, and communication	International co-operation

(continued on page 96)

Canadian residuals
Conservation of resources

Systems analysis; automation; computers

Efficiency of service industries; of hospital care; development of devices to perform menial acts; computer-based aids for education

SOURCE: The Canadian list is from SC report no. 4, 1968; that of the Netherlands was in a report to Parliament by the Science Policy Council of that country, as quoted in *Science Policy News*, vol. 1, (1969) no. 2.
NOTE: Major goals are given in italics followed by a list of the contributions of science and technology to each. The Canadian list is in its original order, except for some condensations; that of the Netherlands has been reordered to exhibit similarities. Where appropriate the reader should include one or more of these connecting words; increase, develop, reduce cost of, understand better, continue, apply, study, innovate, improve, maintain.

Research on labour-saving devices is the one dominant Canadian aim which has no parallel in the Netherlands list. It is included under four of our six national goals, viz:

– effective use of computers by management,
– improvement of efficiency of service industries,
– application of systems science to medical, health, and hospital services,
– application of systems science to education,
– development of computer-based educational aids,
– increased automation to permit greater leisure,
– development of devices to perform menial tasks.

The potential of computer communications systems is already the stuff of after-dinner speech making, and it is said that the development of electronic information transfer will have an impact more sudden and more drastic than the Industrial Revolution. It is believed by advocates that Canada, now second only to the USA, can attain industrial leadership in this field.

The Science Council's preoccupation with efficiency reflects three Canadian facts: we have continuous opportunity to compare ourselves with our more efficient neighbours to the south; we have a wage scale so high that, at our level of efficiency, our exports are only marginally viable; and the service industries, including education, have not yielded to assembly-line methods. Canada's attitude here would be shared by other countries in similar wage and labour situations; it would not be shared by, say, South Africa.

The only other Canadian recommendation without a Netherlands equivalent is development of sound programs for the use, conservation, and replenishment of resources. This inclusion, perhaps, reflects a view that our resources are sufficiently varied, extensive, and little known, to justify reconsideration of the R & D appropriate to them.

We have had in Canada a compulsive desire to give ourselves a national science policy and, in this first formal step, have discovered that we are not very different from the other rich nations of the West. The Canadian imprint will appear only in later stages when priorities are set among the aims, and price tags attached to them.

II COMPONENTS OF A NATIONAL SCIENCE POLICY

At this point I offer a we-hold-these-truths-to-be-self-evident list of determinants from which a formal Canadian science policy must develop. As an introduction to the methodology of social forces acting on science one might compare Russia with the West. The key to our Western political system is the opportunity that we are offered at frequent intervals to turn the government out. This creates the public sensitivity in our legislators that enables us more easily to secure what we personally want in many activities of life, including science. Now what does each of us want? If one took a poll, the verdict would be virtually unanimous for the proposal 'I want science above all to keep me healthy and active longer.' The recognition of our scientific preference is evident from the scale of rewards, in which the medical profession leads all the rest, and in the first rank those who are personally working to keep people alive. Second, and considerably behind in favour, come the researchers who provide the information that the practitioners use. Farther back comes other biological research, which derives its methods and apparatus from the techniques of medicine, and on which some lustre is reflected from that subject through association. Most people believe that the countries of the West are better served with medical science than Russia.

Let us now look for a moment at Russia. Medical science cannot be entirely neglected there, since it is impossible to keep people together in crowded cities without plague unless some attention is paid to public health. The government, however, is not immediately sensitive to voters, and death of the individual is not in the first rank of problems confronting the state. In the realm of biology, food production through improved agriculture would probably have a preferred position. Among medical workers the researchers are best cared for, while the practitioners who attend the dying are less well off.

The dominant fear in Russia is for the death of the state, not of the individual, and the reactions to this today lie in the development of physics and its technological applications. Nobody can say whether or not physics is better in Russia than in the West; to make such a comparison would be an oversimplification. However, it is only in the applications of physics, such as in rocket technology, that a public Soviet challenge has been made to Western science.

In Canada also we are greatly concerned today with the survival of the nation which might be cited as the first determinant of policy. National sovereignty has been with us from the beginning, although the emphasis changes from time to time. The residue at present includes a Canadian scientific presence in the Arctic, the Great Lakes, the continental shelf, and the possible export of water. In a paper before the Royal Society in 1968 Solandt remarked: 'The two programs which seem to us to be the nearest to realization are water and space. They are not necessarily the most important, but research is the art of the possible and they would certainly appear on any list of priorities.'

Under the heading 'Prevention of national disintegration,' one thinks of Bilingualism and Biculturalism and hence the support designed to improve the level of research in French-language universities. Another aspect concerns the equality of opportunity in different regions of the country, through the provision of scientific infrastructure in selected growth centres. The pursuit of both these objectives will operate to modify the merit principle as the basis for supporting university research. Paul Dugal pointed out in a minority supplement to the Macdonald report that 'high merit is not a realistic policy because it does not take into account the present state of university affairs in Canada.'

The maintenance of Canada as a nation also involves communications. In the past this has taken the form of construction of railways and establishment of airlines. At present the emphasis is shifting to broadcasting, and is leading to an increasing emphasis on satellites and outer space as a means of keeping the nation together through information.

There are also some matters for the science of the future: how people are to live together in peace under the conditions of crowded cities. Urban planning will doubtless soon become a recognized university discipline.

At present there is no published breakdown of expenditures which would enable us to put a price tag on national survival as a fraction of the cost of science. We can, however, do this with other priorities. First among these there are three categorical imperatives which dominate our science (table 7). The first is the fear of death. The second has been the fear of the Russians. In the humanities this fear finds an outlet in religious and economic propositions; in science there are, in addition to direct military

TABLE 7

Determinants of Canadian science policy (percentages)

	Federal R & D expenditures 1965–6	Founding members of Science Council
THE NATION Sovereignty, prevention of national disintegration, regional disparity	—	—
THE CATEGORICAL IMPERATIVES		
Fear of death: medicine and health	6	19
Fear of the Russians: military science	33	16
Fear of the Americans: the technology gap and U.S. commercial domination	29	31
NATURAL RESOURCES Renewable resources: agriculture, the Fisheries-Forestry-Wildlife complex Mines and energy: water, power Fitness of the environment	23	16
ACADEMIC University graduate schools and pure science	9	18

SOURCE FOR THE COLUMN ON EXPENDITURES: Table 4 of *Federal Government Expenditures on Scientific Activities, Fiscal Year 1964–5*, DBS Cat. no. 13-401, 1967

NOTE: The assignment of expenditures involves the following assumptions: for problems of the nation there is no available basis for a quantitative breakdown and it has been left out of the calculations; to the fear of death has been attributed expenditures by the MRC, National Health, and Veterans Affairs; fear of the Russians includes expenditures by Canadian forces, DRB, and half of AECL; fear of the Americans includes all intramural NRC, half of AECL, and some minor agencies; natural resources include Agriculture, the components of the Department of the Environment, and EM & R; under the heading 'Academic' are included all university grants other than those to the medical group.
  Total expenditure was $321 million.
  In the final column members of the council have been assigned values in accordance with their interests, in the same way as expenditures. Their backgrounds are described in the text. Obviously some members had mixed interests, so the column does not come out as a simple multiple of the 25 members.

activity, industries such as the building of ships and aircraft, which have been kept alive in Canada for reasons of national security. Death and the Russsians are forces which act on Western nations generally, with Canada among those showing the tendencies most clearly. In its sensitivity to the third force – fear of American industrial domination – Canada is geographically unique. George Grant remarked:

Our very form of life depends on our place as second-class members of the western industrial empire which is centered in the USA. By 'second class,' I do not imply a low status, because it is much nicer to be a Canadian than a Brazilian or a Venezuelan, or for that matter an Englishman.[4]

The development of channels of escape from a permanent branch-plant relationship with our great neighbour forms the heart of contemporary Canadian planning in science and much else. The primary formula offered is to tighten our belts and gain independence through acceptance, if necessary, of a lower standard of living. James Coyne, Walter Gordon, and Melville Watkins have been among the advocates of this course in Canada. From the upshot of their proposals and those of others, it is evident that no Canadian national party believes it could carry the country on curtailment. We have, therefore, sought a second-string solution, namely, the strengthening of technology in order eventually to make our branch plants independent and establish a viable economy.

In any case, Canadians may be out of date in their fear of American industry. The American dominance was caused by the destruction of European and Japanese technology during the Second World War and the expropriation of German and Japanese foreign investments. The present U.S. technology lead is only in military developments, but the industries are so glamorous that the narrowness of their base often passes unnoticed. The Americans have by now destroyed their technological lead through the Vietnam adventure. Their currency has collapsed relative to those of other countries, enabling German, Swiss, Dutch, and Japanese money to buy that much more in dollar assets. Foreign producers now export to the USA such products as automobiles, industrial machinery, and electronic equipment, and the Japanese have established branch plants in the USA to make motor cars and television sets.

The combined effects of the technological revolution, military fear of the Russians, and economic fear of the Americans have all operated to develop engineering and applied physics and to get company-sponsored research under way on a sufficient scale.

The third block of table 7 concerns natural resources. This field, as already noted, would be the beginning of science in any new area, for example, the moon, and has been represented in Canada by such efforts as the geological survey and activities in agriculture, forestry, and fisheries. The survey part of this type of work characteristically declines as the resources become known. The outstanding residue today in Canada is the investigation of the Arctic and the Canadian climate, and the search for oil and gas on the continental shelf. In the mineral field the shift with time is from matter to energy, from the Geological Survey to AECL.

As to the environment, two aspects of science involvement will certainly be pollution and recreation. There will be increasing concern with the maintenance of the wilderness, with wildlife, and with sport fishing.

The fourth claimant for priority is academic science, much of which is basic or curiosity-motivated and carried out in universities. Government planners think of relating its magnitude in future to the supply of what are called good people, outstanding scientists, men of excellence, and so on. Academic work is usually taken as a second order correction on the costs of science, say 10 per cent of the total R & D.

The support of university graduate schools is also likely to be related to the distribution of national needs, which in turn are held to be related to the planned relative costs of pure science, applied science, and development, in the ratios of 10 : 25 : 65. This is an approximation of the U.S.-UK ratios (see chapter 5). The result of applying such a ratio will be to increase technicians and decrease researchers as a fraction of the recruits to science.

As Galbraith has remarked, educators and scientists stand in relation to the industrial system much as did the banking and financial community in the earlier states of industrial development. When capital was decisive, banks multiplied. When qualified manpower became important, colleges multiplied, and so, with a decent time lag, will the academic content of our graduate schools adapt.[5]

By way of summary of this section, the interests of the founding members of the Science Council may be compared with federal expenditures on the determinants for the same year, as indicated in table 7.

Half the council were engineers, surely an indication of the government's intention to go hell-bent for D. Five members were in medicine and medical science; four were in metallurgy; three were in military and aerospace engineering; three were in atomic energy and nuclear physics; four were associated with the natural resource field; and there was one other in academic science (a physical chemist).

Medical predominance in planning springs from first principles of belief; metallurgy is a less plausible contender for the crown of Canadian science. It initial emphasis has not persisted and was presumably a reflection of interests of the first director of the Science Secretariat, a professor of metallurgy on leave from his university.

In the final column of table 7, the council members have been assigned to the determinants in accordance with their interests. The centre column shows federal science expenditures for the founding year, treated in the same way.

The expenditures might be taken as an integration of the government's past views on science policy and the membership of the sc as the intention for the future. Without pushing quantitative analysis too far, it is perhaps legitimate to pay some attention to items where the discrepancy between the columns reaches 100 per cent.

In the areas of medicine and health the federal expenditures were low compared to the sc representation. There are, however, also provincial expenditures such as the fabric of teaching hospitals, and direct support for some research. Good medicine is becoming increasingly good politics, and since 1966 the support for medical research has had a relatively spectacular advance. In fact the health program is one of those items which, if extrapolated to a few years hence at its present growth rate, would occupy our total national budget.

Fear of the Russians would be judged to be declining in 1966. Positive evidence appeared later when the NATO forces were cut. However, military bases in depressed areas continue as major industries to alleviate regional disparity, and there is often a great deal of resistance to closing them, as in the case of the air base at Summerside, Prince Edward Island. (The local resistance was in this instance successful. Donald C. Jamieson, the minister in charge of regional economic expansion, stated recently that the Summerside base had been kept open with encouragement from DREE. He said 'This base is kept open for economic rather than military reasons. On purely military considerations, the base would undoubtedly be closed.' Islanders, although ruffled by the statement, agree that the base is a major economic cornerstone of the community. Two new shopping centre developments are proceeding on the assumption that the base payroll will continue.)[6]

The other item with a large discrepancy is the academic field, where support for R & D is low. However, university financing is too complex to justify deductions. The 9 per cent is about what is intended for pure science. In general professors tend to be well represented on national councils because of their professional qualifications.

The distribution in table 7 represents only the federal government's appraisal of relative scientific importance. The universities are under provincial jurisdiction. It would nevertheless be naïve to suppose that the provinces will not be influenced by such a clear lead.

III TECHNOLOGY AND REGIONAL DISPARITY

The great drive for national identity has ruled the policies of many countries – Ireland for instance. It has been generally on the increase since the War, even where it is often in collision with economic advantage. While the Irish or West Indians might put independence first, Canadians have preferred prosperity. An increase in industrial R & D is seen by planners as a means of stimulating home-grown economy and so 'buying Canada back' while still maintaining prosperity. The hope that industrial technology offers of achieving economic, hence cultural, independence is the basis for its strong promotion in Canada today.

It would be a simple but incorrect view of technology to assume that the more innovation there is the better it is for everybody, on the grounds that once inventions have been made and consequent innovations have been introduced then the benefits which flow from those successes will ultimately derive to everyone's advantage. This appealing argument is not supported by the evidence. Large-scale success has been limited to a few areas and as a result the gap between the 'haves' and the 'have-nots' has broadened at an increasing rate in recent years. This has been observed both between countries and within regions of countries such as Canada.

Another distressing characteristic is that innovations which lead to productivity gains, and thereby tend to come earliest in emerging economies, frequently displace jobs, while those which create new industries, and thereby new employment, tend to occur preferentially in the more industrialized areas. Thus, technological innovation selectively increases the unemployment gap in the underemployed economies.

In Provincial science the beginning of R & D has been in the resource field, dominated by Agriculture, and including Forestry and Mining. Fisheries is constitutionally a federal area but all except the Atlantic provinces have negotiated the operation of their own freshwater fisheries, and Quebec manages all its fisheries. All these activities are carried out by government departments or in colleges.

Following the model of the NRC, all the provinces except Newfoundland and Prince Edward Island have set up, or planned, research councils, beginning with Alberta (1921) and Ontario (1928). Usually each began like the NRC, by supporting research carried out in universities, and later acquired its own laboratories. Those of Ontario and BC obtain most of their revenue by offering their services to Canadian and foreign firms, particularly U.S. ones; those of other provinces receive relatively more from provincial grants. As to policy, the OECD report had this to say:

Provincial governments have so far not established principles of action in the science sector. They have supplemented federal action in fields of special interest, determining objectives of their own among matters inadequately covered by Ottawa, or supporting national objectives with important regional consequences.

The main contribution of the provinces has been the support of the universities, which produce the scientific and technical manpower to operate science. Outside education, the powers of the provinces seemed, at the time of Confederation, to be of secondary importance. More recently such areas of provincial administration as health, social services and welfare, resource development, and the environment have become decisive. This has drawn attention to the inadequacy of the financial resources of the provinces. The cities also have new responsibilities for sewage disposal, urban planning, and transport. So we find the provinces constitutionally competent and the federal government financially competent. Until recently the federal government accepted the provincial position that the payment of bills did not compromise the constitution; now it is tending to ask the provinces to pay their own bills and offering regional aid to the poorer ones. As to R & D, the federal government asserts its right to perform it anywhere on any topic. Its laboratories have traditionally centred on Ottawa but more are now being placed across the country.

The policy problem for the provinces is the same one that has confronted one after another of the universities –the only way to enlarge research is to give it the priority necessary to attach some money to it. For the provinces a choice of topics is also necessary. The universities have not usually made any scrutiny of the kind of knowledge that was to be pursued.

Quebec policy has been to keep its options open, so that, in the event of separation, it would have a self-sufficient scientific apparatus ready to function. In case of continuance as part of Canada, there would be laboratories in which French was the working language at all levels. The tendency, therefore, has been to negotiate for the setting up in Quebec of miniatures of the total English-Canadian effort in branches of interest, rather than to go for specialized research fields which would complement work elsewhere. Recruitment of the scientific leaders for such an effort is a formidable task.

The French-language universities also have had difficulty in trying to recruit senior faculty members. French academics do not settle well in the colonies, especially those in which the educational system is set up, not in imitation of France, but oriented towards American patterns. The world academic pool is also smaller; where some 50 per cent of original science appears in English, less than 5 per cent is in French. Was it not Bismarck who observed that the significant fact of the twentieth century would be that the Americans spoke English? No policy within the power of any Canadian government can make French into an important international language of science. Nor will it be possible to prevent ambitious young French-Canadian researchers from publishing their best work in English.

The Scandinavian countries, which also have language barriers to recruitment, have educational traditions and methods which turn up a surplus of high-class home-grown scholars. In French Canada by contrast, the number of active research scientists per head of population is significantly lower than in other parts of the country. The reasons are historical, resting on a system of education that qualified its products for success in heaven rather than on earth. The system is now changing, and so inevitably will the products, with a necessary time-lag while the old teachers leave the scene. The ultimate solution is to produce home-grown scientists of acceptable quality. Meanwhile the direction of extra federal aid should be to promote inducements in salary and equipment to distinguished Quebecers to return from the USA and other provinces and make their impact at home. The weaker science departments, if they follow the lead of English Canada, will resent the intrusion of good men and try to quarantine them from the main stream of education in special centres set up under some Macdonald type of Strategic Development Grant. Correction of this is not easy and requires forceful policies and often a little blood-letting from above.

Of the French-language universities, the Science Council says: 'The suggestion [of Macdonald] that they must now enter into national competition for funds, where the criterion is entirely the scientific or scholarly merit of the proposal, causes these universities some degree of concern.'[7] It appears that existing grant patterns have already taken into consideration the need to rectify regional disparity. Compared with the Atlantic provinces, French Quebec does quite well, as table 8 shows.

The increasing use of English by French-speaking academics was shown in a recent survey by AUPELF, an association of French-language universities (see table 9). The survey included both humanities and science, teaching and research, other languages and English. The only other foreign language to reach a significant score was German in some European universities.

According to the figures English appears to be the true universal scientific language. As to reading, works in English made up some two-thirds of the sources for some two-thirds of the academics. The tendency to write in English is also strong, but less well-marked than the tendency to read,

TABLE 8

Regional distribution of federal support to university research
1967–8 (dollars)

	Atlantic region	Quebec (French)	Ontario	National average
Total federal support per full-time faculty member	2,600	4,300	5,000	4,700
NRC support per full-time faculty member in science and engineering	6,000	8,000	9,100	8,400

SOURCE: SC report no. 5

no doubt owing to difficulties in preparing or editing texts in English.

The general problem of regional disparity is aggravated by the tendency of talented university graduates to migrate from less developed to more developed areas. Erasmus recorded how bitterly a young Cambridge don complained to him about his inability to get out of that isolated spot and into the centre of culture at Rome.

When regional growth rates are examined the fact emerges that countries with large scientific establishments will not only stay ahead of those with smaller establishments but will in all probability forge even further ahead. The loss of people from less developed to more developed areas occurs not only among countries but also within all countries which have relatively rich and poor areas. Areas with low *per capita* income typically lose talent to areas with higher income, as suggested in this comment by L.V. Berkner:

Only those regions will be economically healthy that have the intellectual power to exploit the new science and the consequent industry. Those regions that fail intellectually will fail economically and become chronically poor and colonial. This is the social certainty that the technological revolution of our century has made clear.[8]

Acceptance of this line of reasoning has led, in the postwar years, to the view that each region of Canada should endeavour to educate scientists to the highest level provided at home before sending them abroad for further

TABLE 9

Language used for publication of scientific articles by faculty members of
French-language universities (percentages)

	Europe (mostly France, some Belgium and Switzerland)	Canada	Africa (Ivory Coast)
French	51	23	59
English	27	62	24
Depends on type of article	22	15	17

SOURCE: Survey by AUPELF (Association des universités partiellement ou
entièrement de langue française) as reported in *le Devoir*, 28 March 1970

training. The longer people remain in science at home, the more realistic
are their expectations of the work which they can carry on successfully at
home. Continuing exposure to higher education within the general cultural
pattern to which students are accustomed is seen as the important thing.

The spread of graduate education has recently produced a backlash from
the University of Toronto, which has protested the formula system of
grants by Ontario, which treats all its universities on the same basis. The
University of Toronto, its leaders say, is the only one with the prestige,
facilities, and access to population to make any claim to being a national
university. Financial recognition should be given to its function of producing the teachers and researchers to staff the lesser universities which are
not able to produce their own faculty members.

IV ATTEMPTS TO ALLEVIATE REGIONAL DISPARITY
IN THE USA AND CANADA

The USA has been going through policy developments in regional support
of science which probably forecast Canadian developments of the seventies.[9]

Up to 1940, in American science, the shifting incidence of basic research
seemed to be merely a matter of institutional prestige, and, for anybody
except an academic scientist, a marginal form of psychological gratification
or chagrin. The situation began to change radically with the coming of the
Second World War and the creation by the federal government of major
research facilities in leading universities. At this point, where the cost of

scientific research was soaring to astronomical heights, the universities saw an opportunity to unload an ever-increasing part of their budget on the federal government. The scientific prestige that would attract federal grants became a ponderable asset on the books of a university.

Even this, however, did not turn the incidence of research into a political issue. For almost twenty years there was a surprising acquiescence by Congress in the unargued proposition that the federal research dollar should go to the best men at the best institutions, and that the only appropriate test was their reputation for 'excellence' in the eyes of their peers. This inevitably entailed a heavy concentration of grants upon a small number of towering institutions, with a conspicuous geographical imbalance. But congressmen did not bestir themselves about it.

This self-restraint – or, more realistically, failure to grasp the political implications of what was happening – began to break down during the sixties. The question is, why this sudden awareness? Part of the answer is evident. The rationalization of the Defense Department in liquidating arsenals and navy yards had hit the politicians where they live – under the steely gaze of their constituents. For the record, congressmen have complained about the closings, but they knew that the only real solution was to get a new grip on the federal budget. Pragmatically speaking, that has meant a big scientific installation or major research and development contracts for local industry, preferably both.

Only one further element was required to perfect the logic of the new politics; the rising conviction that a vigorous scientific program at a major university is an irresistible magnet for the location of government research facilities that have no direct academic affiliations, and more than this, for the location of industrial plants with a scientific or engineering orientation – industrial 'spin-off.' University science is increasingly perceived as the great catalyst for the whole economy of a metropolitan district or geographical region.

Once it was generally accepted that great universities inevitably attract independent federal installations, that became an argument for putting new facilities near the greatest universities.

No politician could fail to read the omens. In the years to come, the raw power grab among cities and regions will have to be camouflaged by persuasive invocations of the towering strength of the local university. There is the rub. If the local university is Harvard or MIT, the case is made to begin with. Yet the prospect of seeing the research dollar virtually monopolized by about two dozen universities (38 per cent of federal grants to ten universities in 1964, 59 per cent to twenty-five universities) became politically intolerable once the distribution of university science was seen as affecting the ultimate distribution of wealth and power in American society. It will be a matter of economic survival for less favoured cities and regions to get federal grants for their universities, to build them up on the scientific side by an infusion of federal money.

Is there anything to stop the Johnsonian Revolution? Probably not. Any favoured region or entrenched academic power would find itself in an inherently false position if it tried to resist the logic of regional and institutional equalization. It would inevitably appear to be cloaking its selfish interests with a specious concern for the general good.

So much for the recent past of the USA. We turn now for a look at Canada's past and future. Since the 'excellence' of the local university is taken to be the core of regional development, it is of some importance that Mr Trudeau, ever since 1954, has been at work demolishing the arguments developed by others to justify federal support for education.[10] The original basis of support, used by Mr St. Laurent, was the right of the Canadian government to use money raised by taxation for the purpose of making gifts or grants-in-aid to individuals, institutions, provincial governments, or even foreign governments. However, a Privy Council decision prohibits such grants when they encroach upon subjects reserved for the provinces, e.g., education. These direct grants, as all know, were gradually abandoned after a few years.

From the faculty side, especially with reference to graduate studies, has come an argument for federal support based on joint jurisdiction and federal competence. Must not the universities in their poverty satisfy their economic needs by maintaining a constant balance of power between the federal and provincial levels? The proposal earlier referred to, that research grants should take into account educational 'health' and 'research training' is an oblique approach. The position of the Macdonald committee is that universities should not fall under any sphere of influence; all decisions should be taken internally regardless of the source of support.

The federal government, on its side, has never overtly acknowledged a share of management. Here is Mr Pearson, followed by Mr Marchand, speaking at a federal-provincial conference in 1966:

The federal government recognizes that education is and must remain within provincial jurisdiction.

Unless you are prepared to argue that the federal government should have the permanent influence on your provincial programs that shared-cost arrangements would give us, you must accept the principle of our withdrawal from technical and vocational training.

But by 1969 the federal government was re-entering the direct support of education to alleviate regional disparity. Support agreements between Mr Marchand's department and New Brunswick, Prince Edward Island, and Manitoba all state that an 'integral part' or 'basic objective' or 'purpose and intent' is to improve the quality of education. Here is a snatch of the debate as Mr Marchand's new department came into existence:

Jean Marchand: When we negotiate with a province both of us have global jurisdiction, and the result is that there is no field with which we cannot deal.
John Lundrigan: If there were some basis whereby the federal government and a provincial government could get involved with education, would this be a possible area of development?
Marchand: I do not believe that we can make an agreement dealing solely with education, but if we have a comprehensive plan these subjects could be dealt with in the agreement. We would have no objection to that.[11]

The government evidently intends to include education in its policy of equalization. As Mr Trudeau put it, the political cohesion of a society depends on its desire to secure the essential minimum for *all* its members regardless of their geographical situation. Consequently, if a province is too poor to provide university services that approach the Canadian average, it has a right to federal grants.*

We have been following the circuitous route of the federal government into support of education, out again, and finally in again on the basis of regional disparity. The negotiations mentioned were with provinces and about schools. From here it is an easy constitutional passage into university support via research and graduate training.

Mr Marchand's plans for regional development have included some provincial science installations, such as the fisheries laboratory in Gaspé. But Canadian political thinking has not caught up with the American pattern. There is little recognition as yet of the potential political mileage of science. Federal members still tend to pin their regional hopes on such standbys as military installations. Negotiators from the disadvantaged provinces have been more successful in getting collaboration with presentations from social scientists than with presentations from natural scientists. Among the

---

* Trudeau, 'Federal grants to universities' in *Federalism and the French Canadians*. Mr Trudeau's 1957 rejection of the argument was on grounds no longer applicable, namely, the practice of the 1950s of direct grants to universities in all provinces, regardless of their respective wealth.

latter, qualified provincial practitioners are not numerous enough to enter the game against the federal team. And there is little effective use made of university scientists, many of whom are, as already mentioned, out of sympathy with the policy trends of the times.

5

The categorical imperatives

In this chapter we discuss the three denominations of science that attempt to keep us alive and nationally independent. They relate to medicine, the military establishment, and industry.

Medicine and biology are, in a way, the most complex, since they involve political efforts to reconcile biological facts and ethical values in the framing of public policies. The impact of biology occurs on a time scale that obscures its effects in the early stages, so that it has been overshadowed in the last half century by the spectacular developments in the physical sciences. But the present population explosion has been under way ever since public health and medicine began to eliminate 'natural' controls over human reproduction. Similarly the replacement of natural selection by the conscious control of heredity, which now seems imminent, is the fruit of many years' research.

These topics and their moral, political, and economic possibilities will not be pursued here because they are questions for the world rather than for Canada. The Canadian policy problem is to determine in how many of the big leagues of science we can afford to participate with any hope of becoming leaders. Should we, for example, make huge expenditures on medical research in the hope of achieving in Canada the cure for cancer or hypertension? Probably not. We must, however, do some good medical research if we are to keep abreast of the advance in knowledge in other countries, in order to make applications quickly to the care of Canadians.

Medical and hospital care are rendered free to the consumer; consequently supply and demand are not kept in balance by price. When resources are limited, while demand is unlimited, supply has to be rationed by means other than price. The most pervasive form of rationing, especially in the hospital service, is the waiting list, which can be viewed as a kind of iceberg. The significant part is that below the surface – the patients who are not on the list at all, either because they are not accepted on grounds that the list is too long already, or because they take a look at the queue and go away.

If people are on a waiting list long enough they will die – usually from some cause other than that for which they joined the queue. Short of dying, however, they frequently vanish from the queue by reason of boredom or recovery. If they live they are irritated with their government; thus rationing, whether deliberate or by default, and always unproclaimed, is a major political abrasive for which the only remedy, outside of vastly increased expenditure, is improved efficiency. The Science Council commented in one of its annual reports:

Industrial engineering and the management sciences have perfected many ways of increasing the productivity of workers and equipment both in industry and business. In our health delivery systems there has never been any competitive element; the taxpayer has complacently said 'the best will be adequate.'

What is needed is a broadening of the concept of medical research to include not only clinical and laboratory research, but also systems research and especially how to integrate the skills of doctors, nurses, dentists and others who make up the system. The Medical Research Council is now beginning to show an interest in health care delivery programs.[1]

In the late sixties Canada was spending some $3 billion annually on health care and nearly $50 million on medical research, which is about 1.6 per cent. This ratio is not out of line with the national average.

Three-quarters of the costs of medical research are provided by the federal government. Provincial governments and other Canadian sources supply most of the rest, leaving 4 per cent to American agencies. Of the federal research funds, about three-quarters come from the MRC, the rest from the Department of National Health and Welfare, the DRB, and the Department of Veterans Affairs.

The US spends on medical research five to seven times as much *per capita* as Canada; this total includes private donors. In the UK the visible total is somewhat higher than Canada's and there is voluntary money in addition.

The Macdonald report (see chapter 7) promotes medical and health research to the status of pure science, not to be stigmatized by tests of practicality. Macdonald proposes that an enlarged MRC take its place with the NRC and a Social Sciences Council, to meet university demands in disciplines which are not of interest to mission-oriented agencies. This ultimate partisan position on health care is not often framed so explicitly.

In the universities the members of the medical faculty carry about half the undergraduate teaching load of other faculties with correspondingly increased opportunities for research (table 10). This was remarked on in the OECD report:

Of all the recipients of Canadian government grants, researchers working on MRC programs are the most favoured. Generous grants are given to the best proposals. It is sometimes affirmed that this practice has led researchers in other fields to shift to activities likely to attract MRC grants to the detriment of their original discipline. Evidence on this point is not available, but there is no doubt that the MRC has been instrumental in the rise of the status of medical research in Canada.

Evidently the MRC has served as a pilot-plant experiment in the use of financial inducements to divert scientists into areas of special interest. Since this is what seems to be in the books for the whole of science, once the priorities are drawn up, one might have expected that the prototype would have been the subject of close analysis. Evidently not, since the only additional conclusion the OECD can draw is that the special status of medical research results in isolation of medical schools, whose researchers do not always participate as much as they might in attempts to establish interdisciplinary groups.

The Medical Research Council has followed the traditional NRC practice of making awards on a merit basis with only minor consideration to the fostering of preferred fields, as this extract from the Senate hearing shows.

Chairman: It has been suggested that Canada could become a world leader in a few years if we were to concentrate, for instance, on virus research. Does the Council have a list of research priorities?
Dr G. Malcolm Brown, chairman, MRC: No; we give support to those applications which are good.
Dr Robert B. Salter: One priority that we consider frequently is the new investigator and the new medical school.
Chairman: Is the Council trying to develop research in certain sectors rather than in others?

TABLE 10

Allocation of faculty salaries in Canadian
universities in the late sixties (percentages)

	Medicine	Other faculties
Undergraduate instruction	24	45
Research and graduate training	46	33
Other activities	30	22

SOURCE: Macdonald report, table 3:10. 'Other
activities' include administration, professional
organizations, community service, etc. 'Other
faculties' were arts, science, engineering,
agriculture, and education.

Brown: This is limited by funds, because when the Council has provided support
on a basis of merit ...
Chairman: You have nothing left.
Brown: There is not all that left with which to manoeuvre.[2]

Research on bedside disciplines (the equivalent of industrial R & D) plays
a quite minor part in the program of the MRC, amounting, according to
insiders, to some 20 per cent of the budget. The rest goes to laboratory science. The chairman of the MRC on being asked about this at the Senate hearings, gave an answer which identified the amount of money spent in clinical
departments rather than the amount of money spent on research on
patients.

Senator Fred A. McGrand: I would like to know the amount of money that is spent
in the observation of patients in the wards of hospitals.
Dr G. Malcolm Brown: Approximately 35 per cent of our grants-in-aid are spent
in clinical departments.
McGrand: I would like to get your views on the importance of more research on
people rather than on laboratory animals.
Brown: It is a fact that laboratory research has a cachet or glamour that has diverted
people from other types of research which are necessary and can be very productive.[3]

The MRC Report for 1967-8 contains fifty pages listing operating grants. The opening page, reproduced in table 11, will serve as an approximate sample of the cash flow: 20% for research involving patients, 40% for laboratory research with a medical slant, and 40% for research in pure science, mainly biochemistry, which would require a professional apologist to relate it to medical interests.

Why does the MRC, which claims to be short of funds, spend 40 per cent of its grants in pure science outside its field? In point of fact the real shortage is not of money but of people qualified and willing to work at legitimate medical research. The public has insisted on giving the MRC and other health agencies more money than they know how to use, partly because of a false analogy from the business world that any research results can be bought at a price. Partly too, the loss of a relative through cancer, or the saving of ourself by a wonder drug has removed our normal critical faculties where medical science is concerned.

The introduction of medicare has greatly assisted the deans in their efforts to bring about a revolution in the quality of medical education. Formerly the clinical professors received $500 annually and, if they felt like it, gave an occasional lecture. Now they receive some 60 per cent of their salaries from the universities and are permitted only enough private practice to keep them in touch with the outside doctors. The change will have a profound effect on the amount of clinical research.

The staff-student ratio imposed on medical schools by U.S. licensing bodies is so high that very little time is required to teach medical classes and members of the faculty can practise pure science.* At the Senate hearing a medical witness said, 'In Canada we would not be able to keep a single person in the pure sciences, say a biochemist, who did only teaching. Eighty per cent of these persons' time is devoted to research.'

And why has biochemistry been so successful? Probably at every point of history some branch of philosophy, theology, or science has seemed to be on the verge of unlocking the secret of life, and for the last quarter-century the spotlight has been on biochemistry. The exciting discoveries of brilliant men have brought in their wake a great multiplication of laboratory acolytes attracted by the *cachet* and glamour of pure science. When you detach a man of ordinary intelligence from the main stream of social objectives and leave him on his own, the research product is likely to be

---

* If U.S. directives were not followed our medical graduates would be inhibited from migrating to the USA to practise. Their difficulties would be equivalent to those of physicians from some European countries coming to Canada.

TABLE 11

Part of list of operating grants of the Medical Research Council in 1967–8

Name, department, university	Grant title	Amount $
Abrahams, V.C. Physiology, Queen's	Organization of the superior collicus	24,000
Abshire, C.J. Biochem., Laval	Synthesis and bacteriological investigation of amino acid analogs and related compounds	10,000
Adamkiewicz, V.W. Microbiol., Montreal	Humoral specificity in glucose	16,200
Adamson, J.D. Psychiatry, Manitoba	Psychophysiology of emotion in psychiatric patients	5,725
Aldous, J.G. Pharmacology, Dal.	Regulatory mechanisms in cell physiology	11,600
Allen, J.R. Carlson, H.C. Vet. Microbiol., Sask.	Allergic phenomena in parasitic diseases, and studies on inflammatory reaction in birds	8,025
Angel, A. Pathology, McGill	Studies on the biochemical and structural pathways of lipid transport	12,000
Anwar, R. Biochem., Toronto	Biosynthetic reactions and the structure of elastin and its mode of breakdown by elastases	18,200
Applegarth, D.A. Paediatrics, BC	Investigation of the cell wall of some fungi	8,250
Archibald, J. Clinical Studies, Guelph	Development and use of germ-free pig techniques	10,000
Archibald, Y.M. Phys. Med., West. Ont.	An evaluation of four nonverbal cognitive tests for use in the differential diagnosis of brain damage	2,075
Ashmore, P.G. Surgery, BC	A study of physical and chemical changes in circulating blood during cardiopulmonary bypass	12,000
Auger, C. Pathology, Laval	Maintenance of electron microscopes during the period 1 April 1967 to 31 March 1968	6,280
Awad, J.A. Caron, W. Surgery, Laval	A study of various methods of respiratory assistance by means of an artificial oxygenator and a pulmonary transplant preserved by isolation perfusion	18,750
Axelrad, A.A. Anatomy, Toronto	Investigation of the G_0 state of stem cells in the hemopoietic and other systems	15,000
Ayengar, R. Biochemistry, Dal.	A comparative study of rabbit hemagglutinating and precipitating antibodies	9,000

(*continued on page 118*)

Babineau, L.M. Biochemistry, Laval	Synthesis of new amino acids and characterization of chemically modified peptides	12,760
Baer, E. Banting and Best Dept. of Med. Res., Toronto	Synthesis of clinically useful phosphatide analogues with long-lasting activity on blood clotting mechanism	16,300
Bailey, J.D. Martin, J.M. Hosp. for Sick Children, Toronto	The role of growth hormone in low birth weight dwarfism	10,000

SOURCE: *MRC Annual Report on Support of University Research, 1967-8*
NOTE: Work with patients is evident in the grants to Adamson, Y.M. Archibald, Ashmore, Awad & Caron, and Bailey & Martin (total 21.5%). Medical orientation appears in the titles of Abrahams, Allen & Carlson, J. Archibald, Auger, Axelrad, Ayengar, and Baer (total 39.2%). The remaining grantees, who receive 39.3% of the money, are doing pure science which only an exercise in semantics could relate to medicine.

negligible, and these biochemists and others are no exception to the rule. The usual accomplishment reminds me of some lines written by a friend:

A mind that grinds and grinds and grinds
When there's nothing in it to grind,
Gnawing itself away in frenzied toil,
And producing ...
Nothing![4]

The accumulation of 'pure' biochemists under the medical umbrella is one of the outstanding misuses of Canadian scientific talent. The MRC should be forced to liberate this excess of talent so that it might become available for areas of manpower shortage, such as food and agricultural chemistry or the study of organic pollutants.

II MILITARY SCIENCE

The second of the categorical imperatives, military science, is known as aggression when carried out by their side and defence when done by our side. By 1984, as Orwell predicts, each national establishment will be known as a Ministry of Peace or Minipax.

The politico-military possibilities of science as a bandwagon are shown in the following plug, offered by W.G. Magnuson, a U.S. senator from Washington, a coastal state with some sea-grant college hopes. It was included in the preface to a generally peaceful paperback explaining marine research.

The USSR could attain control of the world ocean if we stand idly by. Soviet Russia has more submarines than the Free World, more minelayers, minesweepers, naval aircraft – research and survey ships – fishing vessels potentially useful as Soviet Naval Auxiliaries – has massed as many as 200 fishing vessels off New England, with specially trained intelligence officers snooping along our coasts with sophisticated instruments. The challenge dates back to Lenin who brought so much misery on the world. The prevention of Communist domination of the seas is our most pressing problem today.[5]

Canada's formal establishment of military science dates from the end of the Second World War. Until about the middle of the War military officers used to think that civilian scientists should conduct their research only pursuant to 'requirements' defined by military staff work. This notion was exploded as it became apparent that what scientists discovered by unrestricted research might be of greater military importance than the things the military officers thought they wanted – in short that the means might determine the ends.*

Our scientific war effort was entrusted to the NRC, whose staff increased six-fold, and which acquired twenty new laboratories, almost all for military research. In 1947, the Defence Research Board was created within the Department of National Defence, took over military research and, by 1968, was operating eight establishments across the country.

The DRB is essentially a civilian agency, whose management is rather like a board of directors, headed by a chairman and vice-chairman. *Ex-officio* members represent the armed forces, the Department of National Defence, and the NRC. Other members are appointed for three-year terms. Eight members of the board represent the administration and eight come from the universities.

Like the resource agencies, the DRB has the task of recommending new techniques, which lead in turn to the abandonment of old ones. The existing weapons have behind them very strong vested interests among the military, whose skills and careers are tied to their capabilities. There is also a civilian

---

* One research project suggested by a Canadian citizen during the War was to provide multi-spiked contrivances, dropped on the ground to ensnare tanks. The military authorities pointed out in reply that the method has already come into use against the feet of Alexander the Great's elephants.

bias in favour of the preservation of existing systems, for example, an air base on Prince Edward Island or in Newfoundland.

In its early days the DRB was the major supporter of medical research and a large contributor to university science generally. As set up by its first chairman, Omond Solandt, its grant program was the most intelligently conceived of any of the mission agencies. Over the years new granting agencies have been created and civilian industrial research has grown, so that the relative impact of DRB activities has been decreasing.

The desire of the board for good public and university relations is hindered by the fact that military technology remains much less publicly visible, relative to its importance, than other technologies. A considerable proportion of it is either classified or proprietary, with controls in military hands.

Chairman: I wonder, Dr Uffen, if you can tell us what is the approximate proportion of research activities pursued by your institution which can be classified as secret.
Dr R.J. Uffen, chairman, Defence Research Board: Your very question, Mr Chairman, is one that I am unable to answer.
Chairman: You think this proportion should remain secret?
Uffen: We must leave some things unanswered.[6]

In its most discreditable activity, the DRB provides every year $6 million worth of 'health in reverse' for chemical and biological warfare. According to the official euphemism 'the Nato countries look to Canada for a contribution to the development of protection against chemical or biological attack.'[7]

As George Grant remarked, 'Of all the aspects of our society the military is the most directly an errand boy of the Americans.'[8] Five of our alphabet agencies have been supporting industrial R & D.[9] One of them, IRDIA, supports both military and civilian industry; two others, DIP and DIR are for defence industries only; and the final two, PAIT and IRAP, are for civilian technology. These programs are stacked so that the government, attracted by the export opportunities provided by the Vietnam War, has favoured defence industries by a ratio of two to one[10] and has given 82 per cent of defence industry grants to foreign-controlled firms.[11] T.E. Broadbent said in a Commons debate:

By the establishment of a permanent industry based on warfare, the government is promoting a military-industrial elite by means of its R & D programs. If profits from war industries are greater than those derived from production for peace, are industrialists likely to choose the latter?[12]

Canada's success in the export field is also heavily dependent on participation in the u.s. defence pattern, as appeared in the Senate hearings.

Senator Allister Grosart: I am concerned with the question that it is not price in the world market any more, it is that early jump on innovation.
David B. Mundy, ADM, Department of Industry: Our geography, economics and politics give us special access to the most advanced world technology in the United States. By taking advantage of these circumstances we have escaped the outcry which there is in Europe about the technological gap.
Grosart: *Défiez les Américains.*
Mundy: We have a special arrangement with the Americans in the defence field, so that the advanced technology of their giant laboratories is available to us where we enter into joint programs with them. In the civil area we obtain production techniques for air frames and advanced aerospace products from parent companies.[13]

Some research activities performed by the Canadian government in its own establishments have been used in testing for u.s. and European industries. The NRC's aerodynamic laboratories and wind tunnels, and the DRB's hypersonic ranges have been supporting research programs of the u.s. Department of Defence and its contractors. It is apparent that in all of these instances the realities of the technological scene, rather than any desire for national identity, have been in control.

In reply to criticism about subservience to the USA, supporters of military research maintain, with some truth, that the by-products of their activity make a greater contribution to the general advancement of science than much civilian-motivated R & D. Because military activity is a categorical imperative it has an emotional base of support and so is able to undertake peripheral projects that would not, on rational grounds alone, be given the necessary priority.

As a classic example, the British Admiralty carried out the hydrographic measurements from which the oceans were mapped. One ship assigned to this work was HMS *Beagle* which, through the good offices of the captain, took along Charles Darwin as a naturalist. A more modern instance is the great support offered to academic science by the u.s. Office of Naval Research.

In Canada, the DRB built up a large section dealing with satellite communication which developed equipment sold abroad. The group was transferred in the late sixties to the new Department of Communications. The DRB has also developed, among other things, new types of batteries and beacons for aircraft.

III   THE TECHNOLOGY GAP

The third of the categorical imperatives, and the one that gives rise to the largest amount of contemporary discussion by planners, concerns industry and how to bring it up to ever-greater efficiency as an exporter of the products of secondary manufacturing. The problem is usually described as the 'technology gap' which refers to the difference between the capability of advanced nations and that of the world's leading country, the USA. The problem is how to become competitive in world trade and thus attain a standard of living comparable to that of the United States.

The gap, as it appears in Canada, has been subject to a good deal of diagnosis and proposed treatment. We may begin by enquiring what form the disease takes. Professor Frank Forward, when he was in Ottawa, had the habit of offering those to whom he talked his sketch of the progress of Canadian science (figure 3). The development of science with time was assumed to follow the classical maturation pattern of populations, animals, or plants. On this s-shaped curve the government departments had reached almost their final size, universities were behind, and industrial research still farther behind. Consequently, while expansion of government science was about over, the universities should still flourish, and especially should have academic strength added to them in the areas in which industrial research was required. The way to accomplish this would be for the NRC and other bodies to award grants to strengthen approved areas in selected universities in each region. Direct stimulation of industrial research would be concurrent.

No quantitative basis exists for viewing figure 3 as a model of the history of Canadian science. Its interest is as illustration of a view widely held by influential people since the early sixties.

M.P. Bachynski also highlighted the view that in Canada the weakest link is in applied industrial research.[14] Working from the premise that our foremost objective is the translation of research and technology into economic benefits, he set up, in the top panel of figure 4, an ideal relationship for R & D in which each component is fully developed. Although the upper panel does not show it, Bachynski considered that in a balanced

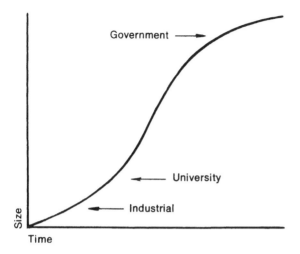

Figure 3 Supposed present position of the components of Canadian science shown on a growth curve of classical form

program the development effort should be greater than the applied research effort, which, in turn, should be greater than basic research. An average ratio (modified American Plan) might be 65%, 25%, 10%.

A point to recognize in the research-to-product cycle is the risk involved at each stage. In basic research only a few results are expected to pay off, and those only in the long term. In applied research the risks are still high. At the development stage feasibility has been proved and preliminary costs and market surveys have been conducted, so the chances of success are good. From all this it follows that government cost-sharing programs should operate on a sliding scale, declining from full support for basic research towards zero at the end of development. Some basic research must be built up in industry in order to provide ground for communication with university and government research.

There is some overlap between the three components which forms the basis of common interest and communication.

In the Canadian position, shown in the lower part of figure 4, pure research is pictured in a reasonably healthy state, but there is an almost total lack of applied research, and inadequate support for development activity. There is also a lack of common interests between the three sectors.

Figure 4, like figure 3, is interesting as representing a point of view held

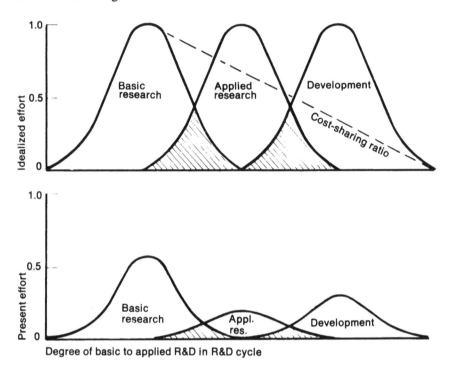

Figure 4 Idealized R & D spectrum of activity (top) compared with the R & D spectrum as it is considered to exist in Canada (bottom). The descending cross line represents the degree of government aid for each segment in industry. Hatched areas represent common interest between the segments.
After Bachynski

by many in industry. We have already noted that the division of research into pure and applied parts is a very subjective operation, and in his presentation of the Canadian position Bachynski has taken an extreme anti-academic posture. Also, as the following paragraphs show, the 'ideal' ratios are not approached by the leading growth country, Japan.

For many years the exploitation of natural resources remained the dominant feature of Canadian economic life. More recently the proportion of finished products has grown and, although still relatively modest, it is comparable with that of Sweden and Belgium. The increase of this secondary industry is felt to be the way to open up the road to prosperity and the first step proposed, as we have just seen, is to readjust the ratios in our R & D cycle.

TABLE 12

Distribution of scientific effort between parts of the
R & D cycle in five countries in 1967 (percentages)

	Basic research	Applied research	Development
UK	11	24	65
USA	14	22	64
Belgium	21	42	37
Canada	23	38	39
Japan	27	31	42

SOURCE: Sen. com. report, table 3, from OECD data
NOTE: This breakdown was not available for any
other leading nation. Charts 10 and 11 of the 1972
Green Book give the total costs of the R & D for
twelve countries, but there is no breakdown such as
is shown here.

Since the cause of our economic disease is said to be faulty circulation
through R & D, it is instructive to look at this feature in countries with supposedly better health. There appear to be only five leading countries for
which quantitative cost relations of the R & D cycle are known (table 12).

The country which most closely approaches the ideal ratio towards
which Canada is supposed to move is the UK, hardly an inspired industrial
performer in recent years. The leading countries in industrial progress, the
USA and Japan, are at opposite ends of the scale. Japan, with the best recent
record of GNP growth, also has the highest component of basic research.

The interpretation of comparisons shown in table 12 is complicated by
the large amount of military development work in the USA. The private-
industry status of U.S. space and defence R & D is about on a par with the
amateur status of Russian hockey players. What is called industry research
in the U.S. defence area is often indistinguishable from government
research, and the 'private' companies are often managed by a retired
general.

In the USA since the War there has developed a whole new complex of
private corporations that are almost solely dependent upon the receipt of
government contracts for research and development services. This complex maintains elaborate contacts with both Congress and the administration, and, since with many of the new organizations the government is the

sole client and awards contracts by negotiations rather than competitive bidding, their status as private commercial concerns is more a façade than a fact. In 1958, a reasonably representative year, in an older industry, the automotive industry, military sales ranged from 5 per cent for General Motors to 15 per cent for Chrysler. In the same year in the aircraft industry, military sales ranged from a low of 67 per cent for Beech Aircraft to a high of 99 per cent for the Martin Company.[15]

But even after the military correction, Canada comes out behind the USA, and as a result industrial R & D is regarded by government planners as the current vixen in heat. The OECD report comments:

Canadians would like to pass from the 'continental model' to the 'American model,' as this would be a good way of making Canadian R & D activities less dependent on the United States' scientific effort. The transfer from one model to the other will require sweeping changes between the various research bodies. It would involve a massive transfer of the research potential from the public sector to industry.

Canadian industry provides for itself nearly three-quarters of the R & D funds it uses; the federal government supplies most of the rest, with some 10 per cent coming from other countries, presumably the parent firms.[16]

Although it is customary to deplore the slow progress of Canadian industry, its science has in fact gone forward about as well as that of the universities. Dr C.J. Mackenzie told the senators:

The total number of scientists employed in industrial research laboratories in 1919 was not more than 50 to 60, whereas to-day there are over 6,000. From 1961 to 1965 the research personnel in R & D increased from 1,000 to 1,500.
Over the years Canadian subsidiary companies have paid their parent companies for research knowledge. From 1962 to 1965 the total so spent has been reduced by $1 million and the percentages from 20 to 9 per cent.[17]

It appears from table 13 that the fields of industrial R & D are largely engineering and chemistry. In the universities these disciplines account for about one-quarter of the research, as judged by federal support which is probably a good relative index (table 16, chapter 7). Some of the work in earth sciences and computers should also be applicable so that perhaps one-third of university research could be considered as directed towards the production of recruits for industry. The kind of industry which interests the federal government is quite clear from the fact that about 90 per cent of its R & D aid goes to the manufacturers of electrical products, aircraft

TABLE 13

R & D carried out by Canadian industries in 1965 (percentages)

Electrical products	22
Aircraft and parts	19
Chemical products, drugs, and medicines	14
Primary metals, metal fabrication, and mineral products (8.7%), mining (4.7%)	13
Paper	9
Petroleum products	8
Machinery and instruments	6
Others, including food and beverages (2.5%), textiles (1.5%), rubber (1.0%)	9

SOURCE: OECD report, table 55, from DBS data
NOTE: The sum expended was $285 million.

and parts, and to the closely allied scientific instrument business (mid sixties).

Canadian planners want a convincing diagnosis and proposed treatment for our sluggish industrial posture compared with the USA. But it is hard to say what are causes and what are symptoms of the national disease. Here is a list based on Lithwick[18] and other sources.

– The inadequacy of university research and the weakness of the link between university and industry. As a result firms have found it easier to borrow ideas and technology from the USA, particularly from parent organizations. Professor L.-P. Bonneau said during the Senate hearings:

The link between industry and the university is still extremely small or non-existent, so that a research worker in mechanical or civil engineering will have considerable freedom. Even if our work is not related to engineering it would still be basic research.

We are not an industrial country. There are whole areas in which the universities do applied research for non-existent industries, with the result that the projects are impractical.[19]

– The relative scarcity of scientists and engineers. Proportionally we only have about half as many of these types as the USA and of those we do have, only about half as many as in USA are in R & D. The managements of purely Canadian firms seem to take little interest in research or in the discoveries made in our Canadian universities.

– A lack of willingness in Canada to use risk capital to finance R & D. Parent firms find that in the USA itself R & D investment pays off, but in Canada they get greater return when investments are in capital terms, such as machinery or construction. Purely Canadian capital is said to be hard to find; also we have entered the era of international firms whose decision centres are located in the United States and Europe.

– A feeling that in Canada the performance of managers is inadequate. In a highly protected economy such as ours, there may be an absence of competitive drive. In the United States the would-be entrepreneur is surrounded by evidences of the simple fact that there are successful entrepreneurs emerging every day in the country. R.A. Charpie describes the type of man that makes an entrepreneur:

The innovator is often an anti-establishment type. His important contributions are made either as an individual, or in a small company which he can dominate. Ordinarily he is stronger technically than in administration, management or marketing. He is usually committed completely to the innovative concept which drives him forward.[20]

IV CANADIAN EFFORTS TO OVERCOME AMERICAN INDUSTRIAL DOMINANCE

In terms of the selling value of the products, U.S. firms control about one-third of all Canadian manufacturing establishments. In some industries, such as petroleum, rubber, and automobiles, the American control reaches three-quarters. At the same time Canadian industrial R & D is running at only one-quarter of the American rate. The question therefore arises whether American control causes the low R & D activity in Canada.

One answer comes from a look at the distribution of R & D in industry. The total was $292 million in 1967. American-owned companies performed 44 per cent, other companies under non-resident control performed 16 per cent, and Canadian-owned companies 35 per cent. The remaining 5 per cent was done by Canadian crown corporations.[21] The American R & D appears to be only a little higher than the level of American ownership.

Further evidence is available in the R & D record of the hundred largest Canadian firms (table 14), of which sixty-nine reported activity. Among the active firms those controlled in Canada showed only about half the R & D level of those under outside management (American or other). Here again

TABLE 14

R & D expenditure in the hundred biggest industrial concerns in Canada in 1966

	Number of firms	Number active in R & D	Percentage of profits devoted to R & D in the 69 active firms
Firms under u.s. control	25	19	15
Control by other non-residents	20	15	16
Canadian firms	55	35	7
Total	100	69	11

SOURCE: OECD report, table 64. See also table 78.
NOTE: The total profits were $1.3 billion and total R & D was $140 million.

there is no evidence to support a thesis of American exploitation of the local peasants.

Another charge, very difficult to analyze, is that outsiders keep the R & D of their Canadian branches at a lower level of quality than those of the parent firms. The OECD report remarked:

In many cases the so-called research staff is mainly employed in furthering sales, its main function being to give technical assistance to the customers. One is sometimes inclined to believe that the research department is little more than a part of the build-up aimed at making a good impression; it is also possible that a far-seeing management seeks to forestall any reproach that the head office is preventing development and research in its Canadian branch.

To sum up: American ownership of Canadian industry has enabled the USA to increase her exports across tariff walls by establishment of subsidiaries. These branch plants have provided us with technological advances at low cost and have been our most intensive performers of R & D. The objections to foreign ownership cannot be supported by evidence that it has had an inhibitory effect on domestic industrial science.

Despite the u.s. foreign aid to our developing national R & D, our own planners are far from satisfied. The stimulation of industrial research is thought by the government to be our first priority in science, and it is at the same time the most complicated. The problem is how to avoid giving most of the money to government laboratories and universities, which is all too easy, and little to industry, which is difficult. The main objective of government planners is to get a high rate of growth in industrial R & D.

In its support of industrial research the United States does not use any incentives; it has depended almost entirely on huge contracts, predominantly for defence and space, which affect only a small segment of its industry. Many of the big industries get no government support for research; these include the chemical industry, which is quite progressive, and the steel industry, which is very backward. Thus the u.s. experience with stimulation of industrial R & D does not provide any model for Canada. The chairman of the Science Council told the senators:

We must begin to pay more attention to how our federal government spends its money – whether for defence equipment which is the traditional way to stimulate industry, or just for ordinary needs such as furniture, buildings, etc. The Government should make it a point every time it orders anything, of putting quality, originality of design, and innovation very high on the list of qualifications, rather than putting low price as the sole qualification.[22]

There were in 1972 three kinds of incentive scheme for industrial research. The first is via expenses deductible from income tax. Section 72 of the Income Tax Act allows R & D costs as deductible expenses in computing corporate tax. The second is a general incentives grant, and the third is through several sharing schemes. Herewith a roll-call of the programs; the dollar values are for 1970-1. The total for that year was $95 million.
– IRDIA Industrial Research and Development Incentives Act – $31 million. This formula-type award provides 25 per cent of the costs of increased R & D over a five-year average.* It was started in 1967 to replace an earlier income tax incentive, the 'cost' of which had not been included in statements of support for previous years. Hence IRDIA was not new money for industry. IRDIA is probably the best of the incentives and it has had its greatest effect in inducing foreign-owned subsidiaries to build labs and do part of their research in Canada, on the ground that it can be done more cheaply here.

The remaining programs offer direct aid and the rules are more like university support, in that the choice and conduct of the research rests with the firm which applies for assistance. Although the methods differ, the

* This used to be called GIRD (General Incentives for Research and Development) and during the hearings Senator Grosart referred to it as Gerda.

agencies are similar in covering about half the costs of the R & D, (as compared with about a quarter for university research).

- DIP   Defence Industrial Productivity Program – $26 million. Set up in 1959 by the Department of Defence Production, it was transferred to the Department of Industry, Trade and Commerce in 1964. It is intended to contribute to military technology and the financing of equipment developed as a result of U.S.-Canadian defence agreements.
- PAIT   Program for the Advancement of Industrial Technology – $25 million. Started by the Department of Industry in 1965, this is a civilian program for larger firms that already have adequate research potential and can carry through their findings to marketing.
- IRAP   Industrial Research Assistance Program – $8.4 million. Launched by the NRC in 1962 as a civilian activity parallel to DIRP, this program is intended to develop viable research teams.
- DIRP   Defence Industrial Research Program – $5 million. Set up in 1961 by the Defence Research Board, it was intended to develop research teams in military science, to participate in the U.S.-Canadian defence agreements.
- In addition there are R & D contracts whose value varies. In relation to the total incentive programs, they might be of the order of 20 per cent for military, and 10 per cent for civilian purposes.
- In 1971 the NRC introduced a program called 'Industrial postdoctoral fellowships' intended to encourage new PH DS to enter industry.

The federal assistance programs are described as having such objects as to: outline major industrial trends; determine desirable directions; foster research on new products; facilitate new procedures; improve efficiency; induce small firms to do research; prompt existing firms to extend their spheres; help sluggish industries to branch out; and support co-operative R & D.*

Government officials from the Department of Industry, Trade and Commerce say that under current incentives industry need pay only 12.5 per cent of the cost of conducting R & D. Companies claim that they are usually fine-printed out of the full benefits, since:

- In order to qualify, they must get a topic of military interest (DIP or DIRP) or else show an increase over the current effort (IRAP). There are also

---

* This list was assembled from the declared aims of the Department of Industry, Trade and Commerce, as cited in the OECD report. One is reminded of Churchill's comment on a wartime document: 'It contains every cliché in the language except "Please adjust your clothes."' ' Or, as Jim Thomas put it, 'One cliche after another bloody cliche.'

restrictions aimed to prevent use of the results by foreign firms (PAIT).
- Income tax relief can be claimed only if the company shows a profit. Furthermore, an increase in sales effort and a corresponding decrease in R & D would qualify for the same corporate tax exemption.
- The IRDIA grant applies only to increases, and thus penalizes companies with established, viable research activities.[23]
- There is also a failure to understand that industrial research is not an end in itself, but merely one of the available means to greater corporate growth and profits. R & D are the initial, least costly, and least risky stages of innovation. Should not assistance be proferred where it would provide the greatest incentive – in tooling up construction, marketing start-up, or design or manufacturing start-up?[24]

As an indirect incentive to industry, the NRC and DRB have for some years offered grants for engineering research.* The limiting factor has been a lack of qualified applicants rather than money. The most energetic engineering professors have traditionally operated a private practice downtown, which left them little leisure for acquisition of new knowledge. However, by the mid sixties the support program had come so far that some 15 per cent of university research was in engineering (table 16, chapter 7).

The University of Toronto Institute for Aerospace Studies began in 1949 with a DRB grant, and now receives support from several sources. In addition to research and teaching, it offers, as a company, consulting services to industry. In 1957, the University of Saskatchewan set up an Institute of Space and Atmospheric Studies, also with DRB aid.

In a further effort to improve university participation, the Department of Industry from 1966 on subsidized several industrial research institutes. One was at the University of Windsor, another at the Nova Scotia Technical College, a third at McMaster and a fourth at Waterloo. McGill opened one in 1971, and more are planned. All are essentially concerned with engineering and its technology. These institutes are envisaged as vehicles for the performance of university-based research in engineering technology for corporate or government clients. The Department of Industry undertakes to fund the start-up costs of such institutes, which are supposed in time to become self-sustaining. The Senate committee was interested in the selections:

Hugh Charles Douglas, deputy industrial research adviser: Grants have been

---

* In the United States the first federal grant for experimental research was made in 1832, for an investigation of the reasons for the explosion of steamboat boilers. See D.K. Price, *Government and Science* (New York University Press, 1954), p. 10.

awarded to four universities to establish industrial research institutes. The total amount is $500,000, of which $230,000 has been paid so far.

Senator Maurice Bourget: Were there other universities than the four mentioned?
Douglas: Well, I don't recall.
Bourget: How do we select these universities? I am interested in Windsor.
Douglas: Paul Martin?
Chairman: That is what I thought.[25]

Critics point to two opposite dangers confronting these new institutes. The first is that non-academic activities will become the dominant concern, to the detriment of the university as a whole; this is made probable by the expectation that they will eventually pay their way via fees for services. The second is that, because they are not supposed to compete with consultant firms or professional laboratories, they will lose their industrial incentive and slip into academic problems. Maintenance of the correct balance in these situations usually depends on the personality of one key individual.

It would have been more sensible if the Department of Industry had channelled its regional funds through the provincial research foundations. These have, in comparison with the universities, fewer operational or administrative difficulties in meeting the R & D needs of industry and government. The work they can undertake is not limited by the interests of staff members and graduate students.

To digress into undergraduate matters, the OECD reported that the present shortages were, in order of demand: production engineers, mathematicians, mechanical engineers, physicists, chemists, electrical engineers, and civil engineers. However, the future holds too many unpredictable elements to permit any rational estimate of shortages.

To conclude this section a word should be said about our private industrial institutes. The best known of these industry-based bodies is the Pulp and Paper Research Institute of Canada, founded in 1913, and for several decades located on McGill premises. In its early stages it was largely indistinguishable from the university and was often run by faculy members. Its board includes industry, McGill, and government representatives. The institute has been successful in developing new mass-production techniques for its sponsors.

The Sheridan Park Corporation, established near Toronto, with the Ontario Research Foundation as its nucleus, is a community of industrial R & D agencies, mostly private companies. The hope is that the components will have an autocatalytic effect resulting in a strong national centre of industrial research. So far, the hopes have not been realized.

Any one of the categorical imperatives, discussed above can, under favourable circumstances, develop a take-over bid for the economy of a country, with corresponding orientation of science. All too familiar in recent times have been the military take-overs in Germany and Japan. At present either the USA or Russia could easily slip into military domination. Canada seems at this time to have a declining interest in military prowess.

In the USA the money easily available for military purposes has brought with it a substantial fall-out into university science. The Office of Naval Research set the pattern for military and NASA sponsorship of most of the university R & D. Recently Congress has been challenging the tradition and in 1970 put in a requirement that support must be restricted to studies which had 'a direct and apparent relationship to a specific military function.' This was later loosened to 'potential relationship.'

In medicine, the objectives are often as clear-cut as in military science. In fact there is a certain grim family resemblance. This gives edge and sharpness to the deployment of medical research. For it is not the nature of the objective that makes for speedy action, whether it is destructive or on the side of life. All that matters is that there should be an objective at all. Everybody knows that health costs are rising in Canada. According to the Economic Council, a few years ago we were spending 3 per cent of the GNP on health; with the new medical plans this has sailed past 5 per cent and by 1975 is expected to reach 6.5 per cent.

Medicine has replaced religion as the hope for extended life, especially as belief in the afterlife has declined and heaven is now known to be located in Miami. The appeal of medicine lies in its visible and daily proven results. There is hardly a family in the country where lives have not been extended by the use of recent discoveries. In past times there have been many countries in which the church has made a successful take-over bid. Today its successor is health science, offering the same promise, in less extravagant but more believable terms. It may very well, in Canada and elsewhere, come to dominate our economy.

Eventually, for each of us except Elijah and Jacob, the medical promise fails however and the clergy take over with the point blank defences. The integrated system is seen to advantage inside a hospital. Recently I was a hospital patient and one day as I lay on my bed a head appeared at the door, surmounting a clerical uniform. 'Mr Dodgson?' he enquired anxiously. I said 'No, my name is Hayes.' 'So sorry,' he said, 'they must have given me the wrong room. Oh dear! Oh dear! I shall be too late.' He took a watch out of his waistcoat pocket, looked at it and then hurried on down the corridor. I hope he arrived in time to escort Mr Dodgson into Paradise.

Medicine and the military make their claims with some subtlety: 'The best is none too good,' etc. But the third take-over bid, by industry, is loudly trumpeted by planners and opposed only by the thin squeak of the environmentalists. Efforts of Canadian planners to promote a great leap forward in industrial R & D have not so far had much success. Perhaps, therefore, I might offer a suggestion or two as to where the trouble lies.

In some industries, for example, steel, there is great internal conservatism, centred at the level of the plant foreman. In my view the best federal policy here would be to work through the provincial research foundations, which are close to the needs and can integrate financial stimulation with direct help.

The provincial area of applied research and monitoring would itself benefit from a clean-up. Take, for example, my own province of Nova Scotia. There is, first of all, a research foundation set up after the Second World War, supported by provincial funds and grants and contracts from the NRC and other government departments and private companies. Then a few years ago the federal Department of Industry decided to start up a rival outfit based on the local technical college which, predictably, competed for staff with its competitor. This second group, called the Atlantic Industrial Research Institute, has a Madison Avenue approach, with probably as high a ratio of advertising per unit of science effort as any laboratory in the country. Surprisingly, the NRC has begun to subsidize the AIRI as well as the research foundation.

Finally, the province has a series of loan boards to subsidize various industries and natural resources. The subsidies have been traditionally independent of any science input, but have recently been gathered together in the same ministry as the research foundation. The Nova Scotia government is currently considering the possibility of fusing the research foundation with its counterpart in New Brunswick.

No doubt other provinces exhibit similar disorganization. In such cases, where a province has been sloppy and the federal authority has lacked coordination, there is an obvious area for the Minister of State for Science & Technology to intervene. For a start the federal government should prevent its own agencies from acting as contenders for prestige.

The proposal made here to harmonize applied research and monitoring is not difficult to understand and is not primarily dependent on future studies and reports. The federal part would involve a decision repugnant to the Treasury Board mentality, namely, to enquire, before 'restructuring,' which agencies are good and which are bad. Those laboratories and other organizations which are good in achieving their scientific objective should be made dominant. Their internal working arrangements are not really important and may exhibit as much variability as the methods used by good teachers and good researchers.

Since final decisions are political it is of interest to note that each of the categorical imperatives has its political following. Parties of the right and chauvinists favour the military establishment; the left favours take-over by the social services and health. Economic nationalism is a prerogative of the have-nots, usually identified with the left, and of intellectuals.

6
Resources

The exploitation of natural resources was once the core of Canadian science. Resources are administered by Ottawa in the three broad divisions of Renewable Resources, (except water which is the only non-living renewable resource), Agriculture, and Mines and Energy. This section offers some general remarks on renewable resources and makes comparisons with Agriculture.

After Agriculture the first agency in the renewable resource field was the Fisheries Research Board which arose out of a recommendation of the British Association for the Advancement of Science in 1898. In the Trudeau 'restructuring' other components were combined with Fisheries, beginning with Forestry. The 1970-1 session of Parliament created a new Department of the Environment, based on Fisheries and Forestry. Oceanography, meteorology, fresh water, and wildlife are component parts. At the same time the Minister of the Environment stated his intention to set up a National Environmental Council, which is now in operation.

In these days the council form of management is gaining in favour with planners though not, as has been noted, with the Treasury Board. Thus four reports that followed one another in short order during 1970-1 agreed in recommending boards, widely representative of society, to advise the minister.[1] The stable includes: a National Co-ordinating Committee on Forest Resources Research, a Canadian Waterfowl Advisory Board, an Environmental Council of Canada, and a Renewable Resources Research

Council. There is also to be an Agricultural Research Board, so named by B.N. Smallman, which the Science Council prefers to call the Agricultural Research Co-ordinating Council or ARCC. The acronym is evidently not intended to be pronounced.

It is a problem of natural resources that their technology has had quite a different origin from that of the newer adaptive industries. It has come down to us from an uncritical synthesis of experience and was represented by guilds or by highly specialized groups of men who passed on their accumulated skills and judgments to apprentices. They staffed the industries of the necessities – food, shelter, clothing. For a given population there is a limit, within a factor of two or three, on the amount of the necessities which society requires or can accept. The limit on food has already been reached in Canada (although not of world food in the foreseeable future) and may explain why there is a declining interest in the application of science to natural resources here.

The operation of modern science on a guild, say fishing, requires the dismantling of existing methods as well as the introduction of new ones. Conservatism offers great resistance to both processes and makes necessary a supporting group of middlemen or interpreters. They have to be dedicated as well as energetic, for they tend to be denounced by academic researchers as inadequately trained, and by the guild as too academic. The industries of necessity are clearly more difficult to bring under science than adaptive industries which spring directly out of the laboratory.

Of the latter, power, transportation, and communications are typical examples. These adaptive industries have the characteristic, not of providing necessities but of making the individual more effective in his environment. They are usually created directly from the most advanced science of our time. There is no core of conservatism obstructing their practitioners; the problem is, through advertising, to get users for them. This, together with the rate of technical innovation, is the only limit to their expansion.

It has been stated that the mid-century marked approximately the crossover time from empirical to science-based technologies, which now make up more than half the whole. By the end of the century, technology will be almost completely science-based. Presumably the residual activities will disappear or be engaged in only by the poorest people in remote areas.

Those not intelligent enough to participate will have a hard time in a science-based world. They would be most useful and most comfortable as domestic servants if such an occupation could be made socially acceptable.

Turning to costs, renewable resource research, like military and space research, is expensive. The infrastructure may include vessels, aircraft, and the opening up of the Arctic with stores, communications, and ice-breakers. And because of undependable weather and rough seas, there are many lost days in field work. A university field worker (like a medical researcher) is much more dependent on support in kind (ships, aircraft, and so on) than is a laboratory worker, a fact which has until recently been better understood by the mission-oriented agencies than by the NRC. Research costs are also high because of the time scale and inherent variability of biological material, as affected by good and bad breeding seasons, climatic adversity, diseases, etc. The cost of establishing the effect of an experiment or treatment on a variable biological system is comparable to well-known examples in medicine such as the relation of cigarettes to lung cancer.

To take an example, consider the Greenland salmon fishery which resulted in closure of commercial fishing by Canadians in their own waters in 1972, and which has raised international antagonism in every interested country, except Denmark. To find out whether this fishery was having any effect on salmon stocks would require an investigation of the same order of cost as the cigarette-cancer one. While society would pay the costs for cancer research, it certainly would not do so in fisheries. Thus the Greenland problem is insoluble. The action which was taken was equivalent to prohibiting cigarette smoking in 1900 on a hunch. This same observation applies to all studies of salmon populations on both coasts. We know little more now than we did when the first white man put a net in the water. This is one of the failures of science on which work should be discontinued.[2]

Table 15 shows the distribution of resource R & D by performer. The situation in Agriculture is discussed in the next section. Forestry is remarkable for the large share undertaken by industry, largely in forest product laboratories. Since the forests are private property or leaseholds, there is some private field work as well. General aspects of forestry such as diseases and pests do not receive much attention from industry.

Fisheries and wildlife are common property resources; hence individual Canadians have no adequate incentive to invest in the husbandry of their wealth and potential. For this reason, and because of the fragmented nature of the industries, there has been no alternative to government domination of their research. It is probable that the distribution shown in table 15 will continue, except for some increase in the university segment, perhaps to 10 per cent.

I will refer here to a form of inertia which leads to repetitive observations. This is characteristic of all research fields, but is especially notice-

TABLE 15

Expenditures on renewable resources R & D in a typical year in the late sixties arranged by performer

	Agriculture %	Forestry %	Fisheries %	Wildlife %
Federal	53	38	85	41
Provincial	11	6	13	50
Industry	7	51	—	5
University	29	5	2	4
Dollar total in millions	75	57	26	8

SOURCE: SC special study no. 10 and reports nos 8 and 9 (all 1970)
NOTE: The university component in agriculture includes the appropriate fraction of salaries and administrative costs, while the others include grants only.

able in resource science. It has a legitimate origin, arising out of the great variability in the speed at which natural events occur. A generation of bacteria requires an hour, of fruit flies a week, of salmon and spruce trees several years. The study of natural populations and the effect of human and environmental pressures on them may therefore be a lengthy operation. Forecasts are necessary as to which attempts are likely to be worth the long investment in time and money.

Once started, each long program acquires a team who become interested in it and wish it to continue indefinitely. Observations which have been repeated for a few years, take on a momentum of their own until, gradually, the resources of the organization become committed to repetitive routine.

With expanding budgets since the War, the government agencies have been able to finance new work with new money, and so lacked incentive to eliminate obsolete routines. More recently the Trudeau restraints have had the healthy effect of forcing re-consideration of low-priority research. The Senate committee was also concerned about the question.

Senator Harry Hays (a former minister of agriculture): How do you wash out old programs? How do you get rid of them? When do you say, well, this is enough? I do not know whether you are still trying to make Holstein cows out of chromosomes and genes or not. I am kind of relating it to that.
Dr Bert B. Migicovsky: The dairy cattle breeding project goes back to the early

fifties; the plan is to increase the efficiency of milk production through selection. Any genetic project with a large animal is, of necessity, a long term project. The success to date is under review and we will see whether it should be eliminated. *Sydney B. Williams, deputy minister*: We are trying to approach the question of priorities, first through the development of cost-benefit techniques; and secondly we are developing a group within our Economics Branch who will be located on our stations and will bring the economic philosophy to our research people.[3]

II AGRICULTURE

Among the natural resources agriculture has been historically and remains today the most important primary industry in Canada, providing employment for three times as many persons as all other primary industries combined. The research Branch of the department is correspondingly large, with twenty six research stations, fourteen experimental farms, eight research institutes and three research services, manned by more than 700 research scientists.

As the rich man of Canadian science, Agriculture has attracted envious glances from its associates. Its position is paradoxical because the charge against it is that it is, except perhaps for medicine, the most successful example we have of R & D in action. The increased productivity resulting from research effort has enabled progressively fewer workers to pile up embarrassing quantities of food.* The deduction from this that agricultural research should be turned off is a special case of the frequently heard proposal to turn off science because the world is out of joint.

It is also paradoxical that agriculture's greatest achievement, the control of pests and diseases by chemicals, has been a main target of criticism. The federal department reacted to Rachel Carson in about the same way that General Motors reacted to Ralph Nader. As various chemicals have successively given rise to public concern, its posture has been one of scepticism slowly yielding in the face of unwelcome evidence. This has brought the department into poor public relations with anti-pollutionists.

The contemporary problems of Canadian agriculture are rural slums and marketing, neither of which is amenable to attack through natural science.

---

* One result of such food surpluses is that people can afford to indulge their whims and prejudices. Hence antipathies to such food as pork and mackerel. On the Grand Banks, one of our choicest food fishes, the hake, is fished by the Russians and Portuguese but not by Canadians. And we are prohibited by our fish inspection service from eating any part except the main muscle of the scallop, although the rest (about three times as much) is equally delicious.

Hence the trend of proposals to shift the emphasis to economics and sociology. The world problems, however, remain in the field of natural science, and so, in the long run, do those of Canada.

The BNA Act gave concurrent jurisdiction for agriculture to the provinces and the federal government. There have been attempts to coordinate the work of the agencies, but during the past half-century the tendency has been for the 'have-not' provinces to surrender programs to the federal people, which has led to the present federal dominant 53 per cent of national research (table 15). Current thinking is that the provinces will play a more prominent role in the research of the future than their present 11 per cent.

The industry share of agriculture, like other activities, exhibits the branch-plant economy. Whereas in the United States 53 per cent of the R & D is performed by industry, the figure for Canada is 7 per cent. The results of research by the parent companies become available as Canadian manufacturing licences. Thus agriculture joins the rest of manufacturing as a contributor to the technology gap between Canada and the USA.

Agriculture was the first professional faculty in the western universities; together with forestry it accomplished in its early days what it is now the fashion to advocate – it made use of existing principles of science for technological advances. The science was primitive and so were some of the applications. Irreverent students used to quote as the motto of the Ontario Agricultural College: *'Omnia Aroma Cowbarniensis*: if it can't be done with a manure fork it isn't worth doing.' After the Second World War a determined and successful effort was made to bring to dominance in agriculture the experimental approaches which had advanced other branches of science.

The university share of the national effort (table 15) is 29 per cent, much the highest in the resource field. The authors of the special study have not examined the possibility that agriculture may have outlived its time as an independent university discipline. Their suggestion is to attach to one or other of the existing faculties of agriculture each of their five proposed new national research programs. But only one of these (for cold and drought resistance of plants) is agricultural; the others relate to renewable resources generally. They are: bioeconomics, population ecology, rural adjustment, and Atlantic resource management.

In the universities the history of agriculture can be compared to the course taken later by medicine. As the west was opened up, the new universities were build around their faculties of agriculture. With time the system tended to split into two sections; one of relatively short and simple courses for young farmers (like paramedical work in nursing, physiotheraphy, and so on), the other of graduate training and research whose products did not in general return to the farms but were instead ploughed back into the government or university system (like medical researchers). Within the faculties of agriculture, the large plant-science and animal-science departments quite eclipsed their equivalents in arts and science.

Agriculture, despite its long history, never rivalled the social position of medicine in the universities and in recent years several things have conspired to undermine its dominance. One is the growth of other parts of the university; another is the decline of interest and numbers of candidates from the farms, because of increased efficiency and overproduction of food. Also the science problems of today lie with the multiple use of resources and the land-water complex, rather than with farming alone. Hence my prognosis for the faculties, at the graduate level, is that they will either adapt to the broader problems of the environment or wither away.

Turning from agricultural doers to agricultural disciplines, according to Smallman most of the work in the natural sciences and half the economics is done by the federal government; industry does nearly half of the national total for engineering; and the universities stand practically alone in the field of sociology. The overwhelming 82 per cent of R & D devoted to the natural sciences led to the following comment:

Agricultural science, a pioneer of multidisciplinary approach to practical problems, has developed a curious hiatus to the extension of its expertise into economics and engineering, while the effort devoted to rural sociology is both minuscule and fortuitous.[4]

Smallman proposed a five-year adjustment in which all other subjects increase at the expense of the natural sciences, which would be accomplished by attrition of workers in the latter field. At the same time there would be a transfer of some of the smaller research stations and of soil surveys to the provinces. It is hoped that industry too would increase its share.

For a list of high- and low-priority subjects in the fields of renewable resources and agriculture, see table 18, chapter 7.

The feeling that they are no longer necessary has not improved the morale in our agricultural colleges, some of which have become rather defensive and grumpy as they wonder whether they will survive as components of resource or environmental agencies.

III ENERGY

The Department of Energy, Mines and Resources is responsible for non-renewable resources and power.* One of its branches, the Geological Survey, dates from 1841 when the first United Parliament of the Province of Canada resolved 'that a sum not exceeding 1,500 pounds sterling be granted to defray the probable expenses in causing a Geological Survey of the Province to be made.'

The ministry used to be called Mines and Technical Surveys and most of its work today is in this area. It is also concerned with policy regarding the export of water, power, oil, and gas to the USA.

Among the energy sources coal mining, which formerly presented formidable scientific problems, is changing to the sociological question of how to phase out displaced miners. The research aspects of oil as a source of energy are to a large extent in the hands of the large American companies. As to the great new water-power proposals like Fundy and James Bay, the technical assessments are made by private consulting firms with EM & R pronouncing on economic feasibility. All these are activities of great national importance, but to go into them in detail would be beyond the scope of this book. Their impact on the public consciousness derives chiefly from their potential capacity to destroy the environment.

For the future the hope and focus of research interest is atomic power, centred in the crown corporation, Atomic Energy of Canada Ltd. It will be convenient to comment on this corporation first as a scientific enterprise, then as a business enterprise.

Nuclear fission, the basis of atomic power, was first reported in Berlin in 1939.[5] The German high command considered its potential and decided (correctly as it turned out) that it could not be developed as a weapon in time to affect the outcome of the European War. The Americans took it up with the well-known result at Hiroshima.

A fission reaction occurs when a uranium atom is split into two by bombardment with a neutron. In the process a small amount of mass is transformed into energy or nuclear power. Some of the fission products eject further superfluous neutrons which strike other uranium atoms and institute a chain reaction, which produces more energy, and so on.

---

* The Dominion Observatory, formerly a part of EM & R, was transferred to the NRC in 1970; radio-astronomy has always been with the NRC. An observatory founded in Fredericton in 1851 is said to have ushered in the first pure science practised in Canada.

Once a chain reaction had been achieved the problem was to produce enough of the right kind of fissionable material to construct a bomb. Canada's initial research effort was directed towards the production of material for atomic weapons and was carried out in great secrecy. The people of Canada were very surprised to learn, in August 1945, that by far the largest organization ever created in this country to carry out a research project had been engaged in atomic research in Montreal, and that construction of the Chalk River plant was well advanced.*

The decision which then had to be made was whether the Chalk River project should be continued or be run down along with the rest of the war machine. The decision to continue was a crucial one because it ushered in Big Science in Canada.

It was also a rather easy decision. One must remember that, as a result of their war contributions (radar, mines, the bomb) the physicists had become white-haired boys and little was to be denied them; they emerged from the Second World War with much the same sort of social status which chemists (explosives, poison gas, synthetic products) had achieved in the First. And as a result their numbers had rapidly increased. The many young physicists who had been recruited to the nuclear program returned to university work, which became heavily weighted towards their interests.

In 1947 the world's most powerful research reactor, the NRX, was commissioned at Chalk River. Ten years later came NRU with ten times the initial power of NRX and with experimental facilities that kept Canada in the forefront of world nuclear science.

The use of the letters NR in the names of the instruments is a reminder that the program was at first a part of the NRC.

A few years later some other countries had developed instruments that out-performed the NRU. As Dr W.B. Lewis, one of the key figures in AECL, put it to the senators: 'With United States in the lead, France and Germany having a combined effort, and the United Kingdom talking about it, they have gone to new reactors to get higher fluxes than the NRU reactor.'

The physicists proposed to build an Intense Neutron Generator, or ING, which would be, among other things a factory for producing particles called mesons. Compared with its United States counterpart it would cost three times as much but would have sixty times the power. The new reactor was

---

* A few members of the public knew. When a station attendant at Montreal was approached by a shabby looking Englishman in grey flannels he would tell the man which platform to take for Chalk River before being asked.

not conceived for purposes of international competition but the statement of Dr Lewis was a make-weight designed to impress politicians.

The ING proposal became the most contentious scientific issue of its time.[6] Discussion stemmed from its high cost – $25 million annually for ever. The suggested capital cost of $155 million was taken on all sides *cum grano salis*. AECL refused to adjust any other part of its program to help find funds for ING The AECL board of directors stated that they would have hesitated to recommend ING if it meant cutting back on R & D in industry or in the universities.

Criticism of ING developed among some physicists, who were unhappy lest it absorb too much of the money available for their work. Others believed that nuclear physics was relatively overdeveloped already, especially in the universities. If there has been ample funds for university research, some of the academic criticism might have been forestalled.

The SC was asked for an opinion by AECL's minister. The council had, of course, no budgetary responsibility; its position, as Senator Lamontagne remarked, was analogous to a cabinet meeting without the Minister of Finance; it could easily endorse all projects. One of its members was the head of AECL, whose presence would tend to mute the comments of his colleagues from other government science agencies. The SC was not happy about its assignment; as its chairman stated later, 'We were asked to advise on a detail, but a very big detail, in a picture that we had not yet begun to paint, we could not even see.'

What the SC recommended, in brief, was complete scientific approval, but no funding except for design studies, feasibility experiments, studies on alternative systems, and a search for a site other than Chalk River.[7] In two years they would review the project again. The recommendations were so worded that they were variously understood as follows by concerned people, speaking in Senate hearings:

Senator Allister Grosart (addressing Dr Solandt): I have never seen anything quite as explicit in a complete recommendation of anything as you gave to ING.

Dr J.L. Gray, president, AECL, and an SC member: There was no criticism that this was not a good, well-founded project. The decision of the Government not to go ahead was entirely due to non-availability of funds.

Simon Reisman, secretary, Treasury Board, and a member of SC: The recommendation by the Science Council was hedged by qualifications; there never was a clean cut recommendation from the Science Council.

In the midst of the ING discussion, there was an Ottawa meeting on the subject, attended by the heads of federal science agencies. After Dr Gray had made an introductory statement, some questions about costs and benefits were addressed to the vice-president and chief promoter, Dr W.B. Lewis. Dr Lewis became impatient and said something to this effect: 'Of course this discussion is really just a waste of time since the physicists have decided to go ahead with ING and that's that.'

This remark, on 20 February 1968, seems in retrospect to signal a change in Canadian science policy. It was the first time that a nuclear deterrent (or rather nuclear facilitator) aimed by the physicists failed to go off. Four months later the Trudeau government was elected and, on advice of the Treasury Board, cancelled ING.

I have devoted considerable space to the nuclear program and ING because it had several important policy results.

– It dealt a body blow to the credibility of the Science Council. The SC considered ING on its scientific merits only, without looking at alternatives. There was no attempt at an estimate of whether this investment of public funds might yield more value if used elsewhere.
– It revealed to the scientific community and to the public the naked power of Treasury Board officials. As Senator Grosart said: 'What is going to happen in the future? What is the use of the Science Council? We are back where we started. The Treasury Board is making science decisions.'
– It finished the successful promotion of Big Science by scientists (the Queen Elizabeth Telescope was blacked out at the same time). Since then no scientific promotor has had any luck in the Big Science field. The new big deals such as the environment and health and the International Development Research Centre are political in origin.
– It cut the physicists down from super-power status to great-power status.

And now we may turn to consideration of AECL as a business enterprise. But first the intrusion of one more item of nuclear science.

Central to the problem of a chain reaction is the ability of uranium to capture neutrons. As it happens its ability to capture slow neutrons is very good, but if the neutrons are travelling at high speed it is downright indifferent to them. Since the neutrons released in fission are primarily of the fast variety they must be slowed down, or moderated, before there is much hope of their capture.

The slowing down of neutrons is achieved by allowing them to lose their energy in collision with certain light atoms. (Duckworth has compared it to a shopper in a department store using up most of her money by a series of small disbursements.)[8] One of the suitable light atoms is carbon, which was used in the first chain reaction in the form of highly purified graphite blocks. Another is the heavy isotope of hydrogen, deuterium, in the form of heavy water. The latter has been the Canadian choice and results in a power plant which is expensive to buy but cheap to operate. A third moderator is ordinary hydrogen in the form of ordinary water. This has been the American choice and results in a power plant which is cheap to build but expensive to operate, because it cannot accept 'ordinary' uranium but must use enriched uranium.* The costs as quoted by Dr Gray at the Senate hearings are:

	American	Canadian
Capital costs in dollars per kilowatt	200	240
Operating costs in mills per kilowatt hour	1.4	0.7

Originally a research and development agency, AECL finds itself today competing commercially in world markets. Its present goals are to produce a reactor system that is economically viable and competitive, to produce low cost energy for Canadian utilities, and to offer an economic plant for export. Parallel to the nuclear power program there has been extensive research, development, and application of isotopes.

The Senate report attacked our atomic energy program on several grounds. At the outset, it said the AECL was influenced on its selection of a method by a nationalistic desire to be independent of the USA. The CANDU (Canadian Deuterium-Uranium) process, it was thought, could be carried out totally in Canada. As it turned out, however, because of the Nova Scotia fiasco resulting from a political decision, we have had to rely exclusively on others for our supply of heavy water. Canada's technical difficulties are shared by other countries with other reactors, and it will be some years yet before an objective judgment can be made as to the best commercial design.

A valuable by-product of the CANDU process has been the production of Cobalt-60 therapy units for the treatment of cancer. There are now thousands of these units throughout the world, developed from Canadian effort between 1945 and 1951 and they may in the long run be the most important part of our atomic energy development.†

---

* Cost analysis is difficult to apply to American enriched fuels because they appear as by-products in the construction of nuclear weapons and the process is secret.

† In somewhat similar vein the famous statistician, Karl Pearson, remarked that while the outcome of discoveries was usually unpredictable, he could say with certainty that the newly discovered x-rays would be of no use to mankind.

The most serious criticism by the Senators was that, in the absence of proper federal mechanisms, the strategy of the Canadian nuclear program was exercised by Ontario Hydro. AECL had intended, on the basis of its Chalk River experience, to place the design of commercial reactors with private industry, and manufacture of a small one was started with Canadian General Electric. However, Ontario Hydro was in a hurry and did not wish to deal with a private company which might later get a monopoly, so AECL undertook to build a commercial reactor for them without waiting for completion of the CGE experiment. They thus lost both the relation with private industry and the experience gained in building the prototype.

The Ontario experience suggests that our technological reach has exceeded our grasp. AECL was able to specify economic reactors but the design and fabrication problems were beyond existing Canadian skills. Thus the first plant built for Ontario Hydro in 1964 was not in satisfactory performance until after 1969. The second plant is not in operation yet because of the lack of heavy water.

It would be unfair to finish with the impression that Canada is stumbling along behind its competitors. Here, for instance, is a recent comment from the *New Statesman* on the British effort.

As industry picks itself up after the miners' strike it may well be wondering whatever happened to Britain's great 'peaceful atom' breakthrough that scientists were telling us 20 years ago would be producing much of the electric power the country needed by the Seventies. The harsh truth is that our national nuclear power programme faces a crisis. Expensive to build, late in delivery, occasionally unreliable in operation, the technological child of the Fifties has grown into a very awkward adolescent.[9]

IV POLLUTION

All the pursuits of science that we have been discussing so far (except medicine) have the common feature that they are destructive to the environment. The list of the detrimental effects of technology is infinitely long; from the growth of suburbia and decay of city centres under the influence of the automobile, pollution of all kinds, congestion in the metropolitan areas, and lack of convenient mass transportation, to the abuse of chemical poisons. They all reflect the fact that the artificial environment lacks built-in mechanisms that would assure its stability, and that the rate of growth of this artificial environment is so high as to preclude adaptation – characteristics diametrically opposed to those of the natural environment, which exhibits a high degree of stability and a slow evolution.

Federal government action has been largely aimed at the prevention of specific environmental abuses which annoy or harm the public. One thinks, for example, of electric shavers interfering with radio sets; safety measures for air travel; thalidomide babies; assignment of channels for TV. The common quality of these efforts is their negative character. They do not involve any science planning, they are essentially a response to pressures. As technology advances, the controls may be expected to increase.

The historic aspects of pollution control were concerned with the spread of epidemics such as typhoid by infected water. This has led to chlorination and other practices developed by sanitary engineers, which have had such success that epidemics are quite rare today. Unfortunately the classical techniques of the engineers are not effective against the contemporary assaults. In fact a recent book lists the self-duplicating tendencies of engineers and economists in government pollution control agencies among the harmful effects of pollution.[10]

Our knowledge of contemporary pollutants is turned into tattle-tale gray by the efforts of the soap lobby, the oil and gas lobby, and many others. Predictably, the word 'ecology' is now being used to promote products which a militant environmentalist would prefer to see banished by law. The Shell Oil TV commercials present that company as a leader in the fight to preserve the Arctic in its natural state and to clean up the car exhaust problem. And now various magazines are running ads devoted to Westinghouse's new 'Homecology' products – including a pop-up toaster. A Westinghouse official admitted that home ecology may be at the expense of general ecology.[11]

Leaving advertising aside, there are two major classes of pollutants which are under the most active assault today. The first kind is poisons. They generally get into water in areas where the populations are sparse, and include sulphite and mercury from paper mills, mine tailings, and, until very recently DDT. Proposals for monitoring environmental poisons have not generally been treated as urgent. As humans we have not been much concerned with misfortunes that are ten years off, let alone a couple of generations away. That is what we leave to the government.

Take for example, radioactive fallout, which was looked on in the years after the war as the most serious threat to the environment that had ever overtaken mankind. Atmospheric radioactivity was increasing year by year, culminating in the enormous blasts by Russia in 1962. It was becoming evident that the government should have available to it sound advice on the hazards of ionizing radiation and on methods of protection in peace or war. With these things in mind a concerned biologist, H.B. Newcombe of Chalk River, documented the case for an increase in Canada's research efforts. Newcombe's ideas, put forth in 1957, required a decade to incubate, as shown in this extract from the Senate hearings:

1957   AECL turned down Newcombe's proposals. They pointed out that their prime responsibility was engineering for nuclear power.

1960   Newcombe induced the Genetics Society of Canada to form a Committee on Radiation Biology, which organized a symposium. The NRC formed an Associate Committee.

1961   The NRC Associate Committee recommended (a) special university support and (b) establishment of a central research institute.

1961   A House of Commons Research Committee, after inspecting NRC and AECL, recommended stronger effort in radiation biology.

1962   The project having been cleared with AECL, DRB and Health, the Cabinet approved establishment of a Radiation Biology Division of NRC, provided Treasury Board would allot funds.

1964   Public Works began to design a laboratory and staff recruitment began.

1966   Construction of building began.

1968   Division of Radiation Biology occupies new building.

1968   Radiation Biology group incorporated into NRC Division of Biology.[12]

This formal record indicates an orderly, if slow, progression. My own recollection is that the beginning of action in the early sixties was an incidental by-product of cabinet changes. In 1959, following the death of Sidney Smith, Howard Green took over the portfolio of External Affairs. He attended the United Nations and was there made conscious of the problem of radioactive fallout. He returned to Ottawa convinced that Canada ought to be doing something and communicated his views to the NRC. Thus the effective action was to reach the ear of someone with power. This has been the method since Babylon and it is not likely to be superseded by technical developments in the field of cost-benefit analysis.

A further reason for delay, characteristic of environmental problems generally, was that radiation biology research is interdisciplinary. It lies outside the boundaries staked out for the half-dozen concerned federal agencies. These included, in addition to those already mentioned, the Atomic Energy Control Board and the Emergency Measures Organization.

Radiation biology is also outside regular university structures. The NRC did not have much success with its special support program. Biologists tend to say 'How does radiation biology differ from any other kind of basic biology? Radiation is only a tool for studying genetic effects and mutations, and geneticists might as well be using some other tool. This is not a separate discipline.'

Following the Test Ban Treaty of 1963, public interest in pollution has transferred gradually from radiation to detergents and other agents, so the NRC group, formed with such effort, will probably be left quietly to its work. It is depressing to add that the annual rate of nuclear weapons tests in the world has increased since the Test Ban Treaty from forty to forty-eight. Those of France and China are carried out above ground and many by the USA and the USSR release radioactive material into the atmosphere.[13]

The second contemporary concern is eutrophication. This refers to the enrichment of water by nutrients, whether intentionally or unintentionally, and without reference to the desirability or otherwise of its effects. Although the word is usually used by environmental well-wishers as a synonym for pollution, it was not intended by its coiners to make an offensive appeal, or indeed to evoke any emotional response. In most parts of the world, eutrophication would be considered beneficial since it leads to higher production capacity for fish. When extreme, however, it eliminates game fish, makes the water look and smell unpleasant, and contributes to nuisance growths of algae. Even so the yield of a lake after eutrophication is often greater than before, and centuries ago monks used to add horse manure to their carp ponds to build up the amount of fish protein for their Friday dinners.

Some of our streams and lakes are receiving large quantities of phosphates and nitrates, originating in sewage and in waste from synthetic chemicals such as detergents. The drains of a city carry away both rain-water and used water from houses and industries. During fine weather the sanitary drainage can be managed and treated, but during storms the rain-water overflows the system and carries raw waste into the river or lake.

Separate drainage systems should be set up, one for rain-water and one for raw human leftovers, which would not then be washed into the river during storms. But separate systems are expensive, comparable perhaps to the national defence budget, and the costs frighten governments. The public too, although becoming increasingly disquieted about alterations in the environment, is not yet ready to accept the financial consequences of improvement.

The public likes environmental rapes to be treated like the ordinary kind, with only one being presented in the headlines at a time. Not long ago the overnutrition of the Great Lakes was the centre of interest. The condition arose from the combination of a large concentration of people and a high standard of living. It has recently become acute from the excess addition of detergents. All at once treatment pioneered and demonstrated in several centres was recognized as a valuable means of reversing the trend towards unwanted algal growth in Lake Erie and the rest. Over an uproar from the Canadian soap lobby, the Minister of Energy, Mines and Resources ordered a reduction in the phosphate content of detergents. The u.s. soap lobby has so far been successful in preventing action on their side. Meanwhile the public as been set to clamouring against phosphates in rural Nova Scotia where the lakes would, in fact, benefit from an increased supply of nutrients. Thus a regional need evokes a national policy.

Since this is rather a melancholy recital it may be well to conclude it with a joke. Our antipathy to phosphates is based on research carried out on lakes. The practical result has been the substitution of nitrogen compounds for phosphorus compounds in detergents. But it is now reported that in the coastal environment nitrogen, not phosphorus, is the limiting factor.[14] And the coastal area forms a much larger part of the environment than lakes.

V THE FITNESS OF THE ENVIRONMENT
VERSUS 'PROGRESS'

In the current index of science, the most emotionally charged entry is: Environment, Rape of. Between the silent spring and the dying ocean the pathway to the future looks bleak indeed. The confrontation of biological facts, political exigencies, and ethical values has given a new twist to the subject of biopolitics.

Biopolitics has been defined as the science of proving that what must be done for political or economic reasons is biologically safe for the human race. The definition raises one of the most difficult questions of our time; are science and politics really compatible? One thinks of claims that the radioactive by-products of nuclear testing are not harmful; that the levels of DDT in animals are nothing to worry about; and that industrial wastes can safely go into our waters.

The protagonists of the *status quo* are Men of Standing. They are officers of the Atlantic Salmon Association, and heads of oil companies, shipping companies, and pulp mills. Above all they carry a certainty of rightness, both in engineering and economics. They can visit Ottawa and buy the Prime Minister lunch at the Rideau Club. They are the main contributors to party campaign funds.

By contrast, the attackers of government for (as Ralph Nader put it) allowing companies to relieve themselves in public view, are not, except incidentally, professional scientists. They are, collectively, one of our great inheritances from England, namely the small, independent, usually bankrupt societies which set out to look after one or other of our liberties or to champion some great cause. Among the prominent subspecies *canadensis* flourishing today, the defenders of the environment range all the way from study groups to sue-the-bastards activists. It is the neighbourhood bands who have stirred up enough of a political storm to make our governments aware that clean air, clean water, and so on, are good politics. These defenders of the environment are seen by government expeditors and political leaders as bunches of local nuts and professors, who offer no program beyond parading outside the premier's office with placards. If they are asked to assess the effect of a proposed environmental change, they are likely to reply that the answer would require a team investigation stretching over ten years with the untreated system, followed by a further decade of study with removable installations. Even then the decision would not be firm. Faced with this sort of prospect, the politician is troubled indeed.

The conflict is not new; Ibsen wrote *An Enemy of the People* on the theme in 1882, in which a doctor was hounded to destruction because he reported that in a tourist town the water supply was carrying typhoid and the town council would not face the expense of purification.

Governments have always been reluctant to act on the side of conserving aesthetic values in natural landscapes and wildlife. Sometimes the disagreement of 'experts' invites continued inaction, and there are contradictions between scientific and popular opinion. When a pulp mill or a mine starts up, there is usually a conflict between wealth and beauty, progress and solitude, the export trade and the tourist trade, employment and enjoyment, efficiency and happiness. Are these desirables mutually incompatible or can the conflicts be resolved and, if so, how?

The offending industry is usually the biggest economic force in its district; it competes locally with a peasant economy of fishermen and farmers. It is far more centralized and single-minded than its real economic opponent, tourism. It can make its weight felt at any level from the local union branch right up to the provincial or federal cabinet. It can threaten to go out of business if asked to bear clean-up costs. Underlying all local comments is the fear that the industry might suffer if the conservationists' cause is conceded. Public relations officers of the industry find it easy to represent biologists as sentimental nuisances, whose concern with wildlife and nature chips into the profit structure which efficient engineers have set up for alert business men.

Although the balance between pollution and industrial development is one of the most difficult problems of the age in which we live, the concept of 'environment quality' does not provide a very useful focus for assessing the value of proposals in technology. The combination of concerns as wide-ranging as solid-waste disposal, occupational hygiene, highway beautification, mental health, urban design, animal life, and smog prevention is usually too broad to be operational.

Water pollution presents a political problem rather than one of scientific structure. Not only the federal and provincial governments are involved, but many municipal governments, and then many conservation authorities and others. In addition there is the International Joint Commission and agencies of the United States, because water pollution, as well as that of the atmosphere, extends across international boundaries. A Canadian count in 1968 showed 228 committees dealing with water problems.[15]

Except in the Great Lakes and other international waters, the federal government has very limited powers to reduce pollution and is unlikely to get any more by consent of the provinces. One thing it does is to prohibit ships from dumping refuse into navigable waters. The only other federal basis for action stems from an ancient law that waters must be fit for fish to live in. Powers under this law are expanded by the doctrine that what's good for the fish is good for the country.

The administration of the 1970 Water Act has been placed in the Ministry of the Environment. This department has a lot of money to trade off against the constitutional powers which rest with the provinces. Ontario and Quebec will likely do most of their own R & D in the pollution area, but the have-not provinces will be grateful to the federal agencies for taking over.

One of the inducements offered to prospective new industries by the have-not provinces is the right to save money on pollution control. The daily press reports mounting public pressure against this practice which must eventually find political expression. It has also been politically difficult for the provinces to clean up economically marginal industries, such as fisheries in the Atlantic area. This industry survives because of low wage scales and a low standard of living, and it has traditionally discharged its crude wastes into the harbours. Governments, confronted with a conflict between economic and aesthetic considerations, have traditionally declared for economics.

But not even provincial governments seem to be pretending any longer that the white heat of the technological revolution is quite so white after all. Many have become aware of the twin tendencies that operate in advanced countries – on the one hand the need they feel to go on relentlessly producing more and more goods, on the other the contamination problems that are the inevitable consequence of that process.

At the global level the conflict between the fitness of the environment and 'progress' disappears. On the one hand an extension of technology which would lift the Third World to the level of consumption of the rich nations would have dire consequences, in that we should soon reach a point of serious depletion of some of the most elementary resources needed for human life. The obvious alternative, namely, restraint and redistribution of income by the rich nations, has so far made no impact on them; they continue with plans to finance Third World technology.

On the other hand the complementary crisis, namely the destruction of the environment, is perceived clearly by the rich nations as well as by the Third World. Poverty abroad may be somewhat intangible, but smog at home is very real. The environmental problem will become politically important as the rich nations realize that they have to define their own development goals as clearly as the poor nations or all will be in the soup together.

The foregoing paragraph was written before the 1972 Stockholm conference on pollution. From that conference it emerged that the Third World awaited development regardless of the ensuing damage of the environment. 'The poor nations want development now – at (almost) any price.[16]

7

Education

I THE GRADUATE CURRICULUM IN SCIENCE

When president of the University of California, Clark Kerr identified not two but three educational cultures in conflict, and traced each to its Greek roots.* One goes back to Plato's Academy, devoted to truth for its own sake, and to the philosophers who were to be kings. The Sophists, whom Plato detested so much, had their schools too, teaching rhetoric and other useful skills to enhance the wealth and power of the privileged. Sophists were thought able 'to make the worse appear the better reason.' The Pythagoreans were concerned, among other things, with mathematics and astronomy. In the modern university, according to Kerr,

a kind of unlikely consensus has been reached. Undergraduate life seeks to follow the British who have done the best with it, and an historical line that goes back to Plato; the humanists often find their sympathies here. Graduate life and research follow the Germans, who once did best with them, and an historical line that goes back to Pythagoras; the scientists lend their support to all this. The 'lesser' professions (lesser than law and medicine) and the service activities follow the American

---

* Clark Kerr, *The Uses of the University* (Harvard, 1964). These are the Godkin Lectures for 1963, later reprinted as a paperback. Kerr's classification is oversimplified, since the Greeks did not recognize the distinction which we make between the natural sciences and the humanities, and since the rivalries between the movements were as much political as academic.

pattern, since the Americans have been best at them, and an historical line that goes back to the Sophists; the social scientists are most likely to be sympathetic.[1]

Here are comments on the three cultures by Canadians with whom we are already acquainted:

From George Grant, a humanist's lament:
There is nothing phonier in our universities than the exaltation of scholarship as an end in itself. Scholarship has always been a means through which men could come into the presence of the most serious questions. But when the thought that there are such questions becomes dim, research becomes little more than an excuse for avoiding the ardours of teaching.

From E.W.R. Steacie, a scientists's plea for the ancient purity:
There is a great danger that the trend towards more research by industry may destroy the dominant position of the university in science, and that the increased emphasis on technology may destroy the character of the universities themselves.

From Omond Solandt, a latter day Sophist:
We must evolve some system of guiding people to where opportunities will be available. A student will have to be closer to the top of his class to receive support for a field that is oversupplied than if he is going into a field where there is a shortage.

If the conflict of cultures goes back to the roots of civilization, it is unlikely that any clear and final solutions will emerge during the 1970s. An ecologist might compare a university to his front lawn with its main equilibrium of grass, chickweed, and clover, together with a variety of lesser odds and ends. He knows that there never was a golden age when the landscape was pure grass. He knows that by selective treatment with fertilizers and weed-killers, and some climatic luck, it is possible to approach an idealized mix, but never to achieve it. And he knows that there is, over the whole zone, a mean distribution into which the system is being continually manipulated by its environment.

The academic equilibrium has been under pressure from the changing social environment during the past century. With the Second World War the disturbance greatly increased, and in the years after there began to emerge what Clark Kerr calls the 'federal grant' universities. The adjustments to the change from the training of gentlemen to the service of technology have developed more by force of circumstance than by conscious design. The adaptation of the universities to their new role has been quick and effective, calling to mind a limerick:

There was a young lady from Kent
Who said that she knew what it meant
   When men took her to dine,
   Gave her cocktails and wine;
She knew what it meant, but she went.

Clark Kerr commented, 'I am not sure that the universities and their presidents always know what it meant, but one thing is certain – they went.'

What it meant, in our context, was the promotion of research and graduate work in science. Most of the grants in the early stages went to the strongest universities, so that regional disparities became more pronounced. Latterly more attention is coming to be paid to regional support.

As one university after another began to develop its graduate program and as the student count became a prestige item, the supply of qualified Canadians ran out, and supplements had to be sought, especially from the limitless numbers in Asia. University expansion absorbed the largest share of its output and thus nourished its own growth. By the late 1960s, the output of PH DS in science exceeded the employment opportunities. Not many, however, were going into industry, which failed to get into close working relations with the universities.

The OECD report has this to say about university-industry relations:

The superficial nature of this relationship when it exists at all, struck us as one of the most regettable features of the Canadian scientific scene. Throughout the country we heard accusations from the academics, concerning the naivety and lack of research-appreciation of the industrialists, and from the latter denunciations of the excessive academicism of the universities. Probably this situation is no worse than in many European countries but it is certainly dramatized by proximity to the United States where it is quite otherwise. Of all the federally constructed countries with which we are familiar, Canada has made the least attempt to coordinate educational policies or establish common action.

The report goes on to note the two exceptions to its strictures.

The Fisheries Research Board and the National Research Council have actively encouraged their laboratories to form closer links with the universities. Dalhousie, Saskatchewan and Manitoba have undertaken to give special rights to members of the staff of neighbouring Federal laboratories to teach and take part in the life of their establishments.[2]

The most serious stumbling block towards the development of flexibility in science is the rigidity of the departmental system. A man wanting to get his PH D in say, urban renewal, space research, northern development, scientific and technical information systems, or water pollution, cannot do so. He will have to enrol in physics or economics or engineering or biology. The disciplines fight vigorously for their prerogatives and for their right to control everything that goes on in the university. Clark Kerr commented:

Few institutions are so conservative as the universities and important changes take place largely outside the 'veto groups' of the academic community – in the new department, the new project, the new campus. The institute has been as much the vehicle of innovation as the department has been the vault of tradition.*

Frozen into the classical divisions of science – biology, physics, and so on – the universities have been reluctant to experiment with the newer fields. According to L.A. DuBridge:

No one knows just how to proceed with the task of bringing to bear on our social problems the resources of science, social science and technology. The methods and traditions of research which we take for granted in the natural sciences do not exist in these new interdisciplinary areas. If even a few of the great universities could initiate or accelerate their efforts in research and education in the urban and environmental fields an enormous contribution would be made.[3]

Paradoxically, the department system is also a stumbling block for prospective employers, who have so instinctively accepted it that they look with suspicion on an unlabelled graduate trained in an interdisciplinary field. Thus, a colleague of mine in a dual field feels that he has to turn out his PH D s so that they can declare themselves to be either oceanographers or geophysists according to the whim of the employers.

But, for all its fumbles, university growth is, according to Galbraith, still to be treated as a response to the needs of capitalism.[4] According to him it is a function of the state to provide the specialized and trained manpower which the industrial system cannot supply to itself. The great expansion in education is rarely pictured as an aspect of modern economic development; it is the vanity of educators that they have the initiating power in the

---

* Kerr, *The Uses of the University,* pp. 99 and 102. Kerr went on: '"Nothing should ever be done for the first time" was the wry conclusion of F.M. Cornford from his vantage point as a classicist at Cambridge at the turn of the century. He added that "Nothing is ever done until everyone is convinced that it ought to be done, and has been convinced for so long that it is now time to do something else."'

new enlightenment. But when industry required for its purposes millions of unlettered proletarians, that is what the educational system supplied. As industry has come to need engineers, scientists, computer programmers, and executives, that is what the education system has come to provide.

As to the future of the graduate schools, the difference in outlook between the NRC and the SC shows in their predictions. The former, basing its figures on continuation of present employment patterns, predicted three years ago a production surplus of PH D s in the seventies, and expressed concern as to what will happen to young scientists who will have been misguided by government incentive programs for graduate schools:

The university sector will take up more of the PH D graduates, increasing from 53% in 1960 to about 70% in 1973. The figure for government laboratories will be halved from 33% to 17% while there will be virtually no relative change in the industrial sector.[5]

This projection of manpower trends, now proven all to true, was regarded by the SC heads as pessimistic in that it showed for future years very little increase in the employment of PH D s by the universities and none by industry. The number of Canadian university graduates in the labour force today is less than half that of the USA, particularly in management and entrepreneur jobs. Our lower average level of education is given as a reason why our productivity is lower than that in the USA and is the basis for investing so much money in education.*

Of the PH D s who enter large companies in Europe, for instance pharmaceutical laboratories, only a very few stay in research. They go into production or sales, and this puts drive into these organizations. This is what we should look forward to in Canada. The fresh PH D of the future is going to have to look for a job and sell himself to somebody in industry. The integration of these people into the labour force will be one of the biggest elements in improving our situation over the next ten years. The message we should get from the sudden upsurge of PH D s is that at least we have faced the first step in upgrading the quality of our labour force, and now we are entering the second stage of integrating them, which is going to be more difficult.

With their rapid expansion in recent years, the universities have been absorbing a large number of the PH D s that they were producing. Because of this they have tended to train their graduate students for the academic

* I am following the reasoning used by Drs Solandt and Gaudry, chairman and vice-chairman of the SC, Sen. com. proc. 68–9, 8.

life which most of them followed. In the future a substantial number of these people will leave the universities and be available for employment outside. This will make necessary a reorientation of graduate training, under which some of the 'pure' disciplines that flourish today will follow the road of Greek and Latin.

To the planners, it appears that even engineering has become too pure. We shall have to train more people to be engineer-managers and to follow the less exotic kinds of engineering that are so important to industry. Large industries are short of people who can design a gear box, and over supplied with people who can do theoretical physics or advanced mathematics. Canadian universities have placed little emphasis on design or production engineering, and it has not been possible to get support for research in these fields unless it is switched round to make it look something like physics.

It has been argued that the universities, having saturated the research field with the products of their graduate schools, will either have to retool for the production of future monitors, or reduce the numbers of graduate students. Probably the resolution of this dilemma will vary from place to place.

Planners, on their side, tend to oversimplify their problem of manipulating the curriculum, by thinking of students as babies who will swallow any formula that their elders decide is good for them. But students are not wholly absorbent; in fact they show quite strong preferences. In engineering it is observed these days that many of the better students prefer the more difficult subdisciplines of engineering physics and electrical engineering. The 'useful' subdisciplines (mining, mechanical, civil) seem not to be attractive. In fact mining engineering departments are tending to disappear. A final limit on planning will be determined by what youth agrees to do, and universities may find it impossible to go over wholly to production engineering.

Solandt, however, remained optimistic. As he put it to the Senate committee; 'Probably the governments will have to come back to the universities and say: The people you are training are not quite the people we want. We regard the beginning surplus of PH D s with satisfaction. That is what we have invested our money for. Now that we have got the plan going, let us evolve some system of subject restraint.'

While attempts to control graduate work would be regarded with disfavour by many people in universities, a mechanism could be designed and possibly operated. It is much more difficult to develop an information mechanism to tell us where shortages are likely to occur five years from now. The habit of the federal government in turning its demand on and off like the tap can cause, for example, oceanographers to change from a desperate deficit to a worrisome surplus in one year.

Working scientists often take an intermediate position on modern sophistry. Here is the president of the Royal Society of Canada, C.E. Dolman addressing the Senate science committee:

Senator Chesley W. Carter: The pendulum swings during war to give tremendous emphasis to science; then the war is over and we realize that our main problems are social problems. Do you think that a national science policy should follow or attempt to modify trends of this kind?

Dr C.E. Dolman: University people are dedicated to their own fields and will obstruct directives that seek to detract from their student enrolment. I am in favour of a compromise, whereby we distribute the information but do not attempt to issue directives.

Chairman: Would you say that this information should also be used by granting institutions in developing their programs?

Senator Allister Grosart: Which is a directive.

Chairman: It is not a directive.

Grosart: It is a velvet glove.

Chairman: It may be a corrective.

Dolman: Yes, it would be a corrective; I would think this is perfectly permissible.

Table 16 takes two different looks at university research – one is the subject distribution of projects which departments stated they were carrying out, and the other is the distribution of federal financial aid. One is not surprised to find the columns in general agreement; indeed survival would be difficult in the face of much deviation. The apparent size of programs does show some variability; thus under physics fewer projects are reported, apparently at greater unit cost than the average. On the other hand, agriculture, which received only 1 per cent of federal funds reported 7 per cent of the research programs (had I accepted Guelph at reported value, it would have been 10 per cent). The difference may be partly due to relatively heavy provincial support for agriculture and partly to the more elementary nature of the average project.

If the trends of the late sixties continue there will be a marked change in the distribution of science students during the present decade.

Senator Andrew Thompson: Has there ever been a study done on the attitude towards science of young people who are planning to go to university? I have a suspicion that some really able minds on moral grounds are not going into science.

TABLE 16

Research programs carried out by Canadian universities (percentages)

	Projects reported for 1964–5	Federal support 1967–8
Medicine	(25)	33
Engineering	16	14
Biological sciences	16	14
Physics, including astronomy	9	14
Chemistry	10	10
Earth sciences	6	7
Mathematics, including computers	5	3
Psychology	4	3
Agriculture	7	1
Others, e.g., dentistry and/or pharmacy	2	1

SOURCES: Report on programs taken from OECD report, table 46, with Guelph agriculture projects reduced from a reported 122 to 40, and with a medical value of 25% assumed from financial relations reported by DBS. Report on federal aid from DBS tables supplemented by NRC data.
NOTE: Total number of projects reported for 1964–5 was 3,100, and total federal support in 1967–8 was $71 million.

Senator Allister Grosart: Probably writing poetry.
Dr P.D. McTaggart-Cowan, executive director, SC: There is no question but that the percentage enrolment in physics is dropping in every country in the western world and is still rising in the Soviet Union. Chemistry has been less spectacular but shows the same trend. The life sciences are going up fast. Engineering has fallen but there is an indication that it is past the bend and on the way up.
Thompson: Was there a reason for physics falling off?
McTaggart-Cowan: Yes. One reason is that in high school, physics and chemistry are looked on as tough subjects, and therefore the administrations of the schools tend to encourage students away from the tough subjects, so that the school gets a high rating.
The other is that the students feel that the life sciences are constructive. It has captured the imagination, that these research fields are looking into a greater understanding of life.
Dr Omond Solandt: Mathematics has also started up spectacularly. If the trend continues in the US it will only be two or three years before more people will be taking

TABLE 17

NRC university support by field (operating and major equipment grants) (percentages)

	1961–2	1968–9	Gain or loss
Mathematics, including computing and information science	1	6	+385
Space and astronomy	1	5	+269
Psychology	2	5	+187
Engineering	15	23	+51
Biology	24	24	−4
Earth sciences	10	9	−8
Physics	16	10	−37
Dentistry	2	1	−38
Chemistry	29	17	−40

SOURCE: Table furnished by the SC for the use of a seminar on basic research held in December 1969. Percentage figures were calculated before rounding.
NOTE: The total of support in 1961–2 was $5.4 million, and in 1968–9 $36 million.

mathematics than physics and chemistry combined. These are applied mathematicians, attracted by the opportunities for employment and interesting careers in relation to computers.[6]

The changing pattern of NRC grants during the sixties is shown in table 17. Mathematics, space, and psychology have moved ahead spectacularly. Engineering, which started up a little earlier has made a strong absolute gain. At the other end chemistry and physics have sharply declined. The remaining disciplines have been relatively unchanged.

Anybody acquainted with the realities of science will recognize that a considerable share of the support identified for medicine or engineering could properly be called chemistry or physics. What the table tells us is not that these subjects are declining in importance, but that the university departments have become conservative in their attitude towards the opportunities and demands of contemporary science.

And what is the prognosis for biology? Some of its branches, of course, have been appropriated by medical science and flourish there. For an outlook on some others, consider three reports on renewable resources, whose priorities are summed up in table 18.[7] The message is clear. In the resource field the only biology likely to be in brisk demand is that concerned with the quality of the environment and the survival of living populations in it. The other high priorities are for engineering and the social sciences.

II SOURCES OF RESEARCH SUPPORT

It is common knowledge that the universities did not participate in the general prosperity which followed the Second World War. Against the increasing costs of providing undergraduate training, with enrolments overstretched by returning veterans, graduate study and research simply did not rate a place in the budget.*

Meanwhile the NRC and other federal agencies were beginning to offer research support on a scale which was impressive at the time. Because of the BNA Act these grants were made to individuals, not to organizations, and this practice ushered in the hunting licence era of university research. A professor who approached his president with a request for support would be told, 'Look here, I can't offer you any money, but what I will do is write a letter stating that our university is specializing in your field of interest. If you can get anything out of that, good luck to you.'

The resultant flowering of the free-enterprise system in the academic world led to a large number of one-man science operations across the country. It also blocked anything in the nature of planning or specialization among universities. Everybody was doing everything, and since the professors were raising their research funds independently, the administration had no voice in policy. Deans in general are supposed to be involved in the policy-making functions of their respective faculties. The new deans of graduate studies, however, were to consider themselves fortunate to be allowed to act as expediters of the plans of professors whose primary appointments were in other faculties.

Since the university salary scales were low, the right to seek grants and the hope of getting them were the inducements offered to prospective staff. A good money earner also had a better prospect of being appointed. The

---

* In Dalhousie, for example, the Faculty of Graduate Studies was established in 1949 with a directive from the administration that it was not to cost anything and the dean was to have no budget.

TABLE 18

Recommendations for changes in direction of natural resources R & D

	Agriculture	Forestry	Fisheries and Wildlife
HIGH PRIORITIES	Population ecology	Environmental quality	Environmental science
	Cold and drought resistance	Engineering	Long-term ecosystem studies
	Engineering	Economics, marketing	Chemicals and biocides
	Economics and bio-economics	Genetics	Social and economic research
		Fire protection	Resource use
			Arctic
LOW PRIORITIES	Natural sciences (which are 90% bio-science) to decline within 5 years from 82% to 69%	Biology and ecology	By 1988 Fisheries bioscience to decline from 52% to 29%
		Hydrology insects, diseases soils	Wildlife bioscience to decline from 93% to 31%

SOURCE: SC special study no. 10 and reports nos 8 and 9

new young men who started under these rules were not much interested in teaching and contributed to its deterioration.

The policy of offering research support on an individual basis was also a factor in the decay of authority within departments. The New World had never taken well to the European idea of a Regius professor or *Ordinarius* with his subservient team. There had, however, been permanent heads of departments, who enjoyed some prerogatives. The title came to be changed from head to chairman and the office was made a short-term one.

To recipients of grants the decay of authority and enhancement of the individual were side benefits to the main objective of advancing 'little science' on a wide front. The task of national planners in redirecting research after a quarter-century of independence is likely to be difficult.

Under the NRC support plan, awards were made to indivudual researchers on the basis of their quality. The universities still submit to a quality test, because they have become used to it, but it is doubtful if they will continue to accept the system very much longer. There is some feeling that research policy should be made administratively within the university, and that research funds should be given to those places which are deficient in quality and therefore need help, rather than to those which are already excellent. This last consideration is especially voiced among the French-language universities.

In the future we may expect those universities which feel that they can meet a quality test to exploit their advantage; the rest will not. It is notable that the government of Quebec has been specifically discriminating against McGill in the matter of grants, because McGill is said to be of such high quality that it no longer needs the same level of assistance, as for example, Laval.

Members of university faculties will tend to favour grants on a basis of quality, because these come to individuals for individual merit. Administrators are more likely to favour formula grants, which place the control of policy in the hands of the administration. The function of the university administration to bring up the weak parts of the system to some minimum acceptable standard conflicts with the idea of reinforcing the best. Thus the submission of the graduate deans to the Bladen Commission pointed out that it was disrupting to have the direction of research regulated by support 'won by professors in national competitions.' The control, it was submitted, should be with the deans via formula grants. The OECD report commented:

The 'award of prizes' system leads the recipients to lose sight of the ultimate social and economic purpose and to see in the distribution of federal grants nothing more than an internal mechanism of the scientific community enabling it to reward the quality of its work.

However, the NRC and like agencies would have no reason to continue with grants if they abandoned their quality tests; they could turn over support to a formula granting agency which might make a direct federal-provincial adjustment.

Ninety per cent of university research costs come from internal sources (including working quarters and salaries) and from the federal or provincial government (table 19). However, because of their importance in earlier days, the private donors continue to exert considerable leverage over policy; certainly they have not come to be thought of by management as second- and third-order corrections to the budget. On the contrary, their personal preferences are of great concern.

It is surprising that more general attention has not been paid to the

TABLE 19

Sources of funds for research in Canadian
universities, 1964–5 (percentages)

University funds	54
Federal government agencies	27
Provincial governments	8
Other Canadian sources, including endowments, private foundations, and industry	5
u.s. government agencies	4
Other non-Canadian agencies, including u.s. private foundations	2

SOURCE: OECD report, table 48, from NRC data

frailties and foibles of the federal patron. While his total fortune, like that of the private donor, is limited, he has considerable latitude in its distribution. An astute petitioner can distort the grant pattern to his own advantage, an example being McMaster University in the postwar years.*

Finance from abroad, particularly from the United States, played a relatively important part in the past, particularly in the development of medical research. In the last few years these contributions have become much less substantial, partly because of the internal situation in the United States, which has obliged that country to limit its support for foreign research, but also because the increase in Canadian federal aid has rapidly made it the principal factor of growth.

Over half of the federal research support for universities comes from the NRC and about one-third from the MRC and National Health. The residual 15 per cent is from a variety of agencies, chief among which is the DRB.

In the United States, the distribution of university support is quite different. The three agencies of Defense, Health, and Space Research account for almost three-fourths of the grants. Other mission-oriented R & D takes the total up to seven-eighths. The National Science Foundation which, like our NRC, has the objective of supporting science without regard to a specific mission, was responsible for the remaining one-eighth of federal university support.

---

* The appointment of John Anderson of the FRB as president of UNB is a recognition that a main qualification of a president is knowing how the government thinks.

I have given the pattern as it existed before the cuts of the late sixties. At that time the annual total for university R & D was about 1 billion. Since this figure did not include contract research centres, most of the money was in fact for research.

The military component of support is much more prominent in the USA than in Canada. Thus the top five U.S. universities have been getting about $100 million annually in Defense Department awards. Even Harvard is fairly heavily supported by the military. According to a ninety-page booklet called *How Harvard Rules,* produced by students during the 1969 strike, the Defense Department awards about $5 million annually in prime contracts to that university.

In addition to awards, some U.S. universities bid for military development contracts much like private firms. In the Massachusetts Institute of Technology war research fired-up a faction of students and young professors in 1969 to enough disorder to cause a formal review by the administration. The annual Defense Department contracts were running by 1968 to nearly half the university budget. One laboratory, working on gunsights and guidance systems, received $54 million; another one doing research on air defence spent $66 million. Attempts are being made to restrict military sponsored research to basic problems while avoiding advanced development of weaponry; whether such a partial transformation can be made is doubtful.

In Canada it is unlikely that the military will be come dominant in university support. Medical or industrial research, derivatives of the other two categorical imperatives, are more pressing national aims. The important way in which we are likely to follow the United States is in the manipulation of university research by whatever groups establish themselves as the *élite* in Canadian policy making.

III UNIVERSITY SUPPORT BY FEDERAL AGENCIES

Along with DRB, the federal departments of Agriculture, Fisheries, and so on have been making grants to our universities for specific purposes. In these areas the federal government has concurrent constitutional jurisdiction, so there has been no question of denying its right to make grants or even to legislate in these areas any more than in establishing military colleges.[8]

The mission agencies judge applications for grants a little differently from the NRC. They try to maintain the same criteria for excellence, but in addition each has to make a subjective assessment whether it is in the defence interest, fisheries interest, medical interest, and so on. For example the DRB states that its university grants have three objectives. The first is to acquire new scientific knowledge that may prove applicable to the solution of defence problems; the second is to develop in the scientific community an interest in defence science; the third is to assist in staffing DRB establishments.

Grants to professors often have a negative public relations value since those turned down are resentful and those cut off are angry. A case history will illustrate. The FRB made a three-year grant to a researcher mainly supported from agricultural sources whose work was supposed to have relevance to animal breeding. He was, however, using fish tissues rather than the more usual hens or pigs. After a year's notice and explanation of the conditions under which his program might qualify for a renewed grant, the Grants Committee discontinued support, thereby evoking the following letter:

I am unable to understand why the grant to my group is discontinued. My group is highly productive and its work is recognized as not only unique in Canada but without parallel elsewhere in the world.

If my work is not relevant to the mission of the FRB, I wonder what is. This must surely be an error of judgment by the academic advisors of the Board. I doubt that the Grants Committee could be aware of recent developments in my field. The question of relevance of research to a mission will not be solved by administrators in Ottawa.

One more enemy, probably for life. This letter explains why government agencies are often attracted to formula grants rather than merit grants. It also illustrates the dilemma that would face any agency which undertook to operate a large segment of its program in a university. It would be unacceptable to a university to be under the same policy scrutiny that a board gives to its own operations, or to be subject to discontinuance of support because the work had lost its quality or interest.

A question that will never be cleanly solved is how to support basic research. Harvey Brooks estimated that perhaps 5 per cent of those engaged in U.S. pure science are truly outstanding but adds that others should be supported to provide background for the top 5 per cent, for cultural reasons, and to provide trained manpower.[9] Carl Kayson suggests that basic research should be an overhead on applied research and development and set, in the U.S., at its historical level of 9 per cent.[10] From the UK, P.M.S. Blackett, president of the Royal Society, stated to the senators:

'I doubt if there are enough good people available in most countries to justify spending much more, say than 0.5 per cent of the GNP on pure curiosity directed science.'

Thus the general proposal is that basic research should be of the order of 10 per cent of the total R & D. The current Canadian policy trend is to centre it in universities rather than in government laboratories. But within the universities the correct selection of grantees presents difficulties. There is a disposition today to lose faith in the academic sacred cows that any young man with brains enough to secure a university post is also good enough to go it alone in the choice of research topics (usually a continuation of the thesis that was assigned to him by a professor in another university) and that pure science is better than applied science for training. The time and place of emergence of superior research types is not within the control of granting agencies. The hope of a well-designed plan for financial aid is to spot the Bobby Orrs of science early and offer them adequate support.

Somerset Maugham recalled that after graduation he lived among a group of young men whose talents seemed much superior to his own. He envied them their ability to write, compose music, and criticize art. In later life, however, none of them fulfilled the promise or attained distinction.

Any youth who has worked in a good laboratory can recall similar friends of brilliant promise. Young people begin research because of exuberance, because they admire some professor, or because they want a job qualification. Opinions that seem original are only second-hand and their creative research owes more to memory than to imagination. Youth is the inspiration for this facility, which, if not universal, is so common that one can draw no conclusions from it. One of the tragedies of science is the spectacle of persons who have been misled by this passing fertility to commit their lives to undirected research. As they grow older, harassed for new ideas which fail to appear, they become unfitted for ordinary jobs. The lucky ones find a satisfactory life in teaching or administration.

It is from among those who possess by nature this youthful creativity that the original researcher is produced. It is only one part of his talent; more important is that he sees some part of the world differently from other men. Unfortunately no research supervisor can tell which of his gifted students will retain originality and which will drop out. The more talented the supervisor, the more likely he is to be the source of the candidate's apparent ideas. Naturally he wants all his pupils to have a chance to attempt the race so he recommends each highly.*

* Dr Steacie used to recall a professor who wrote of each applicant 'This is the best student I have ever had.'

The age at which true originality can be identified is apparently related to the field of study. Those in mathematics and theoretical physics mature earliest, say by 20 to 25. Laboratory workers can be graded rather later, say at 30 to 35, the slower ones being in areas like biochemistry where the mathematical content declines and the mass of information increases. Finally at 35 to 40 come the field workers, students of the environment, enormously complex and primitively quantitative.

While these last have a longer wait before being judged and can sometimes substitute physical prowess for mental agility, the good ones may also have a shorter working life afterwards in which to display their superiority. As an extension of the sequence, the social science-researchers are even more difficult to judge, which is one reason why subjects like sociology lend themselves so readily to dubious scholarship. The development of an elaborate technical vocabulary also wards off critical examination.

Special pleaders, among whom medicine is well represented, often say that the inadequancy of research grants is to be measured by the percentage of applicants who are turned down. But the fact is that granting bodies, like hockey clubs, have their farm teams of young hopefuls, most of whom will drop out before reaching the major league. No better way to test candidates than the experimental grant has so far been discovered.

Universities attempt to make their faculty appointments from among those whose research talents look as though they might last. Before the War and after about 1967, they usually got the men they sought. In the interval, during the market shortage of labour and the wretched salary scales, the bag was mixed. Even under favourable conditions only a few professors, perhaps one tenth to one quarter, will continue to be productive in research. The policy of granting bodies like the NRC has been to support moderately any new faculty member who could write an application. A weeding out process follows by reason of drop-out and the competition for limited funds. Since the judgment of applicants is made by their peers, the process is really quite efficient. It would be improved by a grant policy under which, at a certain stage, applicants either go up or out. This would centre the large grants for fundamental research around a few men of distinction, who would attract a few junior academics. These young men would be trained to conduct experiments and evaluate results and to work as a team. They would have a useful role to fill later on.

It will be objected that this is a return to the bad old days of the Herr Professor or the Regius professor who controlled the research of his staff. From those days we have had an extreme reaction to the point where the chairman of a department is but a temporary gentleman who arranges staff meetings and orders supplies. Administrative power rests with the dean; academic power is absent, for every man is a king. There is only one way the pendulum can swing now and that is back towards an academic power structure.

If granting bodies encouraged an academic power structure by support of a few, these leaders might only incidentally happen to be chairmen of departments. In large university departments, the chairman is too fully occupied with administration even to pretend to have personal research interests. He is in fact very much like the director of a government laboratory, minus its mission.

What would new universities, or universities in remote places, do pending their ability to get men of distinction on their faculties? They would in the first place have some support offered to the young men still under observation. And they could be supported in applied research by some mission. The prospect of federal support, pure or applied, often induces good men to move to a new place. Finally, the university itself, in order to get things going, has latitude in the use of its funds.

As the pattern of the future, I predict that the NRC will remain at about its present level, offering support largely on a merit basis. I would hope for a trend towards the grouping of grants around leaders rather than dispersing them over thousands of one-man operations. New money will come from the several mission-oriented agencies on the pattern of the MRC. These would develop competitive attempts to distort the pattern of university science into desired directions. Faculty members who can get under one of the mission umbrellas will do so; others will take their chance with the NRC. Universities will be able to arrange for larger, more formal efforts, comparable to, say, the Institute for Aerospace Studies at Toronto.

From the early days, government laboratories were, wherever possible, located near Ottawa in order to ensure what later came to be called a 'critical mass.' An additional pressing reason was that agencies looking towards survival found it prudent to keep as many of their experts as possible within easy reach of the Treasury Board.

Some laboratories, however, have been dispersed, especially those working with regional resources such as forestry, fisheries, or agriculture, and among these some have been set up in proximity to universities. The universities have welcomed the arrangements because of the supposed prestige or advertising value and have often donated land. The teaching relationship, if any, has rarely gone further than some spare-time lecturing and supervision of graduate students by government men. The experiment has now been tried often enough to warrant two conclusions: government and university laboratories, when placed in proximity, will not spontaneously mate, and formal arrangements hinge on personal inclinations and tend to fall into disuse when one of the key principals departs.[11]

Some of the most expensive branches of science are also among the most progressive and interesting, and the only way for a university to participate in them is through shared facilities and staff. Nuclear reactors, radiotelescopes, and sea-going ships come to mind.

The obstacles are formidable, the largest perhaps arising out of the character, fears and ambitions of individuals, which are reinforced by genuine differences in attitudes; out of different approaches to science (interdisciplinary versus departmental); and out of the need to reconcile academic freedom with the fiscal responsibility required by governments. Fortunately we have as a model the long-standing partnership between medical schools and their teaching hospitals to prove that the obstacles can be surmounted.

IV REPORTS ON UNIVERSITY SUPPORT

I turn now to the recent reports about university support. The first of these, by Bladen et al (1965) has already been mentioned. It is a product of management, originating from the Association of Universities and Colleges of Canada. The authors set the tone for their successors with their statement: 'We have not thought fit to examine the internal management of the universities.' Their recommendations for research funding are a model of simplicity and directness; an immediate 'great increase' in grants from the NRC, MRC, Canada Council and other agencies, followed by a 20 per cent annual escalation in perpetuity. These recommendations were largely accepted by the federal government and continued until the slump of the late sixties.

The largest defence of universities, a 361-page tome, is the Macdonald report, which was one of the special studies sponsored by the Science Council.[12] Its text is supported by 118 tables on all aspects of students, staffing, disciplines, and the financing of all branches of research. It has the material for a strong defence of the importance of research in universities. Unfortunately it is also such a hard sell as to be self-defeating among university friends in government and academic circles. The Science Council in its official commentary repudiated most of its conclusions.[13]

According to Macdonald, all the support policies of the federal government agencies can be divided into two classes. The first includes those concerned primarily with the welfare of the universities and the promotion of research in them, as administered by the NRC and MRC. When each university has determined in which fields it wishes to conduct research, the councils, in a responsive role, are to react promptly to the requirements. They should not, however, attempt to stimulate interest in particular fields beyond circulating forecasts about manpower requirements. Councils such as the NRC should have a balance-wheel function, that is, they should support those disciplines not of interest to the mission-oriented agencies, and they should, when taken together, encompass all disciplines recognized by Canadian universities.

It might be difficult to convince the federal government that much larger sums of money should be poured into university research on Macdonald's ivory-tower basis. It has not been the federal government's overt object to support universities but to support research and graduate training. If the object were simply university support an institutional grant would do. With the NRC Macdonald includes the Medical Research Council as non-mission oriented; this is a little too close to the truth to fit comfortably into the joke column.

His second class of federal support comes from agencies concerned primarily with the accomplishment of some mission important to the government to which the university can contribute, for example, the DRB or FRB. In short, one class of support serves primarily the university and the other class serves primarily the mission.

Efficiency-wise, it is a common belief among scientists that the way to quantify, optimize, and consolidate the humanities is to administer them as though they were branches of science. Macdonald (a dentist) recommends identical organizational policies for research support in fields as diverse as science, medicine, social science, and the humanities. For this symmetrical pattern the Science Council is to be expanded to provide for representation of the social sciences. The inclusion of the humanities as well, to make a broader 'knowledge council,' he regarded as premature at this time.

The arts point of view in these matters was expressed by the Warden of All Souls, commenting on a recommendation regarding changes in Oxford University.* Procedure suggested for filling 'posts,' he said, may

---

* John Sparrow, 'Oxford: the idea and the machine,' *Sunday Times Weekly Review,* 10 July 1966. However, on the current Canadian scene, it is the 'lesser professions,' especially sociology, which seek to impress their organizational patterns on the natural sciences as well as on the humanities. Examples are the development of student management looking to 'relevance' and antagonism to the employment of American faculty members. The charge that these imports give a national slant to their teaching may be true in the social sciences, but hardly in the natural sciences.

be valid in the field of science, but it is not valid for the humanities. The language – 'creation of research job,' 'permanent research posts,' 'planning research on the departmental basis,' the 'setting up of major research programs,' 'the provision of equipment on a large scale' – is appropriate to posts in the laboratory or programs for the teamwork of a science department, but such language and the outlook and attitude that it implies is inappropriate to most research in the humanities. A scholar at work on a historical biography is not the 'incumbent' of a 'post'; the editor of a classical text is not 'fulfilling' a 'program'; the philosopher has no need of expensive 'equipment'.

The Macdonald report also recommends that research grants and contracts should be replaced in Canada by a new legal instrument called a research agreement, which was designed by the United States Bureau of the Budget for use in that country. This, it is said, would assist the Treasury Board in evaluating the involvement of agencies in university research support.

The report shows no awareness that some provinces, and especially Quebec, do not acknowledge federal priority in university support; it proposes the creation of centralized federal structures without provincial consultation. One also doubts the political feasibility of the recommendation that the federal government should make direct grants for research buildings, study quarters for students, library buildings and contents, and so on.

The main emphasis of the report is on administration rather than policy and parts might serve as advice to Biafra on how to start up an academic support program. As an example, take the section on grants in the chapter 'Policies for research councils':

The applicant should be requested to specify the purpose of his investigation, the method he proposes to use, the facilities available to him, his qualifications and the qualifications of others participating in the project, the time required for the study, and an annual budget, listing personnel and salaries, materials and supplies, equipment, travel and other expenses. The project should be refereed, in general by two referees independently and should be judged by an expert committee covering applications in the discipline of the applicant and perhaps related fields. The adjudicating committee should have available to it the application and the referees' reports. It should judge the project on its merits and the applicant's qualifications to carry it out.

The number of review committees should be related to the number of applications. A committee cannot deal adequately with more than perhaps 50 applications a day. Each member of the committee would need to receive all the relevant documentation well in advance of the meeting.

In its conclusions the Macdonald report contrasts quite strongly with another dissertation, the Hurtubise-Rowat report.[14] This study, published in 1970, was set up by the national association of university teachers, of administrators, and of students. Public hearings were held across Canada and ninety-three briefs were submitted. The report took a more rigid position even than Macdonald for university independence from its federal patron, and from its provincial patron too. University distrust of governments has been so great as to break even their tradition of individual autonomy. As A.D. Dunton, President of Carleton, put it:

The universities are trying to develop a central machinery before the government develops its own. This is going to be the race. We are trying to develop among ourselves the research capacity to know what we are doing, which nobody knows at present.

Hurtubise and Rowat considered it essential to repartriate university autonomy in the research field. To this end the report made these proposals:

- Research support should be considered part of regular university funding and, in accordance with the BNA Act, should be taken over by the provinces, following federal-provincial financial arrangements.
- A large share of the research allocation should be in the form of general, unconditional grants, so that the universities and their scholars could decide on the balance between the fields of research.
- The federal research councils should withdraw from the familiar NRC system of grants to individuals. They could continue to make grants for costly proposals.
- Mission-oriented research support by government agencies should be discontinued. Particularly deplored is the distortion in university planning and building programs caused by the medical and health science grants.

It is implicit in the report that the natural sciences should be diminished and that this could be more easily achieved by internal faculty control than under the system of outside grants. Of the latter, the social sciences and humanities have been receiving 7.4 per cent (the rest goes to health, natural science, and engineering). The universities themselves allocate their small research funds in quite different proportions with about 40 per cent going to the social sciences and humanities.

Somewhat inconsistently, the authors also argue that governments should intervene directly in favour of the social sciences: 'Governments may be able to control the magnitude of social problems through shifting the general balance of research support from the natural sciences to the social sciences and humanities.'

One more report remains to be considered, that of Bonneau and Corry.[15] Sponsored by the AUCC, this commission held seminars, public hearings, and consultations across Canada, and internationally with OECD and UNESCO officials. Eight studies were prepared for the commissioners by Canadian academics, and they received about 340 briefs. Most of the briefs were descriptions of activity and support (or its lack) in particular enterprises of universities. One, by E.H. Anthony of Guelph, was entitled 'The stockings were hung by the lab-bench with care.'

The first volume of the report develops the argument and contains the recommendations. The second volume includes a report on the work of the commission by its secretary and a bibliography. It also has a report by a 'Task Force' on library rationalisation which the AUCC had previously set up, and which eventually became associated with the commission.

Bonneau and Corry adopt a more scholarly and conciliatory approach than the authors of the two preceding reports. At the same time they look wistfully at the good old days of 1939 or 1914 when the academic mix was less adulterated with worldliness. Their tone is one of praise for the traditional pattern of pure inquiry which, as they recommend, should continue its domination. But they are resigned to some necessary modern intrusion of mission-oriented activity arising out of national and provincial policies and supported internally as well.

It is very important for the university to keep at work on the problems of the world around it. How else can universities hold the respect of students who know there is a great deal wrong with the world? Universities need the moral support of the communities they serve. That will be hard to get if university researchers pass by the problems of the day.

Also a significant portion of the younger staff are finding their interest kindled by applied research and less excited about basic research where the findings have little relation to urgent social issues.[16]

Bonneau and Corry identify two kinds of mental activity. The first they call frontier research, in which the experimenter tries, as Bacon said, to 'put nature on the rack and interrogate her.' Frontier research, which predominates in the natural sciences, is to become increasingly basic, with R & D missions to be carried out largely by government agencies.

Secondly, there is reflective inquiry, which is to be the new name for some of what is done by social scientists and most of what is done by humanists. The report deplores the use of the word research for prestige purposes, for instance to decribe the activity of a classics professor preparing a lecture, not to mention a school child looking up an item in the encyclopaedia. The authors would like reflective inquiry to replace research as the OK words and to attract a much larger portion of the funds, especially in the social sciences. In fact they want seven to nine universities beefed up by government to 'international quality' in basic social research. An additional ten or fifteen graduate schools are to be strengthened to prepare social scientists for the essental work of the country. Whether social scientists will accept their role as either animals or vermin more readily than natural scientists have done remains to be seen (see page 47). Even when dealing with one individual the classification of mental activity bristles with difficulty and may eventually require the services of a psycho-analyst. As the report puts it:

J.M. Keynes' *General Theory of Employment, Interest and Money* was clearly the result of reflective inquiry. If his dominating motive was curiosity, it was equally clearly basic research. If his ruling motive was to find ways to control economic fluctuations, it was a form of applied research. But it would still remain reflective inquiry because of the kind of mental operations which dominated the exercise. Was it curiosity-oriented basic, or was it applied research which involved problem-oriented basic, looking for a solution for booms and depressions?[17]

Throughout the report the key word is rationalization. Of the eleven central chapters, five have rationalization mentioned in their titles: of graduate studies; important steps in; within one university; between several universities; at the national level. Rationalization is to determine the appropriate role of the universities in a global policy on research. It is to answer the question as to what research is compatible with the universities' larger service to society. It is to search for the best combination of teaching and research to maximize faculty morale, effort, and service. It is, in brief, the academic answer to PPB. As the beginning of planning

we recognise that governments provide the funds for research, and must determine what the balance between basic and applied research for the country as a whole should be, and what share of each they would like the universities to carry.[18]

Hitherto the federal agencies which pay direct research costs have called the tune in university planning and have largely opted for basic research. The provinces, which pay the overhead, have had little authority in determining research directions, a situation which Bonneau and Corry are sure the provinces will not continue to accept. Hence the university strategy should be to manovure into a position to influence provincial as well as federal policy.

Since much of the public concern about sharply rising costs of the sixties is focused on the large sums devoted to PH D work, the first question is how to prevent and eliminate undue proliferation of PH D programs. The report favours a new Ontario plan under university control rather than a more sweeping new Quebec plan under government control.* Under the Ontario plan, which could apply to other provinces or to regions, the universities have set up discipline groups who will decide what universities are good enough to offer PH D work in which fields. The universities have agreed to co-operate with the assessments and will be under pressure to acquiesce to them. Also the provincial government is likely to base its support policy on the findings so that each university will be pushed towards graduate work in fields in which it has the most advantages.

The difficulties in succeeding with such a voluntary plan are nearly as formidable as the achievement of a Soviet-U.S. disarmament agreement. If the plan fails, something like the Quebec scheme is likely to be imposed on each regional university system.

The *Operations Sectorielles,* launched in the Province of Quebec recently, is more embracing than the Ontario proposal, and more government-directed and government-oriented. It takes into account undergraduate as well as graduate programs. As a first step the government of Quebec has expressed the wish that its universities secure provincial approval before undertaking projects funded by the federal agencies.

First casualties are likely to be the negotiated development grants of $100,000 or more introduced several years ago by the NRC and the MRC. They require an undertaking by the university to pick up the enterprise when the grant expires after three to five years. Now the slow-down in provincial support is preventing the universities from honouring their commitments. Provincial governments have mostly been unaware of the existence of the grants and are tending to refuse to take responsibility for them.

Another organization, established in 1969, is the Quebec Industrial Research Centre, which is intended to link the universities with industry.

---

* The Ontario plan is outlined in pp. 60–7 of the Bonneau-Corry report. The Quebec plan, which they do not like, remains virtually undescribed.

Agreements between the centre and the universities will permit interchange of human and material resources between government and university laboratories and are expected to ensure strong liaison of the latter with industry.

Professors who are still riding in the research traditions which began in Germany a century and a half ago had better fasten their seat belts.

The final quarter of the Bonneau-Corry narrative (fifty pages) is devoted to a detailed description of the nuts and bolts of rationalization, complete with elaborate 'flow charts' intended to show the universities how to proceed internally and how to develop outside relations with each other and with governments. An earlier comment will bear repetition here 'One wonders for whom this elaborate taxonomy was necessary and to whom it is useful.'[19]

V PROGNOSIS ON FUTURE DIRECTIONS

The university, in its research activities, is assigned different priorities by each group of planners. To the Lamontagne committee, focusing on national aims which accord with the 'new wisdom,' our first step should be to make industry prosperous. It follows that the function of the university is to prepare technologists. To Lamontagne, an unregenerate Sophist, what's good for Massey-Ferguson is good for the country. However, being a social scientist himself, Lamontagne would throw a bone to his colleagues in this field in the interests of the hoped-for good life.

Macdonald, a former university president, is concerned to get money and keep administrative autonomy. He is not concerned with what the money is for or from whom it comes, or with federal-provincial jurisdiction. He is not particultarly interested in pushing industrial aspects.

Hurtubise and Rowat are spokesmen for faculty autonomy (as distinct from administrative autonomy) and for the have-not social sciences and humanities. What the university does should be decided by the scholars, who will 're-establish the equilibrium which has been lost between the pure sciences and the health sciences on the one hand, and the humanities and social sciences on the other, rejecting the confusion between the means and the end.'

Bonneau and Corry want the universities to develop some policy about dividing up the areas of research interest, and to relate them sufficiently to provincial needs so that the federal agencies will not continue to generate all the plans. Rather inconsistently, they hope that this will turn out to tip the balance in favour of basic research and against mission-orientation, and in favour of reflective inquiry with consequent improved funding for the humanities. They also want the relative position of the social sciences to improve. They hope that governments will consult the universities before deciding how to apportion the funds for academic priorities.

In all four reports the social sciences are presented as candidates for increased support, and may be expected to challenge the natural sciences in the universities. The recommendations of the latter two reports that the humanities should also join the haves is less apt to succeed. It is more probable that as the social sciences increase in power and cease to be have-nots, they will loosen their identification with the humanities, leaving the latter to their small vocation. Also, there is hardly a chance that the trend towards increased applied research can be reversed. Bread and butter considerations in the universities will intervene to prevent it. A more likely outcome is that, just as the humanities will be carried as a kind of ornament to the social sciences, so will basic natural science assume a minor role in its relation to industry-oriented science and engineering, which will be the focus of expansion. Finally, the health sciences, built on the deepest of our personal fears, will survive the slings and arrows and continue to prosper. It is doubtful whether even Hurtubise or Rowat, if he needed his gall bladder removed, would prefer an incompetent doctor.

8
A personal appraisal of the
strategic possibilities

Through this book my own point of view on science policy has been implicit in the direction of the argument. It may be useful now to make it explicit, and to offer some personal opinions on the manipulation of science. But before doing so it will be well to restate the conflict which is at the core of our discussion. It is simply the issue of reconciling the objectivity and independence of science with the responsibility of government. The disparity of views has been leading towards a deadlock in which the politician and administrator want a system in which they can direct science to practical ends by control of the purse strings, and the scientist wants the purse held open without strings.

The planners have been set up, or have set themselves up, from the government side, and naturally they look to the government way of doing things for a pattern. Their essence of planning is an organization chart or model of a hierarchy. They want to have pyramids with the issues of most general significance at the top. At the bottom they combine increasingly dissimilar things until they have established an artificial and arbitrary unity. D.K. Price has remarked:

If the organization chart is the model of government, a university curriculm is the model of science. Here the process works, not by artificial integration, but by natural division and subdivision. The scientist breaks each discipline down into sub-disciplines and multiplies their subordinate specialities. What he learns about each part of a problem opens up a tremendous number of further questions that call for solution. If you start a scientist on a simple problem he can build on top of it an inverted pyramid of abstract and refined research projects.

When you try to match up the pyramid of government organization with the inverted pyramid of science you are bound to run into trouble. Even at the lowest level the government must deal with problems, each of which could be solved perfectly only by a considerable number of scientists. In the process of solution each scientist would open up enough new questions, all needing to be answered before final solution could be obtained, to keep their research going indefinitely.[1]

Price goes on to say that the scientist's response to a government request is to propose a complete study of what you ought to study; and then a complete study of the methods that you ought to use in making the study; and then a complete study of the way in which the results of your study should be applied.[2] By that time, of course, you would need to study the extent to which changes in the situation had made the original question obsolete.

In any other branch of the labour force this tendency would be described as working to rule, or practising a slow-down, or going into a study session. The attitude, unaccompanied by any adequate defence from the scientists, has gradually exasperated the politicians and planners to react, and over-react, with proposals which are sometimes beyond reason.

It might be thought that the scientists, finding themselves under attack, would, as they say in the military, attempt some regrouping of their forces. Not at all. Jacob Bronowski, for instance, adopted an extreme anti-government position.[3] He reasoned that since power over our environment comes from the work of scientists, responsiblity for the use of the power of science should be pinned on them. Hence there should be a separation between science and government. This he called the disestablishment of science, in the same sense that the churces have become disestablished and have become independent of the state.

Under Bronowski's plan the choice of priorities would be taken from the state and given to the scientists, together with a single and overall fund or grant to be divided by all the scientists of the country. Bronowski thinks his plan would compel the scientists to assign priorities, judge the balance of importance of the different branches of science and the main lines of research in each, and arrive at a scale of priorities with which it would divide its overall grant.

Now, as the Laurence report on physics showed, it has proved impossible for a group of scientists, however hard they try, to agree that any part of their field is of low priority.[4] The Bronowski proposal would amount in practice to an extension to the whole of science of the method of judgment by peers, which was developed by the NRC and similar organizations. This would please many academic scientists but would be unacceptable to planners, who would see it as a device to extend further the proportion of pure science in the system.

Bronowski is offering a special case of the proposition that man is fundamentally good and needs only to remove the artificial constraints of government in order to reach an ultimate state of perfection. This general idea was, paradoxically, at the root of the philosophy of both the *laissez-faire* economists and their extreme opponents, the Marxists, who thought that man would have no more political troubles when the state had withered away. The idea is not acceptable to any major party in Canada, or for that matter in the world.

II BIAS IN PLANNING AND REPORTING

In earlier chapters we have examined many reports which offer plans from which to construct a model science policy. The feature that they conspicuously hold in common is that in writing them each team or author came out by the same door as in he went. Each author, according to his character and point of view, had drawn his own conclusions before the hearing of evidence was begun. While evidence might moderate to some degree the extremity of the leader's initial intentions, it did not change their direction.

Obviously a cynical government could, by selection of the right authors, obtain whatever directives about science it wished to hear. I do not suggest that this was consiously done in Canada; the government's views did not go much further than to make science policy an appendage to finance. It is a coincidence that we may discern, in the three major reports, a progression from a business man's solution, through an expert analysis, to an attempt at a master plan.

The first of the national reports, by Glassco, dealt with science policy as seen through the eyes of a chartered accountant; it was a product of the simple days when good organization was thought to be synonymous with good science. In my opinion (and I was there) the structural changes which resulted have been largely irrelevant to the advancement of research.

The second, or OECD review, was one of a series which now covers about a dozen nations. Each review is a massive collection of information, together with a critical report, on which the country concerned, or any country, can draw in its search for a science policy or for improved international co-operation. It is an OECD assumption that each country is looking for a master plan which will meet some such requirements as the following: improved relations between researchers and administrators, promotion of research in medium and small industries, and closer relations between university fundamental research and that in industrial and government laboratories.[5] The OECD report on Canada has stimulated a more or less agonizing reappraisal and some change in the emphasis of government science. It has not so far had any visible effect on industry or the universities.

As for the third major report, that of Lamontagne et al., the senator outlined his conclusions in advance during the speech in which he proposed the special committee.

The creation of a dynamic and balanced science organization is an urgent and absolute necessity. A main centre of co-ordination and financing of scientific policy is extremely desirable. The time has come to create a federal department of scientific affairs.[6]

He went on in the speech to give, in considerable detail, the arrangements and duties of the councils which were to be part of the coming ministry of science.

Before continuing with my own opinions, I should perhaps expose my personal bias. My research career began with the study of chemical embryology, in which field a Nobel prize had just been awarded for experiments which showed the location in developing eggs of an 'organizer.' The organizer was able to turn a mass of haphazard cells into a well-formed little frog. We all expected that within a short time the chemical structure of the organizer would be worked out and an era of great scientific expansion would follow including the cure of cancer. Now, nearly half a century later, no additional progress has been made and the organizer is moving from science into philosophy to take its place beside entelechy.

Similarly in the matter of science policy it is quite easy to propose a control formula or organizer, from which science progress is expected to flow in beneficient directions, but when the phenomenon is of great complexity a central control is not likely to be effective; the web is too wide for the spider to manipulate all the threads. I do not believe that a control mechanism will in itself change significantly the rate at which science moves in the direction desired by Senator Lamontagne. Any central planning body such as a ministry supported by a council has the limitiations that the force is not available to bring the nation's scientists into line, and that we do not possess the information necessary to lay out the line which we propose to make them toe.

There is, of course, in the climate of our times, no prospect for a diminution in the machinery of central organization; my purpose is only to testify that 'restructuring' is amongst the easiest, but at the same time most irrelevant, appendages of science policy.

We arrived at our present national position of faith in organization through the work of successive committees which assumed a false similarity between science and business. Hence what made business prosperous would also make science prosperous.

But the divisions of the research-development spectrum are strongly held, more like churches than business arrangements. There are three Canadian denominations – government, industry and university. Very roughly the universities have tended to be high church (pure science) and industry low church (development) with government laboratories in between. Now Senator Lamontagne proposes to get the universities into revivalist low-church practices. Nobody acquainted with religious history should expect easy conversions. Rather, what we have before us is a discouragingly slow ecumenical movement.

In any ecumenical movement, whether of religion, international affairs, or science policy, the greatest difficulty arises out of the character and ambitions of individuals. There are great differences in philosophies, attitudes, and policies. Both science and education are changing so rapidly that it is imprudent to plan science more than a decade ahead, and even this projection is subject to continuation of the same individuals in power.

In past times policy has ranged from Mr Howe's 'okay, let's go' on atomic power to Mr Diefenbaker's 'Vision of the North' on the Arctic, or an abrupt negative act such as the cancellation of the Arrow project. This system is likely to continue. There is no real hope that some mechanical method such as systems analysis will be refined to such a degree that future science policy will emerge from a computer. System analysis is designed to deal only with the secondary, tertiary, and quaternary derivatives of policy.

At present the view is widely held that to increase industrial innovation is a first priority, some would say *the* first priority. How is this to be done? Rapid changes are brought about by a blend of force and persuasive oratory, neither of which is available for use in transforming Canadian science. We must, therefore, accept slower progress, working within the framework of the oldest and best-understood technique, namely the influence on the young. E.W.R. Steacie remarked:

If it were decided to-morrow that there was a vital need for ten million horses, the problem would not be solved by budgeting for them, or by appointing committees or having conferences. The important thing would be to start breeding more horses. Similarly, the development of industrial research involves first the strengthening of post-graduate schools, and secondly ensuring that the best graduates remain in the universities.[7]

Steacie's method, which is that used through the ages, has already brought Canadian basic science to a respected international level, and it has launched various branches which were mentioned in chapter 2. Industrial research, which is currently understood to mean engineering activity in secondary industry, can in theory yield to the same techniques; in practice its variations in form, its international overtones, and the attempts to relate university research to not-yet-developed industries have placed difficulties in design of a university-business linkage.

The universities will look for a broadening of the definition of industrial research. To them the term goes beyond the promotion of innovation to include the welfare of workers and the maintenance of the environment.

III THE TWO KINDS OF SCIENCE

Turning now to the two kinds of science, Dr Gerhard Herzberg I hope will not object to my use of his name as the personification of the anti-Lamontagne forces. One hears today from university scientists, and even in NRC circles, that Herzberg's Nobel Prize will save us all. 'They' won't dare to go ahead with 'their' plans in the face of such a distinguished award to a Canadian.

This solace I find hard to accept. As we have seen in earlier chapters, Herzberg has been a vocal critic of the prevailing trend towards socialism in science ever since the Glassco report. His future views or precepts are not likely to be more or less effective than those of the past.

The Herzberg doctrine, as it is usually articulated in university departments, assumes a sort of laying on of hands, so that anyone who can get a job in a university is in a consecrated position. Lord Rothschild identified this as the Pedestalisation of Science, which polarises society into scientific and technical on the one hand, and 'lay' on the other.[8] He noted that applied science, and even some technology, get into the sanctified class by virtue of the reverence we have for pure science.

Rothschild distinguished between basic research, which is an occupation in its own right, and applied research plus development, which is not. The latter is one of the human activities which may be necessary if we are to achieve a practical objective, and it must be geared specifically to that objective. For if we can not have a single science policy, we must deal separately with resources, pollution, food, manufacturing, and the rest.

With the wisdom of hindsight, it is evident that in Canada we have not faced up to the realities of the two segments of science. Traditionally, university research support was almost wholly administered by the NRC, which at first made its grants on the basis of the quality of the applicant. Had this policy been continued, the strong would have been increasingly strengthened, and the weak left to starve. After the second World War the nominal policy was increasingly distorted by regional pressures, first by new English-language universities and departments wanting development grants; later by the French-language universities demanding to be brought into equality. Hence the NRC got into programs whose aims belonged more properly to the Department of Regional Economic Expansion rather than to a pure science agency.

The NRC suffered further constriction of its original purpose in that more and more of its funds became committed on a permanent basis to universities and programs, so that it had diminishing resources with which to manoeuvre into new situations. This locked-in escalation is one we frequently hear about in provinces and municipal bodies where fixed charges on streets, schools, hospitals, and so on, use up practically all the funds.

For the NRC I do not see any way out of the dilemma except to get back to its original aim of supporting pure science on the basis of the quality of the applicant. In addition, programs should have a time limit, under which the grant diminishes annually by, say, 20 per cent. This practice is very common in foundations like Ford and Donner. The method would also tend to force the universities to look into their own priorities and abandon the pretence that every university is prepared to become a specialist in anything with a dollar sign attached to it. It would, in addition, permit the NRC to experiment with new support patterns.

But what about the universities which cannot produce applicants of sufficient distinction to qualify for NRC grants? First of all, if the provinces so wished, there is no evident constitutional reason why they should not come under Ottawa's regional development plans, being considered as necessary infrastructures like highways or power plants. In addition, we should award most of our federal research grants, say, four-fifths, through mission-oriented agencies rather than the NRC. Then the prime qualification for support would be the national value of the program, and the secondary requirement would be to find a man available to undertake it. The relative allotment of funds to the several agencies is obviously a political decision on which the pressures are likely to be subject to continuous change.

I cannot agree with Senator Lamontagne that the economical way to rearrange our national academic support patterns is to destroy the NRC and immediately set up a facsimile in its place.

IV FEDERAL LABORATORIES AND FEDERAL SUPPORT MECHANISMS

The one area that the government does control, and in which it can use coercion to make sure its policies are carried out, is in its own laboratories. The absence of coherent policy here has been due to the lack of interest of successive governments, which have allowed numerous local empires to grow up, often in competition. Governments have had two or three chances to place the NRC in policy control and have backed off each time under pressure, usually originating from interested deputy ministers.

It must also be remembered that once the multiple authority system got going, Canada had no adequate body of opinion outside its own government scientists, from which advice on science policy could be sought. The university community was small, weak, and dependent. Also the outside scientists were, and still are, in agreement with the NRC policy of building scientific infrastructures as a first step.

It was right and inevitable, half a century ago, to plan on some fundamental science in government labs. But with the recent advance in the universities the needs have changed, and much of the basic science can be phased out. However, Big Science, including much of neutron physics, requires such extensive facilities that it cannot be done competitively in universities. To bring about scientific (as distinct from book-keeping) rearrangements of the government program, one possibility is to vest real power in a science council. Real power, that is, over government laboratories. One of our mistakes has been to reason that because the government has no coercive machinery over the industrial and academic sectors, it has to abstain from the application of general policy in its own operations.

Another mistake has been to assume that the provincial and private sectors, over which no coercive powers exist, would make a significant response to federal preaching. The same error is illustrated in the failure of the Economic Council to influence capital and labour.

There is also the persistent problem of getting federal recipients of expert advice to pay attention. We have a half-century of observation of the level of attentiveness of the cabinet to science policy. It has been close to zero. Can we expect anything better in the future? I think not. Ministers have no time to contemplate long-term policies.

Added to the constitutional barrier and cabinet frailty, there is the complexity of government science, which may be too great to be regulated effectively by any standing committee. Perhaps, therefore, we should use in the future the method that has been most successful in the past, namely, the commission for a special purpose. These commissions have brought about most of the changes and they have the merit of freshness, enthusiasm, and lack of permanence.

In the third segment of science, industrial innovation, federal support has grown more recently, but also in an air of unreality. One illusion here is that the industrial area is too important to have scientists fooling around with its management. So most of its grants are handled by administrators in the Department of Industry, Trade and Commerce. Eventually the planners hope to gather the whole system into one grand national organization with a uniform pattern.

Such centralization, I suggest, is the opposite of what is needed in a new field, where no policy has yet been shown to work. What we need is rather experimentation by several systems to see what combination will work best. The planners look to something equivalent to the well planned Panzer attack which overran France in 1940. I would look rather towards the guerilla type of action by smaller units which defeated the u.s. forces in Vietnam.

Dispersal and attention to local variability are much more important than central uniformity. To provide regional sensitivity, the ready-made agents are the provincial research foundations, which offer a uniquely Canadian mechanism. They could reach large and small industries directly with suitable development contracts. They could also succeed with a policy to alleviate regional disparity, which has been intensified by failure of the central agencies to place support successfully in the industries of the poorer regions.

Support of industrial innovation is also hindered by a tendency to think in terms of watertight compartments. In the real world outstanding scientists may contribute freely to both pure and applied science. A classic example is Pasteur, who spent his whole life solving practical problems, but who is known to students today for his contributions to pure science, rather than for his improvements in wine-making or for finding out how to keep silkworms healthy. One of my students who went on to Duke university was asked in her final PH D oral: 'What was Pasteur's most important discovery?' The expected answer was, 'He discovered that yeast was alive.' Could such a milestone of science progress have been anticipated from a government support program in applied research to the brewing industry? (According to the *New York Times* of 6 September 1972, the Soviet Union is introducing new rules for graduate degrees for 1972-3. There will be no final oral defence of the thesis which will be read in private by a board of experts. Theses will be limited to 150 pages. A spokesman pointed out that Einstein's thesis occupied twenty-one pages. The number of candidates will be sharply cut. The defence of theses is a German invention which the Americans cubed and over-organized. It was the era of the land-grant colleges and over much of the country the thinking about higher education was based on farming needs. Canada, out of step and out of breath, adopted the American plan. My own PH D taken in England forty years ago was assessed by exactly the method that the Russians are now adopting.)

To come back to the main theme, this is not to say that I am advocating a return to the exploded notion that all fanciful proposals should be supported because of imagined potential spin-off or fall-out. The point is rather that the quality of the man cannot be overlooked even in the most applied fields. When you see a Bobby Orr of science you let him develop his own style of play. Centralized planners, with their organization charts, do not like these exceptions because they do not lend themselves to administration by computers. The superior types will emerge from the farm teams and their level of originality can be watched from there on.

Unfortunately there will be very few with superior brains and for the rest applied research should be subject to advance scrutiny by non-scientists as well as professional scientists. For major proposals there is no reason why the method of the law courts could not be used, with advocates for and against the proposal, and a judge who should, of course, have the same standard of objectivity as in the courts. Certainly the Treasury Board should not act as judge.

It will be difficult to assemble a roster of scientists who are prepared to act as prosecutors and make a case adverse to a proposal by a colleague. Indeed it would have been impossible in Canada a few years ago because of our small science community. But now there are a few old boys appearing who are not themselves hoping for future grants from their adversaries, and would be truthful as critics.

Our failure to place the test of national utility on so-called applied science has been the core of the criticism by investigating bodies during the past decade. The worst offender is medical science which, if subject to objective standards, would throw out some 40 per cent of its expenditure as not truly medical. Other examples come readily to mind. Take fisheries, where population studies on our banks are proceeding at such a leisurely rate that the stocks under consideration are long dead before the report on their abundance gets into print. Such work usually has no claim to be in the care of researchers of distinction, no claim as pure science, and no claim as applied science.

To sum up, the government should indeed centralize its control over its own laboratories. But both industrial innovation and university support should be fostered by a variety of federal and provincial organizations, working independently. A single central control office for the three denominations, modelled on business and characterized primarily by a detailed accounting system, would probably hinder rather than help imaginative work.

> For the snark's a peculiar creature that won't
> Be caught in a commonplace way.
> Do all that you know, and try all that you don't:
> Not a chance must be wasted today!

V THE MINISTER OF STATE FOR SCIENCE AND TECHNOLOGY

C.M. Drury used to be fond of saying that there was no reason to appoint a minister for science policy since there was one on hand already, namely himself. His real job, however, was that of president of the Treasury Board and he regarded the management of science much as a prostitute might regard a marriage ceremony. It added a touch of class without interfering with his professional activities.

His assistant for some months had been Alastair Gillespie. When Mr Gillespie succeeded to the Ministry of State for Science and Technology, Mr Drury handed on to him the tablets containing his sacred laws of science. Here are the commandments:

1 Thou shalt have no other gods before the Treasury Board.
2 Thou shalt not bow down thyself to any other board or council nor serve them; for we of the Treasury Board are a jealous god visiting the iniquities of the fathers upon the children and showing mercy to those who keep our commandments.
3 Thou shalt not take the name of the Treasury Board in vain.
4 Remember the Budget Day to keep it holy.
5 Honour thy father and thy mother, the Minister of Finance, and the president of the Treasury Board.

6 Thou shalt not kill any government department or agency.

7 Thou shalt not commit adultery with the universities.

8 Thou shalt not steal any authority or control.

9 Thou shalt not bear witness against the Department of Industry, Trade and Commerce.

10 Thou shalt not covet the prerogatives of other ministers.

The dilemma of any science policy minister is that he cannot move in any direction without breaking one or more of the commandments. His influence in the cabinet is weak because his department has no muscle.[9] His position is illustrated by the wartime story in which Stalin, in reply to a suggestion that the Vatican be consulted, asked 'How many divisions has the pope?' What would happen to a science minister if he tangled with the Minister of Agriculture over agrarian science policy? To ask the question is to answer it.

Under present conditions the success of a science policy minister depends on his ability to appease the Treasury Board, with the help of the Science Secretariat. This latter comprises a group of full-time government employees with a science background, who are in truth a part of the TB. They are subject to the normal human instincts of self-preservation, and soon discover that they had better pass on to the minister a judicious blend of what he wants to hear and what the TB wants him to hear. We have already seen in earlier chapters the direction which such advice is likely to take.

The reason that TB control has not collapsed before now has been nation-wide inertia. Most of the science action has been in federal government laboratories. But now, with the increasing importance of university research, the national determination to stimulate private industry, and the exercise of constitutional rights by the provinces, the segment of national science amenable to TB control is diminishing. So when the minister makes enquiry from his ss men he will get increasingly inadequate advice.

No doubt there are readers who will say that I am making all this up, that there is no *bête noire* hidden in the TB. Fortunately we had direct evidence on the point from an interview in 1971 with the secretary of the newly created science policy ministry, who said:

The Treasury Board has been doing its job of developing criteria for the assessment of science and technology and taking very important decisions. The Treasury Board will continue to have the key role in assessing the efficiency of individual programs and will continue its attempt to have each of the departments spend its budget wisely. We must not give the impression that we are taking over a responsibility of the Treasury Board. We are not here to implement changes, but to recommend as advisors to the Treasury Board and the Privy Council.[10]

What chance would a minister of science policy have if he wished to steer a course between the TB-Lamontagne Scylla and the Herzberg Charybdis? The prime minister will not fire a shot to help him. The Science Council will name no order of priority. Hence the minister would have to develop his own strategy.

What he (or she) would have to recognize is that Lamontagne and the Treasury Board are proposing essentially the Russian system of science policy, although they have never compared the reality with their idealized version of it. They are like somebody who believes he has stumbled on the principles of Marxism but has never heard of Marx, and does not know that his precepts have been under test for many years.

The duty of Mrs Sauvé is that of any scientist confronted with a hypothesis, namely to examine the existing evidence from the half-century of trial which the system has received in Russia. An even better model might be Czechoslovakia, an industrialized country comparable to Canada, which used our scientific methods between the wars and then, after the Second World War, switched to complete state control. When the minister has some evidence she will be in a position to confront the Treasury Board with facts which even they will find difficult to brush off.

The appraisal must be done by people who are not committed to their conclusions in advance, and who must be predominantly working scientists. Learning about natural science policy from economists and accountants is like learning about love in a brothel; the lessons are clear enough but rather oversimplified.

What a science policy minister should obtain from Russia is direct evidence on how far socialism can be carried into applied research without becoming counterproductive. Eventually there is an undesirable multiplication of commissars, co-ordinators, and liaison officers. From this there develops an inability of those in command to devise the necessary plans. J. Polanyi has recently offered an analysis which is a good forecast of what a ministerial team would discover about Russia.

For fifty years governmental structures have been sought that might hasten the realization of Lenin's vision that 'Communism is Soviet government plus the electrification of the whole country' (1920). Gosplan, the State Planning Commission, was founded in 1921. In conjunction with the Soviet Academy of Sciences, it has been responsible for the planning of the national science effort. A little over a decade ago an agreed list of 'thirty basic directions of science' was announced as a guide to the sponsorship of basic research. The thirty basic directions cover all the important growing points of modern science. Since then there has been a division of responsibility, in which the State Committee for Co-ordination looks after what we would call applied research, and the Soviet Academy of Sciences looks after basic research.

This division may appear to be a surprising outcome of an effort to 'strengthen the ties between science and production.' Certainly from an ideological standpoint, Marxism is unfriendly to the idea of a separation between basic and applied research. It seems reasonable to suppose that the realities of the situation forced this outcome.[11]

In 1971–2 the costs of science to the federal government were distributed as follows:

Intramural activities in federal government laboratories	63%
Universities and non-profit institutions	20%
Industry	17%[12]

The task of the minister of state for science and technology, if she takes the direction of the planners, will be, in the next decade, to change these figures to a final equilibrium between the performers and the functions which might look something like this (the figures may be read either as percentages or as tens of millions of dollars at the present annual level of national expenditure):

Government laboratories responsible for defence, most natural resources, and most Big Science	25
Universities, etc. responsible for medicine, environmental research, and some work now done in government laboratories	25
Industry responsible for preventing and cleaning up environmental left-overs, and for most engineering now done in government laboratories.	50

Any real decline in the federal laboratories will obviously be strongly opposed by the agencies concerned and their ministers. The minister of state for science and technology, in her counteroffensive aimed at change, is likely to be driven into steps like the following:

– a little cheating: following the u.s. plan by shifting some government research in military and space topics over to so-called private companies whose only client is the federal government,

- a general closing out of government engineering laboratories,
- a shifting of monitoring operations which should become a provincial responsibility,
- the restriction of federal research to common property, international, and resource areas and some special cases, such as transport.

As well as dividing up the existing appropriations, the new ministry will presumably have to recommend to the cabinet what absolute annual sums are to be spent in future on science, and what price tag is to be placed on basic science. The sum to be set aside for pure research could be an absolute number of dollars, or a fraction of the total science budget. A figure commonly heard is 10 per cent of the total, a number which has now acquired the Lewis Carroll standard of certainty, 'What I tell you three times is true.'

This 10 per cent should go to university scientists of distinction and their young acolytes to form what used to be called 'schools.' The distinguished professor who heads the school will not today usually be the head of a department as was the *Ordinarius* in Germany or the Regius professor in Britain. The schools will be in a continuous state of changing order and leadership, like a flock of birds in migration.

Another fraction of the science budget, used for research on matters of national importance, is conventionally placed at 25 per cent of the total. It is intended to be divided between industry, the universities, and government laboratories, hopefully in that order. Hitherto in the development of Canada a large part of this area has become the perquisite of federal laboratories and there is a huge vested interest opposed to losing it. Industry, with a few exceptions like Bell Telephone, the paper companies, and the oil companies, has so far been unable to mount a significant fraction of Canadian research. The minister's unsolved problem is how to induce industries to accept money for applied research with real intent to use it, while avoiding the side-effect of siphoning the results into the USA.

Everybody (apart from the workers in federal laboratories and their directors) would like to see a massive transfer of applied research to industry.[13] But the fact is that there is no presently known effective way to accomplish such a transfer. The industries, particularly smaller ones, simply cannot absorb such a program, and the sc report does not open a way, for, as it says characteristically, 'the formulation of a co-ordinated industrial strategy is not the responsibility of the Science Council.' The re-recommendation in the report that federal and provincial governments explore new mechanisms for supplementing capital to new and small companies is (despite its bromidic sound) worthy of the attention of the minister.

The third segment of science is called development or innovation in industry and monitoring or survey work in resource areas, and it is expected by many planners to use up to 65 per cent of the future science budget. Writers from the business world like Bachynski seem to assume that this 65 per cent is all to be expended directly by industrial firms to increase their production – of shoes and ships and sealing wax; of satellites and snowmobiles and arms to use in Vietnam. Some of it, however, may be done in universities, for although ultimate practicality is hardly an academic function, it does provide a good break-in for departments trying to get started, and carries to the public an aroma of usefulness. It is, in fact, the only aspect of science activity that illiterate people can understand which is why university presidents like it so much. Big industry, if forced by society into a clean-up situation, might find it advantageous to support environmental research in the universities.

To sum up: innovation is a rather inclusive term, taking in anti-pollution, medical developments, and improved traffic lights as well as goods export-able to the USA. Also, as the Science Council has pointed out, the service sector of our economy now employs about 60 per cent of our labour force, while the private service sector alone employs about as many Canadians as do the manufacturing and primary resource industries together, and is growing far more rapidly.[14] Innovation in this sector is as badly needed as in manufacturing.

The distribution of the suggested 65 per cent for innovation will have a much wider base than has been assumed by industrialists and planners. It will probably be expended by industry, government laboratories, and universities in that order.

In making recommendations about environmental monitoring the minis-ter will have to make allowance for the odd situation in which the federal authority has the money and the provinces have control of the land, that is, the right to alter the environment. Only the poorest provinces will swal-low their pride and invite the federals to continue the take-over. The others will try to arrange a trade-off of some of their constitutional rights for some federal money to enable provincial officials to participate in the clean-up. Failing that they will pay for it themselves as Ontario and Quebec do now.

Taken together the Western and Canadian pressures and recommenda-tions make up a vector of forces pushing on science. As the forces gain momentum the system of science support that we knew in the sixties is likely to be replaced by trends like the following:

– A diminution of government laboratories, with the result that federal sci-entists will tend to assume the role of expediters of research in universities and in private industry rather than acting as personal practitioners of research.

- The government will find that the best way to bring force to bear on the universities, for the purpose of getting its wishes carried out, will be to greatly increase mission-oriented agency grants. Projects then will be looked at with reduced attention to the quality of the men carrying them out. The outstanding current example of this approach is in medical grants, which likely will respond to further pressures in the direction of hospital research rather than preclinical science.
- Basic research, of the kind which we have traditionally associated with NRC grants, will be available only to really outstanding professors, and to young farm-team prospects for a limited time. The right to state support for freedom of choice in research will have to be earned by previous performance.
- The belief will disappear in the two sacred academic cows (a) that any young man good enough to obtain a university post is also good enough to go it alone in the choice of research topics, and (b) that pure science is better than applied science for training students and for fostering genius.

To conclude with a personal word: I cannot number myself among those well-wishers of science who are waiting for Godot. To them science policy is some magical new thing which, if only we had it, would solve all our problems. And it is an all-or-nothing proposition – you either have it or you have not, and there is no gradation in between.

My view is more pedestrian. I believe that the technique of successive approximations based on trial and error which has determined science policy in the past is the best one we are likely to find for a long time to come. The nation will need, from time to time, a review of the whole system. We have just sustained such a decade of stir-up, from Glassco through OECD to Lamontagne, and are now entitled to a decade of gradualness to test out the new ideas.

Notes

CHAPTER 1

1 Sen. com. report, p. 268
2 *Towards a National Science Policy for Canada* (sc report no. 4, 1968)
3 *Proposed Standard Practice for Surveys of Research and Development* (OECD, Paris, 1964). This is the so-called Frascati manual used by the OECD for its international compilations.
4 M.D. Reagan, *Science and the Federal Patron* (Oxford University Press, 1969). Chapter 2 is an analysis of the justifications for support of basic science.
5 D.N.W. Wilkinson, Convocation address, University of Saskatchewan, 1965
6 G. Herzberg, Convocation address, York University, 7 November 1969
7 *University Research and the Federal Government* (sc report no. 5, 1969)
8 Bladen report, p. 75
9 P.E. Trudeau, 'Federal grants to universities' in *Federalism and the French Canadians* (Macmillan, 1968). The article was originally published in *Cité Libre* in February 1957.
10 Sen. com. proc. 68–9, 3
11 Reagan, *Science and the Federal Patron,* p. 279
12 A.M. Weinberg, 'Criteria for scientific choice,' *Minerva,* 1 (winter 1963). The article is reprinted in Weinberg's book, *Reflections on Big Science* (MIT Press, Cambridge, Mass., 1967), pp. 65–84.
13 N.H. Lithwick, *Canada's Science Policy and the Economy* (Methuen, 1969), chapter 7 and appendix C

14 'Systems analysis in planning, programming, budgeting,' Seminar sponsored by Treasury Board, Ottawa (prepared by Kates, Peat, Marwick & Co., Toronto). These are undated lecture notes, probably prepared in 1967.

15 Sen. com. proc. 68–9, 26 and 36

16 D.K. Price, *Government and Science* (New York University Press, 1954). See p. 120

17 J.K. Galbraith, *The Affluent Society* (New American Library, 1964), p. 102

18 sc report no. 5, 1969

CHAPTER 2

1 Sen. com. proc. 68–9, 16

2 Sen. com. proc. 68–9, 10

3 C.P. Snow, *Science and Government,* Godkin Lectures at Harvard University for 1960 (Oxford University Press, 1961)

4 Sen. com. proc. 68–9, 10. See appendix p. 1152

5 J.K. Galbraith, BBC Reith Lectures, 1966

6 Sen. com. proc. 68–9, 10

7 Sen. com. proc. 68–9, 3

8 Mel Thistle, *The Inner Ring: The Early History of the National Research Council of Canada* (University of Toronto Press, 1966), p. 11. The following sketch of NRC history is largely based on this volume.

9 Thistle, *The Inner Ring,* p. 209

10 OECD report, p. 120

11 See Tory's views on biological field work in Thistle, *The Inner Ring,* p. 408–9

12 For a review of Steacie's career see Leo Marion, *Biographical Memoirs of Fellows,* vol. 10 (Roy. Soc. London, 1964), pp. 257–81. See also J.D. Babbitt (ed.), *Science in Canada: Selections from the Speeches of E.W.R. Steacie* (University of Toronto Press, 1965).

13 Sen. com. report, vol. 1

14 All the quotations are cited from Babbitt, *Science in Canada.*

15 Adapted from an inscription over the door of Staunton Harold Chapel, Leicestershire, in memory of Sir Robert Shirley, who had the audacity to found a church during Cromwell's Commonwealth. He died in the Tower at the age of twenty-seven.

16 The Glassco report, vol. 4, pp. 183–322, deals with science. The quotation is from p. 218.

17 Ibid., pp. 230 and 271

18 C.J. Mackenzie, report to the prime minister on government science, tabled in the House of Commons, 30 April 1964

19 Betty Lee, 'The atom secrets,' *Globe Magazine*, 28 Oct. 1961, quoted in John Porter, *The Vertical Mosaic* (University of Toronto Press, 1965), p. 432

20 Chapter 3, section 2

21 Framework for Government Research and Development, Command 5046

22 H.E. Gunning, 'Canadian science policy and the OECD report: a critical analysis,' *Science Forum*, vol. 2 (1969), no. 6, 3

23 H.E. Gunning, 'The Lamontagne report: a simplistic approach to a complex problem,' *Science Forum*, vol. 4 (1971), no. 2, 7

24 Judy LaMarsh, *Memoirs of a Bird in a Gilded Cage* (McClelland and Stewart, 1969, paperback 1970 by Pocket Books)

25 Sen. com. proc. 68–9, 57 and 58. The appendix to 57 contains the statement by Professor Hare; the rest are from 58.

26 OECD report, table 2, which described the mid 1960s. No figure is given for Germany or Japan.

27 Sen. com. report, vol. 1, table 2

28 Sen. com. report, vol. 1, 189–90

29 Ibid, table 2

30 Ibid., pp. 111–13

31 N. Calder, *Technopolis: Social Control of the Uses of Science* (MacGibbon & Kie, 1969). See chapter 14.

32 Ibid., p. 274

33 Sen. com. report, vol. 2, 334

34 Sen. com. report, vol. 2, 600

35 Ibid., p. 604

36 *Issues in Canadian Science Policy,* sixth annual report of the Science Council (1972)

37 *Science Policy in the USSR* (OECD, Paris, 1969). The account given here is paraphrased from the summary, pp. 559–82.

CHAPTER 3

1 C.P. Snow, *Science and Government,* Godkin Lectures at Harvard University for 1960 (Oxford University Press, 1961)

2 Canada, House of Commons, 1968-9, Standing Com. Fisheries and Forestry, Proc. and Evidence no. 6, 14 November 1968

3 Enoch Powell, *A New Look at Medicine and Politics* (Pitman Medical, 1966)

4 Sen. com. proc. 68–9, 8
5 The sc and ss appeared six times before the Senate committee, and I have drawn freely from the proceedings. The references are Sen. com. proc. 67–8, 3, 7, and 12, and 68–9, 8, 11, and 22
6 Private communication, 7 November 1969. See also his address to Department of Transport Component Convention, Ottawa, 10 May 1969.
7 D.K. Price, *Government and Science* (New York University Press, 1954). See essay I, 'The Republican revolution.'
8 R.J. Uffen, 'Recent changes in government organization for science policy,' *Science Forum*, vol. 2 (1969), no. 5, 3
9 See 'Canada's new ministry of state for science and technology' (interview with Dr Aurèle Beaulnes), *Science Forum*, vol. 4 (1971), no. 6, 16.
10 See more on this subject in chapter 8
11 Martha Ornstein, *The Role of Scientific Societies in the Seventeenth Century*, as cited in chapter 1 of M.D. Reagan, *Science and the Federal Patron* (Oxford, 1969)
12 This and the following citations are taken from the Royal Society brief and evidence of the Society's president, C.E. Dolman and others, Sen. com. proc. 68–9, 54, and from issues of *Newsletter to Fellows*.
13 C.O. Hines, letter to *Science Forum*, vol. 2 (1969), no. 5
14 C.E. Dolman, 1969, presidential address to the Royal Society of Canada, *Proceedings of the Royal Society of Canada*, series 4, vol. 8 (Ottawa, 1970), 31
15 C.E. Dolman, *Newsletter to Fellows*, vol. 2 (1969), no. 7
16 Bob Cohen, 'Below the veneer of union, some bubbling dissent,' *Science Forum*, vol. 2 (1969), no. 5, 19
17 Future of the Canadian Association of Physicists as seen by E.W.R. Steacie, quoted from J.D. Babbitt, ed., *Science in Canada: Selections from the Speeches of E.W.R. Steacie* (University of Toronto Press, 1965), p. 63
18 Snow, *Science and Government*, p. 74
19 *Towards a National Science Policy for Canada* (sc report no. 4, 1968)
20 Sen. com. proc. 68–9, 8

CHAPTER 4

1 *A Space Program for Canada* (sc report no. 1, 1967)
2 Statement of Omond Solandt as witness before the Senate science committee

3 N.H. Lithwick, *Canada's Science Policy and the Economy* (Methuen, 1969). See pp. 5 and 42.
4 George Grant, *Technology and Empire* (House of Anansi, 1969), p. 64
5 J.K. Galbraith, *The New Industrial State* (Houghton Mifflin, 1967), p. 238
6 Halifax *Chronicle-Herald,* 28 February 1973
7 *University Research and the Federal Government* (SC report no. 5, 1969)
8 L.V. Berkner, 'Renaissance in the Southwest,' *Saturday Review,* 3 June 1961
9 This account is based on an article by D.R. Fleming in W.R. Nelson, ed., *The Politics of Science* (Oxford, 1968)
10 P.E. Trudeau, 'Federal grants to universities' in *Federalism and the French Canadians* (Macmillan, 1968). The article first appeared in *Cité Libre* in 1957 and is said to have been developed in a brief to a commission in 1954.
11 Commons debates, 20 & 21 March 1969, dealing with the Government Organization Bill which established the Department of Regional Economic Expansion

CHAPTER 5

1 Annual report of the Science Council, 1969-70
2 Sen. com. proc. 68–9, 30
3 Sen. com. proc. 68–9, 8
4 R. Watson Kerr, *War Daubs: Poems* (John Lane, The Bodley Head, 1919)
5 E.J. Long, *New Worlds of Oceanography* (Pyramid Publications, NY, 1965)
6 Sen. com. proc. 68–9, 4
7 U.M. Franklin, 'Canada's CBW research: unknown territory that scientists don't discuss,' *Science Forum,* vol. 3 (1970), no. 3, 17. See also the government's view in the same issue, p. 32.
8 George Grant, *Technology and Empire* (House of Anansi, 1969)
9 For a description of the agencies see section 3 of this chapter.
10 OECD report, table 67, with proportional attribution of IRDIA assistance in 1967-8. The military and civilian aid by government to R & D were respectively 66% and 34%.
11 J.E. Broadbent, Commons debates, 12 March 1969
12 Ibid., 20 April 1970
13 Sen. com. proc. 68–9, 42
14 M.P. Bachynski, 'How Canada can close the technology gap through R & D,' *Science Forum,* vol. 2 (1969), no. 1, 31–5

15 From Hearings on Systems Development and Management, House Committee on Government Operations, 87th Cong., 2nd Sess., 1962

16 OECD report, table 6, based on Department of Industry figures for 1965

17 Sen. com. proc. 67–8, 2

18 N.H. Lithwick, *Canada's Science Policy and the Economy* (Methuen, 1969). See chapter 4.

19 Evidence of Professor L.-P. Bonneau of Laval University, Sen. com. proc. 68–9, 3

20 R.A. Charpie, 'Technological innovation and the international economy,' *Science Policy News,* vol. 1 (1969), no. 1

21 From information filed under the Corporations and Labor Unions Returns Act, quoted from the Toronto *Globe & Mail,* 10 February 1971

22 Comment by Omond Solandt, Sen. com. proc. 68–9, 11

23 M.P. Bachynski, 'Factors to keep in mind when trying to assess Canada's industrial R & D,' *Science Forum,* vol. 2 (1969), no. 5, 15–17

24 A. Vanterpool, 'Hindrances to innovation in Canadian industry,' *Science Forum,* vol. 3 (1970), no. 4, 14

25 Sen. com. proc. 68–9, 42

CHAPTER 6

1 B.N. Smallman et al., *Agricultural Science in Canada* (SC special study no. 10, 1970); *Seeing the Forest and the Trees: A Report on Forest Resources Research* (SC report no. 8, 1970); *This Land is Their Land: A Report on Fisheries and Wildlife Research in Canada* (SC report no. 9, 1970); and *Two Blades of Grass: The Challenge Facing Agriculture* (SC report no. 12, 1971)

2 For an analysis of the statistical requirements to establish a minimum measurable increment of river stock (MMI) resulting from treatment of a salmon population (e.g. closing a commercial fishery) see: F.R. Hayes, *Artificial Freshets and Other Factors Controlling the Ascent and Population of the LaHave River, Nova Scotia* (Fisheries Research Board Bulletin no. 99, 1953).

3 Sen. com. proc. 68–9, 10

4 Smallman et al., *Agricultural Science in Canada*

5 For a layman's guide to atomic physics see H.E. Duckworth, *Little Men in the Unseen World* (Macmillan, 1963). For the Canadian aspects see Sen. com. proc. 68–9, 5. Included are two days of hearings by AECL witnesses and the AECL brief.

6 See Sen. com. proc. evidence given by AECL, Treasury Board, and Science Council; *The Proposal for an Intense Neutron Generator* (SC report no. 2); and *Science Forum*, vol. 1 (1968), no. 1, which is almost entirely devoted to the pros and cons of ING.

7 The SC report was used as the model for F.R. Hayes, 'Project SWETORE: How Columbus got his grant,' *Science Forum*, vol. 2 (1969), no. 6 11.

8 Duckworth, *Little Men in the Unseen World*

9 *New Statesman*, 28 February 1972, p. 228

10 R.O. Brinkhurst and D.A. Chant, *This Good, Good Earth: Our Fight for Survival* (Macmillan, 1971)

11 *Consumer Reports*, April 1972, p. 194

12 Sen. com. proc. 68–9, 21

13 *Yearbook of World Armaments* (Gerald Duckworth, London, 1970). This is a product of the Stockholm International Peace Research Institute, set up by the Swedish Government, cited from *New Statesman*, 20 November 1970.

14 J.H. Ryther and W.M. Dunstan, *Science*, vol. 171 (1971), 1008

15 Private communication from Dr. W.H. Cook, NRC

16 Peter F.M. McLoughlin, 'The poor nations want development now – at (almost) any price,' *Science Forum*, vol. 5 (1972), no. 5, 7

CHAPTER 7

1 Kerr, *The Uses of the University*, p. 18

2 OECD report, p. 306

3 L.A. DuBridge (science advisor to the president), address to the National Academy of Science, 29 April 1969

4 J.K. Galbraith, BBC Reith Lectures, 1966

5 Statement by Dr W.G. Schneider, president of the NRC, Sen. com. proc. 68–9, 3

6 Sen. com. proc. 68–9, 11

7 SC special study no. 10 and reports nos 8 and 9 (1970)

8 P.E. Trudeau, 'Federal grants to universities' in *Federalism and the French Canadians* (Macmillan, 1968)

9 Cited from the Macdonald report which is discussed later in this chapter

10 Ibid.

11 For an analysis and some examples of joint efforts see F.R. Hayes, 'Co-

operation between universities and government' in *Transactions of the Royal Society of Canada,* series 4, vol. 2 (Ottawa, 1964), 33–8, and H.E. Duckworth, 'University research and governments' in ibid., vol. 6 (1968), 37–46

12 SC special study no. 7 (see 'Abbreviations,' s.v. Macdonald report). See also *University Research and the Federal Government* (SC report no. 5, 1969), which is a commentary and corrective to the Macdonald study.

13 SC report no. 5

14 R. Hurtubise and D.C. Rowat, *The University, Society and Government: Report of the Commission on the Relations between Universities and Governments* (University of Ottawa Press 1970). Chapter 9 deals with the support of university research. There are in addition two volumes of 'studies' prepared for the commission.

15 Louis-Philippe Bonneau and J.A. Corry, *Quest for the Optimum: Research Policy in the Universities of Canada: the Report of a Commission to Study the Rationalisation of University Research* (Association of Universities and Colleges of Canada, vol. 1 1972, vol. 2 1973)

16 Ibid., pp. 47 and 175–8

17 Ibid., pp. 38–9

18 Ibid., p. 40

19 By Lord Rothschild, see note on p. 4.

CHAPTER 8

1 D.K. Price, *Government and Science* (New York University Press, 1954), p. 162–3

2 Ibid., p. 170

3 J. Bronowski, 'The disestablishment of science,' *Encounter,* vol. 37 (1971), no. 1, 9

4 G.C. Laurence et al., 'Purpose and choice in the support of university research in physics,' *Physics in Canada,* vol. 27 (1971), no. 5

5 *Reviews of National Science Policy: Japan* (OECD, Paris, 1967)

6 Senate debates, 29 June 1967. The committee was set up in the following November and hearings began in March 1968.

7 Address by E.W.R. Steacie on 30 October 1956, cited in J.D. Babbitt, ed., *Science in Canada* (University of Toronto Press, 1965), p. 159

8 Lord Victor Rothschild, 'Controlling scientific research,' Trueman Wood Lec-

ture to the Royal Society of Arts, cited in a summary in the *New Statesman,* 31 December 1971

9 Mr Drury emphasized this point at the OECD Paris Confrontation Meeting. See chapter 2, section 6.

10 P. Calamai, 'Canada's new ministry of state for science and technology,' *Science Forum,* vol. 4 (1971), no. 6, 16 (transcript of a taped interview with Dr Aurèle Beaulnes)

11 J. Polanyi, *Science Forum,* vol. 5 (1972), no. 2, 32

12 S.A. Forman, 'Where all the money goes: Federal expenditures on science and technology,' *Science Forum,* vol. 5 (1972), no. 1, 11

13 See, for example, *Innovation in a Cold Climate* (SC report no. 15, 1971)

14 *Issues in Canadian Science Policy,* sixth annual report of the Science Council (1972), p. 27

Index

established by mission agency grants 190; *see also* NRC relations with universities.

USA, industrial domination as determinant of Canadian policy 99–100; domination declining 100; alleviation of regional disparity 107–11; 'private' defence corporations as extensions of government 125–6; control of Canadian industry 128–33; domination of agricultural research 142

USSR, *see* Russian science.

Van Steenburgh, W.E. 81

Waite, P.B. 53–4
Watkins, Melville 100
Weinberg, A.M. 10–11
Weir, Robert 72
Wells, C.M. 54
Wiles, Roy 54
Williams, Sydney B. 141
Woodward, James C. 32, 35

Lightning Source UK Ltd.
Milton Keynes UK
UKHW010002210722
406167UK00001B/188

9 781487 591519